OVER THE CANDLESTICK
On Raising Jack

OVER THE CANDLESTICK
On Raising Jack

Clara Middleton

RED FINCH PRODUCTIONS
San Rafael

Cover design by Laila Parsi.

ISBN: 978-1-940121-06-2

Red Finch Productions
Published by Urtext Media LLC
San Rafael, CA 94901
www.urtext.us

Printed in the United States of America

To mothers who shoulder it alone

She wondered whether the child were a boy or a girl, and therefore she made two things, a pretty ball and a bow and arrows. These things she left alone with the child all the next day. When she returned, she saw that the ball was full of arrows, and she knew then that the child was a boy and that he would be hard to raise.

Kiowa myth
The Way to Rainy Mountain, N. Scott Momaday

Contents

Introduction: Motherhood Made a Man of Me   11

Chapter 1   **Private School**   20
    Scenes From Classroom Q   21

Chapter 2   **Public School**   47
    The Website: Mothers of Bad Boys   50
    The Launch: Why Boys, Why Bad,   56
    Why Mothers?
    The Main Blog: Clara's Clearing   61

Chapter 3   **Homeschooling**   139
    A Great Vanishing Act   140
    Who'da Thunk?   146
    Clara's Clearing, Continued   150

Chapter 4   **The Teaching Part**   232
    Sixth Grade: Educating My Boy   234
    Seventh Grade   277
    Eighth Grade   288

Chapter 5   **Extreme Mothering**   306

Chapter 6   **Monster Moms and Extreme Fathers**   319

Chapter 7   **Community: The Body of the Matter**   323
    Organizers   325
    Educators   330
    Friends   337

Chapter 8   **The Work Of Modern Mothers**   345

Introduction

Motherhood Made a Man of Me

Before I had a kid I lived in a bubble. It had to do with my upbringing. It was a bubble of idealism, high standards, and lofty aspirations, created by generations in my family and validated by the greater environment in which we lived. I suppose those ideals were what people who cared for me wanted for everyone, and they did their best to support it. Now, I was no Prince Siddhartha. I was neither insulated from the evils of life and the world, nor did I develop into Gautama Buddha. In fact, cruelty, injustice, deceit, vulgarity, and other ugliness were pointed out to me. I did learn to survive in a less than ideal world but I always had the choice to retreat into my own bubble. Until I had a kid.

When you have a kid you quickly realize that a lot of things are out of your control. And as luck of the draw would have it I ended up with a kid who was hell-bent to prove it was he who was in control. I believe children are born with temperaments, nascent characters, and existential predicaments. Some call it karma. My kid's whatever-you-want-to-call-it was of the take-matters-into-his-own-hands kind. When you see your toddler taking on two kids twice his size over the ownership of a red polka dot ball, you are impressed but you start to worry.

When he continues to seek challenges and push limits as he grows, your job as a parent does not get any easier. You are aware of the incongruity in the stage of his life and his innate characteristics, but this is not an easy thing to explain to a child. How do you watch over him but not hover? How do you teach but not preach? How do you strike a balance between encouraging confidence and alerting about consequences? I still don't know. What ensued between Jack and me was an interminable fight of me pulling in one direction, and he the other.

Maybe I'm being overly dramatic. Maybe I take things more seriously than they call for. I sure did try to remind myself that it would be wrong of me to think everything outside my own bubble is ugly and hostile. But I guess I even took this too far. I ended up giving benefit of the doubt to things that were far uglier and more brutal than I imagined, thus betraying my son's wellbeing and trust. There are plenty of incongruities within most of us so I'm sure I always was and will remain too much this way and not enough that. Indeed, so are kids and so will they remain. So I'm also pretty sure that no matter what I tried it would still meet with the same resistance and lack of cooperation on Jack's side—the mom, after all, is the first testing ground. It's the safest place to unleash your power and conduct your experiments. In my case, I felt I was turned into some Los Alamos National Laboratory by my bundle of joy, Dr. Strangelove. My own little bubble of beauty and intellectual curiosity did not seem to stand a chance against my son's nuclear experiments.

The infected blanket

After all these years I'll still be damned if I feel any wiser in striking balances. I still can't put things in proper objective perspective, so I am not going to try. My subjective truth is that as my son grew up I started getting a sense that some invisible hand was trying to snatch him away from me and from what I wanted for him. I felt like a Native American who was handed an infected blanket to wrap her child in. I myself, not having developed proper antibodies to the germs in the blanket, was sickened along with my kid. Luckily, neither of us died. And I definitely do believe that what doesn't kill you can make you stronger. Jack will have to tell his story himself but I certainly feel stronger—or as my friend Fahimeh, mother of another strong-willed boy, put it, motherhood made a man of me. And who knows, maybe by being exposed to the germs in that infected blanket at a younger age Jack will have developed better immunity to them in the long run.

Our exposure to the infected blanket started with my son Jack's attendance at a private school in San Francisco. We were eager to secure him a spot in a good school, so once he was accepted to a posh private school that ran from pre- through middle school we pulled him out of his small part-time neighborhood preschool and sent him there fulltime (the school required that). Big mistake, on a number of accounts. This was early 2000s in San Francisco, the beginning of a major cultural and socioeconomic redefinition of the city. The old quirky San Francisco was changing into headquarters of a new breed of company and a playground for the new rich. I had fundamental issues with a certain corporate mentality with its smug lack of social and cultural awareness that was pervading the city, but I had no idea it had spread to schools so quickly.

Chapter 1 describes the year and few months that Jack was in private school. In a nutshell, I found that particular school, and other private schools that I looked into, to be essentially gated communities. Gated communities are ultimately about segregation. At private schools, children and families are heavily screened for admission and kept on their toes (not to mention bled for cash) for the privilege of belonging to the privileged cliques inside the gates. Once we ran into trouble at that school it did not take us long to decide to leave. We most enthusiastically left that scene behind.

Chapter 2 is an account of the next phase in Jack's school experience, in public school. It was a relief sending Jack to a public school; I so detested gated communities. (Idealistic bubbles should not be mistaken for segregated communities.) But we quickly saw what a can of worms public schools are. First off, a group of people lumped together does not make a community. Public school was certainly a more diverse lump than the carefully screened population of private schools. But without a conscious effort to create real communities, public schools remain shapeless and transitory collections of people, albeit with a dose of litigated rights that discourages some degree of segregation. We would have plodded along in our random assemblage of folks in public school and found friends in its pockets of tenacious liberality if a certain dog-eat-dog-mentality, in the form of bullying and forming gangs, had not cut it short. (Education was a small part of school life, I found.) Despite all our efforts to "work" with the school it got to a point that we had to pull Jack out of school before more damage was done to him and our family.

The rest of this book describes our years of homeschooling Jack through middle school. Now, have no illusion, for most people, myself included, homeschooling is difficult. It is labor-intensive, requires sacrifice, and is certainly not easy on the nerves. My report from the trenches of homeschooling is reflected in the blogs and other parts of this book. But... given the facts of life outside my chosen bubble, homeschooling was the best thing that happened to us. It was liberating. It was a significant step in emerging from the enclosure of the infected blanket. It opened my eyes and, as will be clear to the reader plodding through our days and struggles, it changed me.

Nature, community, culture

Raising a child has made me aware of a sad, and indeed quite awful, reality. I think children are increasingly brought up in unhealthy, unhappy and impoverished environments. By high school it is plain to see how unhealthy, unhappy and impoverished a lot of young people have become. By "impoverished" I mean to stress both the spiritual kind (lack of striving for a life worth living) and a very practical and material one. Hooked on consumption as the measure of happiness and success, young people will perhaps sooner than later find out that they cannot sustain their "habits." No real education, no meaningful pursuit, polluted and exploited environments, dwindling family resources, and a future of few, mind-numbing, and poorly paid jobs—how does one rise above this?

I think the way to avoid this sorry and dangerous state of affairs is very simple. The solution, and the salvation, has always been with us: nature, community, culture. Human beings have known the significance of these three things for thousands of years. Homeschooling helped strengthen my family's connection to these crucial basics. I finally felt I was in company of people with whom my ideals found some resonance. At both private and public school I felt myself in a heavily sound-proofed room where my voice was muffled and in fact deadened. People often refer to homeschooling as a form of dropping out. I think of it as a final kick, throwing off the tight wrap of that polluted blanket, and dropping *in*: Hello folks, let's pick up where the lights went out...

Our homeschooling ended with Jack's return to school in ninth grade. As of this writing he has finished his second year in high school. He's done well and is happy enough. My life has certainly gotten easier. But I am grateful and very glad for our homeschooling years. The friends that both Jack and I made in those years are invaluable to us and here to stay. The kids remain close friends even though some have returned to school. The community is strong and healthy and happy; we continue to participate in many homeschoolers' activities . The programs, classes, volunteer work, random pursuits, and even jobs the kids held during their homeschool years have built them solid academic and life resumes. Many of them have taken courses at local community colleges before school kids entered high school.

In the end, this book is an account of the struggles of my son and me with things inside and outside my bubble and with each other. It's been a struggle full of fabulous things and awful things and surprises. It's an account of being alive and kicking in every moment. All's well that ends well enough.

Not to be misunderstood...

Before going any further I feel I should clarify a point. While I am very glad for having had our homeschooling experience I am not proposing that staying clear of schools is a solution to all child-rearing and educational ills. Homeschooling certainly is a viable and growing option for the present. It has produced good and happy results and it surely should remain a choice. But it is only one option. I simply don't believe any one option is the best for everybody. I myself went to school as a preschooler through graduate school and thoroughly enjoyed it. A lot depends on the individual child and his/her life circumstances, including access to alternative schools.

Alternative schools, those operating outside the goals and structures of mainstream schools (both public and private), have existed for a long time. One of the earliest is Summerhill school in England, which has been around since 1921 and is still going strong. Waldorf schools present viable alternatives all across Europe and United States. In the US, Sudbury schools with their ingenious combination of freedom and learning have created a successful and viable model. "Democratic Schools," drawing on the ideas and examples of many alternative approaches have become increasingly popular in Europe. These schools show "school" does not need to be demonized.

It would be especially simplistic to offer homeschooling as the cure for unhealthy, unhappy, and impoverished childhoods. I think these problems run deeper than school per se and the solutions have to be more encompassing and constructive than merely rejecting schools. I think the question of the health and happiness of children, and their right to rich and meaningful lives, merits serious discussion on social, even political, levels.

A word on turning a website into a book

This book came out of a website. The blogs I wrote for my website, MothersOfBadBoys.com, form the main part of it. I will write later about how that website came into being but I want to say a few words about the challenges of turning blogs into a book.

First, blogs have an easy-breezy style that sometimes doesn't quite work on the printed page. So please, overlook stylistic deficiencies. Second, in a book you don't have that lovely thing called hypertext that can link any part of the website to another as well as to other sites. While I was writing blogs I liberally linked to relevant items that shed light on what I was trying to say. The links were to other articles, news reports, video clips, art work, etc., that helped demonstrate my points. Third, an interactive website opens the discussion to readers who make comments. Often interesting conversations developed, inspiring new blogs. I wrote a number of blogs in response to comments to previous blogs. A lot of this digital and interactive texture cannot transfer to a book.

A fourth challenge in converting a website into a book is that in a website you can run multiple blogs at the same time, focusing on different aspects of what you're exploring. For this book I have only used my own two blogs: *Clara's Clearing* and *Educating My Boy*. Another blog, *The OMM Club* ("OMM" for One Mad Mom), was made up mostly of readers' contributions. In this book I have only incorporated my own contributions to that blog. (The only exception is a couple of blogs by one contributor to another blog, *Manners and Morals*.) In the interest of maintaining the narrative continuity of my own story I have had to leave out others' stories. A fifth challenge was posed by the question of repetition. When you write a blog you cannot assume that readers have read all your previous blogs, so sometimes you repeat something. When you're writing in "real time" no two moments are the same, but in book form repetitions stand out sorely. I have tried to minimize them but eliminating all repetitions would require rewriting the whole book and changing its character.

Finally, going back and forth between digital and analog modes of communication has been an interesting experience. A "digital" slice of life can be pictured as a simultaneous group of discrete moments. A particular moment in your life—or experience, or thought, or story—links to discrete moments in others' (life, experience, thought, story) right there and then. But to tell a story with narrative continuity we inevitably fall into the old "analog" mode. This is the mode in which moments blend into one another and produce a narrative continuity of before, while, and after. Stories lend themselves for the most part to this mode.

Life, of course, doesn't exactly unfold in a linear fashion, steadily accumulating meaning and value like numbers. A lot of life is experienced in a series of isolated, here-and-now moments, connecting often randomly to others' here-and-now moments. But it is an odd human character to try to superimpose a coherent narrative over a string of the here-and-now moments of our own or others' lives. The connections of these present moments to past and future ones are not always intelligible but we are determined to find them. I guess we're just not content living our moments, we want to understand *what they mean:* where they're coming from and where they're going to. We want our life to be a coherent story, and, by God, if there isn't one we're going to invent it.

To put it another way, even if our "real time" experience of life has a more digital configuration we can only make sense of it by discerning the analog thread running through. For that, books trump websites any day. They've been around longer and, for telling stories, we return to them.

To tell my story and maintain some narrative continuity I sometimes interrupt blogs to add or explain something. The book also contains chapters that did not appear on the website. To make it easier for the reader to distinguish between what appeared in electronic form and what has been added in the book I have adopted a visual clue.

The parts of the book that appeared on the website as blogs are printed in this font.

The parts that have been added, such as this introduction, appear in this font.

CHAPTER I

Private School

Before we enrolled Jack in a private school with a good reputation in San Francisco he went for one year to a family day care at age two and a preschool at age three. His schedule at both places was a few hours a day, two or three times a week. The day care, Growing Up, was run by Julia Ready, a lovely woman with whom we have remained friends. The preschool, Little Bear School run by Patricia Finnegan, was also a happy "open structure" environment with lots of freedom for kids. They had weekly classes in music, dance, tumbling, martial arts, yoga and lots of other "academic" and nonacademic subjects. Jack was happy in both places.

When Jack turned four we started him at Hillside School where my husband's first two kids had gone and had had a good experience. Hillside, however, did not allow a part time schedule. Jack started going to school full time at age four. The school had a September cut-off date so because of Jack's October birthday he was older than most of the kids in his "class."

I wrote the next piece in article form shortly after we pulled Jack out of the school. A few years later when I had a website I published it as a series of blogs.

Scenes from Classroom Q

This is the account of our experience at a celebrated private school in San Francisco. I write it partly to put an unpleasant experience behind us and partly as a way to complete a story I have been telling other parents and educators in snatches. I believe the public at large would benefit from directing a critical eye toward claims of excellence that justify the funds and labor that private schools require of parents. I have changed the name of the school because this is not an attempt at vindication.

Most importantly, I feel compelled to write this in acknowledgement of the mindlessly cruel and potentially damaging treatment my son received for over a year.

How we ended up at Hillside School

My husband Robert's older kids had gone to Hillside School from preschool through middle school. These are terrific young people through whom I have met other wonderful graduates from the school. These kids are all well educated, with many interests, open and enquiring minds, and a healthy dose of skepticism. Clearly some credit was due to the school.

Furthermore, Robert was on the board of directors of the school for ten years, four as president. He had volunteered a great deal at the school and enjoyed being part of the community. So when we were given sibling status we were optimistic that new good experiences and memories will be added to old. Our almost four-year old son was admitted to the combination preschool/kindergarten classroom with a group of entering three-year olds. Classroom Q, a combination of preschool and kindergarten, was composed of three groups of, roughly, three, four, and five year olds.

On an instinctive level, however, I did not take to the

school. My immediate reservation was the so-called Montessori approach of the preschool and kindergarten. I had majored in developmental psychology as an undergraduate and even back then it was generally agreed that strict application of any theoretical model in an actual learning environment is impractical, if not downright silly. In fact, I was aware that the good name of Maria Montessori needed to be rescued from the contradictory applications and much shoddy work to which her name has become attached. I assumed that Montessori accreditation required learning about the context and constraints of Maria Montessori's work, society, and times. At any rate, by now, the strict application of the Montessori method in the classroom has been critiqued and revised for nearly a century. I just assumed people in early childhood education were up on these developments.

But I put my own instincts and even my education on hold and trusted what was before my eyes: actual evidence that great kids came out of that school. I believed—as I still do—in the futility of expecting a perfect any kind of environment for my son. I was not looking to fall in love.

"Why is Hillside School so important?"

Jack had just turned four and was in his first year at Hillside when he asked me the question above. I knew exactly what he was getting at. Classroom Q was a joyless and humorless environment and I cringed each day when dropping him off. We were driving to school the day he asked that question and I had the sudden urge to reply, "You know what? It ain't," and make a U-turn right there and then. But then again, as parents we need to be in control of our impulses. (We also have work to do.) So I offered him some parental inanity about Hillside being a good school, that he would like it in time, that his brother and sister went there, etc.

But the truth of the matter is that the poor four-year old had hit the nail right on the head. The air of self-importance and the utter lack of spontaneity were out of place for a preschool and kindergarten. The kids had assigned seating where they were supposed to take their "work" and sit, for what I'm sure seemed to them an eternity, pouring beans from one container to another or putting rubber bands around pegs on a board. There was of course time to run outside and play later, but to even introduce the idea of "work" to the three to five year old crowd is really overkill. (It reminded me of a cartoon I saw a few years ago. A little boy dressed in a three piece suit with a briefcase was knocking on a door: "Can Johnny come out to work?")

The first few weeks, the various Montessori learning equipment interested Jack. He checked out each one and figured things out about them. Then it was over. The other kids, the play structure, and pretend games beckoned. He avoided his "work." The teachers were dismayed. "It's boring, Mama," he said to me. "It is not *instereyting* [interesting]." I was ready with another inanity: "Try to find something interesting about them. That's how you learn things." (Somebody should have slapped me.)

"I felt like a supplicant"

This was Robert's comment after our first parent-teacher conference. We encountered a "professional" tone and bearing that was particularly ridiculous sitting on little kiddy chairs around a short table. After we were talked at for a while about our son's progress in various Montessori tasks, we only had time to beg yet again that he be excused from napping in the afternoons. Being four in a class of mostly three-year olds, he did not need the nap and it kept him from falling asleep at a reasonable hour at night. That was driving the whole family crazy. For months we had begged the teachers to allow him to join the four-year group at nap time but had been categorically refused. "Children of x years need x number of hours of sleep," we were informed. Finally, midyear, sitting as supplicants on tiny chairs, our request was benevolently granted.

The nagging unhappiness of the second year

Okay, so the first year was not ideal. For summer school we put Jack back in his old preschool, Little Bear School, because it was a more fun environment and we all liked it more. I was also hoping that being away from his new friends and teachers he might miss them and be happier when Hillside started again. And he was. He started the new school year with excitement to see his teachers even more than his friends.

But the second year was not turning out any better than the first. It was even more of a struggle to get Jack to go to school in the mornings. "I don't want to go to school," and later, "I don't like the teachers," was routine. Again, he said that it was boring. This time, I thought about it. I had noticed during an observation day the previous year that one very bright girl, also a four-year old in the three-year old group, having missed the birthday deadline by days, often sat quietly at her desk with nothing to do. She simply looked bored. By the end of the year her parents took her out of the school to start kindergarten elsewhere—at Hillside she would have had another year of preschool like Jack.

During the summer at Little Bear the head teacher, Patricia, told me that Jack often sat quietly singing to himself and reading a book. "And sometimes he spends quite a bit of time looking up a favorite topic—sharks, right now. That's the beginning of research!" Patricia said with a laugh. We both found it interesting that the high energy and rambunctious little boy was exploring other interests on his own. Mostly, I felt that the teacher took pleasure in watching the directions in which the children at her school grew. It was quite apparent that she and her staff paid attention to the kids individually. Lo and behold, maybe they even enjoyed the differences between them!

I kept suppressing making comparisons between big beautiful Hillside and this unassuming little preschool. "If only we last through preschool and kindergarten then everything will be fine," I kept hoping. (The first grade teacher had a great reputation.) After all, I had heard the Hillside preschool described as a necessary evil to go through to get to the elementary school. I had taken the chance.

"The teachers are not happy to see me"

The second year started with Jack excited to see his teachers but ended with him pointing to their picture on the wall, pale and trembling, saying: "I hate the teachers— all of them..." In a calmer moment the next day he said: "In the mornings I'm happy to see the teachers and I say hello but they're not happy to see me."

Again I knew exactly what he was talking about. I myself had cringed at the way the teachers greeted his enthusiasm in the mornings. His excited, happy hellos were almost always greeted with a reprimand: "Good morning, Jack. Stop running..." "Hello. Put that away..."

I witnessed an unfeeling and gratuitously oppressive exchange one day that made me feel utterly miserable and worthless for putting my son in the care of those teachers. Jack was wearing new sunglasses about which he was very excited.

"Hey, Cindy, do you recognize me...?" he approached a teacher with a mischievous smile.

"That's nice, Jack. Now take them off and put them in your cubby."

"Can I show it to my friends? Maybe they won't

recognize me," he beseeched still smiling.

"I told you to put them away."

Deeply disappointed Jack handed me the glasses to take home. But apparently the bucket of cold water on the poor child's head had not even been enough. The teacher seemed not to have made some point forcefully enough. "I told you to put them in your cubby, Jack, not to hand them to your mother," she said.

The previous year I had tried my utmost to make some kind of warm human contact with the teachers, to no avail. In fact, they seemed pretty good at not allowing any connection to take hold. No comment, no discussion, no joke was acknowledged except with a perfunctory smile and change of subject. I wondered whether I made any sense to them at all.

Developing a relationship with teachers continued to stall in the second year. One morning, trying to entice Jack to go to school, I said that it would be more fun to go to school and play with his friends and teachers than stay at home. He said, "Teachers don't play with you. They just tell you what to do." What about the friends? "Teachers don't let me play with my friends when I want to. They are always saying do this, do that..." Another time: "The teachers don't let me have any time to myself." (This is time that perhaps the teacher at the little preschool would have looked at as opportunity for research!)

Not surprisingly Jack started becoming defiant with the teachers, which did not endear him to them. One afternoon, in the bustle of pickup time, one of the teachers had a quick talk with me about him refusing to do his "work." Jack, who had his ears perked up while hanging around with his friends, turned to us and putting his arm around me looked straight into his teacher's face. "You know why I don't do what you tell me to do?" he asked her. Then he almost shouted: "Because it's boring." Then he ran off not to hear what we might say to him. (I learned later that this was called a "listening problem." I myself call it proper avoidance of teacher reprimand and more parental inanity.)

Things fall apart

One Wednesday morning in the first week of December of the second year, as I dropped Jack off at school, one of the teachers pulled me aside and asked if he had told me of the problems he was having with his friends Neil and James. I knew that Jack loved Neil and Neil was the single most attractive feature of the school for him. I also knew that he quite liked James but that his feelings had been hurt because a couple of play dates with him had been cancelled. "James doesn't want to be my friend," he had said. I had tried to explain to him that it was James's mother who had cancelled because of some problems and that James had nothing to do with it. At any rate, James's mother and I understood each other and our boys, and we knew we would make it up. We knew the two of them had a penchant for butting heads and quibbling. It didn't seem particularly alarming.

That morning the teacher informed me that Jack and James both wanted to play with Neil and that sometimes led to disappointment for Jack. "He can't handle disappointment very well," she said. (In contrast to the rest of humanity, I suppose.) She also added that she and the other teachers were at times "saddened" by how upset Jack got over losing Neil to James, as it were. She suggested individual play dates with both kids. I told her James's mom and I were trying to arrange that but that Neil's mom did not return my calls.

That very afternoon the same teacher dropped a bomb, totally unrelated to anything we had talked about in the morning. "Jack does not listen to the teachers. We have tried everything but he completely shuts us out," she said.

And then: "Do you think Jack has trouble understanding things?"

I was taken aback. I asked if she could give me examples of Jack not understanding things. She mentioned that they had asked him to put on his jacket before going outside and he had ignored the request. She said there were other examples but she couldn't think of any right then. Had we noticed anything at home? She said that the "learning specialist" teacher agreed with her that maybe Jack had "comprehension problems." They would give me examples at first opportunity. "We can't understand it," she said. "He knows so many things...!"

The alarms in my head—no, in my whole being—suddenly went off. There was something dreadfully wrong. I kept Jack at home the next day. He kept throwing anxious glances at me to see if I was mad at him. I reassured him that I wasn't.

Labels fly

By next Monday morning, Jack's list of problems had multiplied. The "learning specialist" had determined that he not only had comprehension, but social, behavioral, and developmental problems too. (A little knowledge is a dangerous thing, and little kids make excellent surfaces for attaching labels.) "Can we talk about it?" I wanted to know. "Yes, yes. As soon as we can schedule a parent teacher conference the third week of January," I was told.

Imagine that! Being told—out of the blue, after over a year of attending school—that your child has serious problems, the details of which will be discussed—nay, revealed—in about two months. This is the stuff of which parental nightmares are made.

The only answer I got when I asked for examples of Jack's "problems" was that he did not listen to the teachers. Sure enough, he was at a point of not even making eye contact with them. ("An understandable response to a hostile environment," Patricia from Little Bear School said later.) But why had we not received any communication about any of this before? When did this problem start? The teachers mumbled incoherently to my questions. They looked pale and frazzled. Clearly, Jack had driven them to their wits' end. I think they completely lost any semblance of professionalism. (Five year-olds are not without their own desperate measures!)

As for Jack's developmental progress, we in fact were quite satisfied enough. He was beginning to read and write easy words and make simple additions and subtractions. He had decent attention span. He sounded out words religiously (this we owed to the school). He had a good vocabulary in English and liked learning words in other languages. He was physically coordinated and musically inclined. He was protective of younger kids and generally kind. He knew the dinosaurs, planets, and The Beatles. He even made incisive political commentary: "I would like to have a talk with George Bush and explain to him what war is."

Just to be on the safe side we got a bunch of K-1 workbooks for "diagnostic" purposes. Friends and family (many of whom are seasoned educators) took turns working with Jack on those. Finally we just let the poor kid go. There was nothing wrong with him.

There was one development, however, that alarmed me. He was increasingly avoiding talking or listening to us, particularly on the subject of school. "I don't want to talk about it," he said every time I, or even he himself, brought up some problem at school.

Behavioral problems

I started racking my brain for behavior problems. Certainly Jack was not the model of exemplary behavior. There were plenty of times when he misbehaved—pushed kids, snatched things, covered his ears and said "blah, blah, blah" when I talked to him, kicked and screamed his way to the bath, etc. He even confided one day that sometimes he acted like a bully at school. (When I asked him if he enjoyed being a bully, he—I don't know exactly how truthfully—said, No.)

I knew that in the classroom there was a group of roughhousing older boys. Jack was attracted to them and longed to be accepted into their group (he was closer in age to them than to most kids in his own group). They were bigger and tougher and made no qualms about showing the younger kids who was in charge. Jack occasionally reported that this one kicked him, or that one punched him. I have the pictures he drew of them doing that. But he never really complained about them. He actually liked them. Once when I asked how come he didn't tell the teachers that those boys were rough with him, he said: "But they're my friends. I don't want to hurt their feelings."

I kept my ears open but did not interfere, apart from reminding Jack that if he didn't like the way those boys treated him he didn't have to hang out with them. For all their roughhousing antics I thought they were perfectly fine boys. I wasn't about to teach my son to tell on his friends or run crying to his mom, especially when he voluntarily got into scrapes.

But were there behavior problems we did not know about? The only example I got was that he was "mean" to James. When I apologized about this to James's mother, she told me that she had explained to James that his words hurt Jack ("I don't want to be your friend," "Neil is my friend, not yours," that sort of thing) and that made Jack mad. I was very sorry about my son being rough with another kid but in this particular case I think James's mother and I saw eye to eye. Our remedy was to try to arrange play dates and generally bide time until the boys got a little older and wiser. We both thought that these kids were going to be together until 8th grade and that there was going to be a lot of time for their friendship to mature.

The afterschool teacher spills the beans

By coincidence, a couple of days after the labeling session with one of the head teachers, I ran into one of the day care teachers on a cigarette break outside of school. (I always knew you could trust a smoker!) When I mentioned what the teachers had said about Jack, he was surprised. He hadn't noticed any particularly bad behavior. He mentioned the James and Neil conflict of interest and that Jack sometimes was rough with James. "But James is no angel either," he said. "We can see that."

Then he casually added: "From the beginning of the year we decided that since Jack is older and bigger than the other kids in his group he should have a leadership role." And what this meant was that bad behavior was going to be "nipped in the bud," and that for Jack "it was not going to be three strikes and you're out, but one strike and you're out."

I will always be grateful to this teacher for his honestly crude words—he captured the spirit of Jack's treatment. (Incidentally, he is the only teacher of whom Jack has good memories.) So it turned out that since the beginning of the second year Jack had been put on strict discipline—to which he had responded very poorly. It was done in the name of making a "leader" out of him. (What next? Military invasion of a country to impose democratic leadership on it?) And again, we had never heard a word of this plan. If we had, perhaps we could have signed an agreement absolving the school from its responsibility to beat leadership into our kid.

The mysterious role of certain parents

An incident that I accidentally witnessed in the classroom was an indication of yet another angle on things—but

I didn't know that at the time.

One morning shortly after that fateful Wednesday when I was told of all the things that were wrong with Jack, I hung around the classroom a few minutes longer than I used to. I was watching Jack and Neil happily putting together a puzzle. Jack had pulled his chair over to Neil's desk. Suddenly one of the teachers descended on Jack and said something to him. I could not see or hear her but I saw Jack look up at her and ask, "Why?" She repeated herself and he repeated, "Why?" Eventually she made him leave Neil's desk to go back to his own. (So much for her sadness over Jack not getting to play with Neil.) Angrily, Jack carried his chair back to his own desk, and looking straight into the teacher's face (the way he had done the day he told her what she was asking him to do was boring), he slammed his chair on the floor. Then the teacher saw that I had seen what had happened. She came over to me and mumbled something to the effect of, "I see that you saw what just happened, but..." Again she was not coherent.

After we left the school, in conversation with other mothers I stumbled upon the fact that there were certain parents in the classroom who strongly disapproved of some kids. (I never was "in" with the right groups.) So when, during the Christmas break, Jack told me that he had heard Neil's mother telling the teachers that she did not want Jack to play with Neil, I put two and two together. The reason the teacher pulled Jack away from Neil that day was probably because she was operating under Neil's mother's instruction. I later learned that Neil's mother had complained (to other mothers as well as the teachers) that the way Jack treated James "traumatized" Neil. ("Traumatize" is such a convenient word—so hard to define and to disprove.) But I think we had displeased her long before Jack started traumatizing James. She had ignored us—birthday invitation, calls to make play dates—long before Jack had shown any particular interest in Neil.

As it turned out, this woman was not the only one who was displeased with Jack and/or the rest of the family. Through the grapevine I heard about another mother, very involved in various capacities at the school, who also took strong dislikes to some kids. In fact, I was told that she was instrumental in getting rid of Thomas (I will come to this) the year before. Hearing this I was reminded of an uneasy feeling I got when talking to her one day. At a picnic at the beginning of the second year I was mildly complaining that the classroom could be a little more spontaneous and joyful. I don't know how she turned the conversation to Jack but she casually commented that with the new "learning specialist" in the classroom that year he might find school more enjoyable. I must say that I am so clueless in gossip and innuendo that after this comment I only felt a bad taste in my mouth but did not make much of it. But after Jack was badgered with a string of "problems" and other mothers filled me in on the influence of this particular woman, I was horrified at the possibility of a connection here. The possible cruelty of this woman astonished me but it did not excuse the ineptitude and unprofessionalism of the teachers to let her wield this kind of influence.

During Jack's last week of school, while I was still in my clueless state, I thought it was appropriate that I mention our impending departure to other mothers I encountered while waiting to pick up our kids. To my surprise, a number of women with whom I was on smiling and chatting terms, suddenly turned cold and hard. One blurted out, "It's because I complained." I didn't quite understand. Her son, Daniel, was older than Jack. Had Jack been traumatizing him too? (As chance would have it, the very next day Jack showed up with a big scrape on his elbow. "Daniel pushed me," he said. I let it go.) The real clue had already been given us by the principal during our talk a few days earlier (I will come to this too) but I was slow to put two and two together. Apparently, the minute word got out that Jack was leaving the school, rumor spread that he was being kicked out. So in fact Daniel's mother was taking responsibility for (or pride in?) the expulsion.

During the winter break, after we had told Jack that he would not be going back to Hillside, and he had told me about Neil's mother telling the teachers that she didn't want him to play with Neil, he said, "Don't get mad at me if I ask a question." I reassured him. "Do you think Neil's mom is stupid?" he asked. Once when he had called some-one stupid I had said that only cruel and disrespectful peo-ple are stupid. "Yes," I told him. "I do think she's stupid."

I think he sighed in relief. After that Jack finally opened up to talking to his father and me and telling us things about the school. After three months we still hear new stories.

Cultural difference is a slippery thing

I want to digress here a little from the strict recounting of events. I think there are some important issues whose bearing on the experience of our particular family may be hard to determine but must be nonetheless brought out in the open.

Jack is bicultural. And let's face it, boys from more "col-ored" cultures tend a bit towards unruliness. For one thing, family life tends to be less structured, less punctual, less strict. This attitude, combined with the typical high energy levels of normal boys, makes for extra capacity for ram-bunctious behavior. The family and community culture, however, has tolerance for this kind of behavior and cer-tainly does not see it as pathological or an imminent threat to the order of things. (Surely we have all seen our share of unconventional and rebellious white boys?!)

What these boys face in "real life" (don't you love this?), however, are two things. First, the "white" culture at large expects behavior that is much more under control. Energy must be harnessed, feelings checked, rules observed, directions followed. These are all good things to learn—it is only that kids, especially boys, will get around them if they can get away with it, and for as long as they can. In my view, this is far from indication of pathology. Second, as Jack's old preschool teacher put it, our school system, at least at the early childhood education level, is really set up more for the way girls learn. We expect boys to do the same calm, fine-motor activities that girls are good at. No wonder that the "problem" children in classrooms are overwhelmingly boys.

What you end up with, then, is an environment that is restrictive particularly to boys of non-white cultures. But then again, in real life—and this is cause for celebration—a teacher with experience, imagination, and love of children can maneuver around all kinds of differences and eccentricities, and work perfectly well with children of all kinds of backgrounds. They do it all the time. This is certainly what I expected from the well-compensated teachers at one of the most sought-after private schools in town.

The African American question

I will digress (or maybe not!) a little more. I recently read in a cover story of a national magazine that it is common knowledge that African American boys are punished more than any other kids in school. This is very disturbing—and was corroborated by what I saw at Hillside School.

In March of our first year at Hillside, Thomas, the only African American boy in our group, was expelled. He had proved too much of a challenge for the teachers and occupied too much of their time. What I saw was a high energy three-year old boy, maybe too young to be in school full time, completely oblivious to classroom rules. I took secret pleasure in watching him drive the complacent teachers to distraction, but the truth is that nobody was having any fun. His poor mother, with a job and a younger child, made heroic efforts to make the situation work. In the end, the school bid them a smug email farewell ("Not a good match... We'll miss Thomas...") fairly late in the year—not only too late for the parents to find another school for Thomas that year, but also too late to apply to most schools for the next.

In the second year, Miles, also African American, joined the group. He too was high energy and very bright. One of the difficulties he faced was to be accepted into a group that had already been together for a year. He was also quite spirited and resisted submission to heavy-handed teacher authority. The offences he committed brought him daily banishment from activities and exclusion from the groups he desperately wanted to join. This was done, I'm sure, in the name of consistency—he was subjected to the same policy as other kids—but it was a glaring misapplication of policy. (I must say, I never saw any kid being banished quite as often as Miles. But then again, I was not around while my kid was being disciplined!)

One day I helplessly watched as a teacher approached Miles, who had happily joined a game with a group of other boys, and yanked him away: "Miles, you know you're excused from the block area..." I suppose he had done something wrong the day before. So much for being accepted into the group.

Another day I watched Miles being banished to his lonely desk during circle time. He had elbowed another child and next thing I knew, he was sitting at his desk, far away from everyone. I could feel the whole room tremble with his rage and the tears he held back. All I could do was go over to him, pat him on the head and say, "You're a good boy, Miles. You're a good boy."

My own son, who looks quite Caucasian, probably received the same treatment ("One strike and he was out..."), so it is hard to say that Miles' exclusion was blatant racism.

But it would take a blithering idiot not to see the effect Miles' repeated expulsions from the group was having on the other children. The day he was banished from circle I watched as all eyes turned toward him. It was done innocently enough of course, but I would neither want that gaze turned toward my son, nor that he should be part of a group directing that gaze toward others. Not surprisingly, to the day we left, Miles was not accepted by the other boys.

The conversations I had over time with both Thomas's and Miles's parents were quite enlightening. At a birthday party the first year, Thomas's father made a comment about the classroom having the atmosphere of "army barracks." In the second year, Miles's mother, virtually in tears, said to me: "What do they want from my kid? Conformity? Docility? They want to break my son's spirit."

Robert and I had been discussing the school in practically the same exact words. ("'Celebrating diversity'" he snorted, "should be 'celebrating docility.'") But we were aware that addressing some issues—boot camp methods, submission, conformity, etc.—especially in the context of race and cultural difference, required a brutal honesty that was beyond the reach of the school's limp liberalism. At any rate, we were quite sure that we did not want to take any chances on what our son was learning from the way African American boys in his class were being treated.

Volunteering at the school

While we're on the topic of culture, a few words about the parent/administration culture are also in order. When my stepchildren were at Hillside, my husband had been very involved. From cleaning up the yard to sitting on the board, he had enjoyed volunteering at the school. It was of course required that we continue volunteering, so in keeping with my background and what I thought I had to offer, I joined the development committee.

The school now had a full time development director and a full time development assistant. (The calculator in my fundraising and development mind was busy making additions and subtractions.) A committee of professionals with an obligation to do grunt work is any development director's dream. (When I told a development director friend about it she nearly gagged with envy.) After meeting a few times one of my fellow committee members gently put a question to the director, "So far we have had annual fundraising drive meetings. When will we get to development?" Well, by the time I left the school, after many a cancelled meeting the first year and no meetings in the second, we still had not gotten around to having a development meeting.

At some point during a meeting I made a suggestion for a new fundraising opportunity for the preschool. It would have been one for which I myself would have put in the bulk of the work. Committee members asked me to run it by the preschool teachers. When I did that the teachers said that they would discuss it and get back to me. I waited and waited, and then I dropped the idea.

The marketing committee, on the other hand, was thriving. In a school with hundreds of applicants for each opening there hardly seemed need for marketing—but then again, I am the clueless sort. A number of marketing and branding "specialists" among the parents—many of them moms whose career ambitions had been interrupted by their devotion to their children—got working toward redefining the school. (Incidentally, the committee was headed by one of the mothers who also kept busy getting rid of kids in the preschool.) The idea was that our school should claim its place among the top elite private schools in town. No more touchy-feely, happy-child hippie-teacher associations here. The crowning achievement of the marketing committee was a new school logo. The old logo showing two happy—and multi-racial—children was replaced by a cluster of abstract and "scientific" looking doodles. No problem. Things change. But sometimes change reflects an unadmitted shift in values.

So it appeared that volunteer work, for people like me at least, was limited to yard and carpool duty.

Damage control: the principal defuses the situation

Within a week of the Wednesday morning talk with Jack's teacher we decided to pull him out by winter break, the end of the following week. It was clear—interestingly, sooner to my husband who had had prior experience with the school than to me—that even though we did not have a lot of information about exactly what was happening in the school, there was something systemically wrong. My husband wrote an email to the principal informing him of our decision, saying that we would follow up by explaining things in a letter. Of course the principal wanted to talk. "After the talk," he gently suggested, "you may not feel like you need to write a letter." (Written words get circulated, you see.)

At our meeting, seasoned professional that he was, the principal let us vent to our heart's content. We told him everything I have written here that was known to me at that time. He listened in great sympathy and concern. At the end, he said that there were of course things he could say in defense of his teachers but since it appeared that we had made up our mind to leave the school there didn't seem to be any need for it. During the conversation, however, he discreetly asked one question.

When I mentioned that I sensed a strange parent culture at the school and that it seemed that undue pressure was put on the teachers by some parents, he asked if I had heard anything or if it was only a feeling. At the time I had not heard what I subsequently learned from more informed mothers, so I told him it was only an intuition. He seemed relieved by that.

He also mentioned that there was a rumor circulating that the school was expelling Jack. (How the rumor had started when even the people to whom we were close at the school had not yet heard, I will never know.) He asked if we could help dispel the rumor by telling people that it was not so, that we were leaving voluntarily. I suppose there was a reason for this technical preference but, not belonging to the gossip circle, I couldn't guess.

Finally the principal asked if we had any suggestions for improvement. The only suggestion that occurred to me was to make the classroom more joyful and inclusive so children would enjoy themselves more and not feel so much on the edge. A less punitive environment would also send a different message to parents and would make the climate less conducive to picking on kids and harassing teachers.

We left it at that.

We decided not to write an open letter for a number of reasons. First, the experience had been so injurious to us that all we wanted to do was to leave it behind. The last thing we wanted was to drag out an unpleasant exchange with all kinds of unpleasant people. Second, we did not feel that the privileged and educated parents at the school needed us to stand up for what their children deserved, and what they paid for. Finally, and most importantly, we did not want any fallout of the situation to affect Jack. We just wanted him out. Period.

Christmas party from hell

The last day of school for Jack was the day of the Christmas party, with many parents present. It was an eye-opening, if dreadfully unpleasant, experience. Up until that time my unhappiness was with the teachers. While I had some misgivings about some parents I did not suspect anything.

At that point many of the parents—new ones, or those, like myself, outside of the gossip loop—did not know that Jack was not coming back after the break. All was normal with them. Of the parents who had heard, many were concerned and were quite supportive and friendly. But, to my great surprise, there were a number of parents who pointedly avoided me. People I was in the habit of greeting pleasantly twice a day for the last year and a half would not even make eye contact with me. That's when I started to get the feeling that perhaps there was more to the story than met the eye.

During the party, I, like most other parents, sat on the periphery of the classroom. The children sat at their desks in the middle of the room. Here and there some parent sat with a younger kid. Neil, flanked by both his parents, sat two rows in front of Jack. Jack, for whom there had been a "closure" ceremony at circle time earlier, was well aware that he would not be going to school with, or even seeing, Neil any more. He so wanted to be with him that day. He kept calling out his name, trying to get his attention. Neil's parents sat on little chairs with their backs unyieldingly turned to Jack, blocking Neil's view and movements. When a couple of upper-class kids came in dressed as elves and distributed tangerines, they by chance missed Neil. Jack yelled out loud above the Christmas music and the chatter: "You forgot Neil." Everyone turned back, smiling, to see where this comradely outburst had come from. Neil's parents did not budge.

It might have been my imagination, but I think the teachers were making more of an effort than usual to be lively and playful that day. I think the children were allowed to sing their songs in louder voices than the customary hushed tones. But at that point all I wanted was to get my son and myself away from a hostile environment.

So what in the world was going on...?

The truth is that we still don't know what exactly was going on. We're also resigned to the fact that we'll never know. Perhaps the only people who know are the teachers and the principal, and it certainly is not in their interest to talk. Telling the truth about what really happened would only incriminate them. In fact, as I mentioned to the principal, I was worried about repercussions to the preschool teacher who had inadvertently given us some information.

We never had a discussion with the teachers. We had seen and heard enough to know that an honest discussion would not be possible. The more we looked at the situation the more we saw that to protect themselves the teachers had no choice but to give excuses for their strangely unprofessional behavior. We also knew that when push came to shove they would not hesitate to blame and label Jack some more. Frankly, at that point both my husband and I felt that if anybody said another bad thing about our kid we would commit a capital crime. Our tolerance for blather was also an all-time low.

The only speculation I would venture now is that the teachers did indeed want to nip certain behaviors in the bud in Jack's group. They had had a hard time with the older group of boys and did not want another group of rambunctious boys coming up. Perhaps they were trying to make an example of Jack (and possibly Thomas and Miles). Sensing this punitive attitude of the teachers, some mothers had stepped in to push the situation to extremes that would result in the expulsion of the kids to whom they had taken a dislike.

At any rate, for whatever reason, the teachers and the principal seemed to have lost control of the classroom. I don't know what went wrong for whom, how, or when. All I know is that things do not go so wrong in a classroom unless there are some fundamental problems with the school.

I also know that there is nothing wrong with any of the children in classroom Q. To place blame on children is the height of professional ineptitude.

The price our son has paid for this ineptitude, however, is still a source of anger and sadness for us. As Jack shares more details of how he was treated we try to explain to him that that is not the way teachers should behave. When he hears us talking about finding a new school he sometimes gets a guilty look on his face like he has somehow let us down. We have to keep reassuring him that even if he sometimes did the wrong things at Hillside it was not he who has made us upset and angry.

What is particularly heartbreaking is the sadness that overcomes Jack when he is reminded of Hillside. Children form strong attachments. He misses the songs they sang, the playground he had made his own, eating lunch with his class. He mostly of course misses his friends. We cannot arrange play dates with everyone—and Neil, of course, is beyond reach. It is very troubling for us to watch the shadow of questions on his face that he cannot articulate. He cannot quite understand why he was the one to have to leave the school. He never asks why he is not to see Neil again. Listening to us tell him that he did nothing wrong, I can see on his face a question for which I have no answer: "So if there was nothing wrong with the way I was, then why was I the one who ended up being punished?"

Classroom Q as of this writing

By now all parents in the class know that we have left. I have since talked to a number of them who are puzzled about why Jack was singled out for disciplinary measures and concerned for their own kids. Many have reservations about the teachers' ability to handle the kids (especially the boys) and are underwhelmed with the kids' "academic" progress (the symbolism of the new logo's "scientific" doodles notwithstanding). Many are disgruntled and feel isolated. The parent-teacher conference is an unpleasant experience they dread. And of course more kids (boys, need I mention?) are now turning into "problem" children who perhaps need to be held back one year (an all too frequent occurrence at Hillside).

Most importantly, I have learned that Miles will be leaving at the end of the year. The parents of another boy from the group are actively looking for another school for him for next year—they are concerned that he is slotted to be held back a year. With Jack, that makes three boys out of a group of seven. Last year, out of our group of twelve, four children left the school.

I am relieved to know that many children, from different groups, miss Jack and are not too traumatized to invite him to their birthday parties. Our friendship with a few families from the school continues and information keeps trickling in. (The other day, I ran into James and his mother. James wanted to know why Jack was not going to his school any more. I told him that Jack had not been happy. "I know," he said. "He was always hiding from the teachers.")

One recurring question among the parents I have talked to is: "Why don't the teachers ever have anything good to say to us about our kids?" Perhaps a search for an answer to this question could answer many others.

A final word of contrast

Things luckily came to a head for us in time not to miss application deadlines for schools for next year. (I still fume when I think of what Thomas's parents went through.) Meanwhile we were also lucky that Jack's old preschool had opened a new location and had space to take him. The contrast between the two schools is instructive.

The first month of our return to the old school I mainly

just basked in the soothing effect it was having on our entire family. Jack was calming down. The children at the school were happy and did not have cliques. The teachers were engaged and attentive, but also relaxed and playful. The parents were not scheming against each other or the kids. They did not hover protectively over their children, but hung out and chatted. At the end of the day younger and older siblings, some of them former students, milled happily about. Jack was allowed time and leeway to make his way into the new routine and the new group.

After the initial pleasure of joining a happy and healthy environment I started comparing the progress of the kids at the two schools. While at Hillside the focus was on endless repetition of Montessori tasks, here the preschoolers were going through a kindergarten curriculum with plenty of time left for free play. In addition to regular dance, music, tumbling, yoga, and tae kwon do classes the kids did plenty of writing, science and art projects. There were regular field trips to museums. The teachers noted each child's strengths, weaknesses, and progress. Heck, after a long day of work, they even found the energy to play tag with a bunch of rambunctious boys cooped up inside on a rainy day.

One teacher out of the blue one day said to me: "It is a pleasure to work with Jack." I could have kissed her hands for that. Not that I think working with my kid, or any kid, is a pleasure every moment of the day—not by a long shot! The comment said more about the teacher, and the school, than about my son. It explained why now Jack not only does not avoid teachers but actively engages with them. One afternoon I watched as he and a teacher had a long talk about some problem. She talked. He talked. Then they arrived at an understanding. The teachers gently but actively worked on undoing the harm done to Jack at Hillside school. But they did not make an issue of it.

Jack now routinely comes home and talks about what

he learned that day from which teacher. I see that he is for the first time developing teacher/student relationships. It is a pleasure and a relief to see that his formal education has finally begun—not at a self-absorbed elite school but an intelligent preschool run by competent and kind people.

CHAPTER 2

Public School

Jack started public school in first grade. Because of his late October birthday he qualified to be in first grade before he turned six (different cut-off dates at private and public schools). Since he not had an official kindergarten year we had a choice to start him in kindergarten or put him in first grade. As we were pondering the question I asked the opinion of Chiara, the twelve year-old daughter of a friend of mine. (I am a firm believer in the insight of children.) Chiara suggested sending him to first grade. "Boys are always immature anyway," she explained.

With my husband and mother agreeing, we opted for first grade because we thought Jack was ready "academically" and he was physically bigger than most kids his age—he would have been a head taller than other kindergarteners. Socially, however, he was less mature, as Chiara had observed about boys in general. I'm still not sure whether we should have held him back one year or not, but off he went to first grade before he was six. Unfortunately there was one aspect we had not foreseen. In first grade he joined a group of kids who had already been together a year in kindergarten. Little did I know this was to be held against him in years to come.

I did not start out in public school with a point to make about the educational system. My idea was that if it is good enough that's good enough for me. I wanted to make it work because frankly I had other priorities than to micromanage my son's education. But I realized the educational system is far from "good enough." In fact there is something fundamental that is broken. And no matter how much positive attitude and support and labor I applied to it I couldn't fix it, not even as far as it applied to our own situation.

Jack stayed in public school through February of his fifth grade. The following sections describe, and sometimes they are almost real time accounts of, what happened in public school and how we came to the decision to pull him out of school. While I was happy to be involved in my son's school I had not anticipated to what degree it would take over my life.

PTA work

I mentioned that I preferred to be in public rather than private school. One reason was that since I knew I would want to be involved in my son's school no matter where he went, I much preferred to donate my time and efforts to kids and families who were not necessarily of the privileged class. The public school my son went to was located in an up-and-coming San Francisco neighborhood and had been turned around by a strong PTA before us. As a good citizen I felt it was my duty to maintain and expand the good work started by parents before me so I joined the PTA and took on various duties at different times.

I have always thought that the afterschool hours are crucial in children's lives. Reforming schools is too daunting and frustrating an undertaking anywhere, so I've always thought you can make up for the shortcomings of schools through afterschool programs. A longstanding idea of mine has been to create an environment for children where they are free to make choices based on their interests, give them some guidance, make no demands on them to prove anything to anybody, and let them have fun. I also knew that the afterschool time is often when children engage in some pretty nasty power experiments and get into trouble. I wanted to fill that time with no-pressure, fun and interesting activities that the kids themselves chose.

Our school had an afterschool "club" program that I took over. Over the years we added a lot of new activities to the basic art and drama clubs: French and German clubs, Spanish language, Italian Carnival, gardening, yoga, knitting, hula hoop, dance, chess, cooking, clay, drumming... Finding space, handling registration (managing fair wait-lists!), hiring club teachers (sometimes out of my own pocket), providing supplies (I made a large purchase of drums for the drumming club) and any number of questions of coordination, supervision and logistics consumed a lot of my time—twice a year, in Fall and Spring. But I really enjoyed it and, watching the kids get into activities, or even sometimes do some club-hopping, I felt deeply rewarded. Unfortunately after we quit school the club program took a nose dive.

The Website: Mothers of Bad Boys

The activity that I did not expect myself to become so involved in was trying to understand and make positive changes in the situation of boys in schools. My experience at the private school had alerted me to a certain intolerance for boys in school settings and the tendency to label them. When Jack's troubles began in second grade of public school I found myself spending more and more time in school and talking to other mothers. While I was trying to improve the situation for my son I realized boys and their mothers need a bit of advocacy if they are to thrive in various hostile environments. My website, *MothersOfBadBoys.com,* was born of this realization.

I will tell the story of the website in more detail in the following chapters. But from the time that the idea of the website occurred to me in second grade to when Jack quit school in fifth, I realized advocating for my kid was not enough. I had to save him. While I continued with the website for a couple more years, I came to the sad realization that in a dog-eat-dog world sometimes you are forced to resort to the every-man-for-himself strategy. Nevertheless, perhaps not all is lost on the advocacy front.

We did make some good friends in public school. I was sad to observe that we would probably drift away after leaving. But then again the ball was in the kids' court. It would be up to them to make their own choices and learn the stamina of loyalty.

I designed the MoBB website as a multi-media, interactive site. It enjoyed modest success but developed a loyal following from many countries. When I was no longer able to run the site I did not take it down. The website is still live although not updated after 2012. To help you envision it, here is the site's structure.

The underlined parts are published in whole or part in this book. Because of copyright issues I have only reproduced my own writing or pieces submitted by friends who have given me their permission.

Blogs
   Clara's Clearing (my own day-to-day blogs)
   Educating My Boy (my blog on homeschooling)
   MoBB Times (contributions by readers)
   The OMM (One Mad Mom) Club (contributions by readers)
   Manners and Morals (contributions by other writers)

In the News
   News items pertaining to children, with links to sources

In the Arts
   YouTube and other clips by or about boys in the arts

What's Out There
   Random, boy-related clips on YouTube

Editor's Choice
   Cool books for, by, and about boys

From the Editor
   Editorials by Clara

Gallery
   Art work by boys

Resources
   Books, websites, organizations

Advocacy
   Contribution by readers

Letters
   Sample of letters to the editor

MoBB Times

The main page of the website was *MoBB Times* to which readers contributed and where I excerpted and linked to articles in other sites. I can't reprint all that here but there was one part that was particularly dear to my heart. At each update the page was headed with a quote from a kid. I collected quotes from kids I encountered here and there, boys and girls. I love these because they reflect the everyday wisdom of kids, a reminder that if we want to understand children we should listen to them.

Kids' Quotes

Overheard in the park:

> Mom, asking her toddler pulling a little frog in his wagon: "What do you want to do with the froggie, honey?"
> Boy: "Hurt him. I wanna hurt the fwoggie."

Overheard on the playground:

> "Freedom rules. School sucks."

> "Long live happiness. Long die badness."

> Boy 1: "Girls get on my nerves. I've got 17 of them on me every day."
> Boy 2: "I've got more than that—18 or more."

Overheard at the zoo:

> Little sister instructing other children: "Look but don't touch."
> Big brother, sarcastically: "She knows all the rules."

"I believe in Mother God who created nature and is nature." —Jack, 5

"Falling asleep feels like a soft shock. It feels like somebody gently lifting you up like an art project." —Leo, 6

"I like girls who are not tomboys—the other kind." —Nigel, 6

Mom: "Stop dawdling. Hurry up and get your homework over with." Boy: "But I don't want to get it over with. I want to enjoy it." —Jack, 6

"Boys are noisy because they like to be seen and they like to torture people." —Omar, 7

"Boys like to fight because if someone wants to fight us we fight back and we like to keep our clothes clean." —Omar, 8

"Boys, when they lose, they get mad." —Jesus, 8

"Sometimes boys can't concentrate because some people tell them what to do and they have a lot on their minds." —Diego, 8

"Boys are smart but sometimes they act dumb because they think homework is boring." —Isaac, 8

"When I saw you the first time, I knew I could trust you. I knew mom equals good." —Neil, 8, to his mother

"What I liked best about the movie Avatar was all the loud noises." —Neil, 8

"I'd like to learn a couple of hard things a week and be free the rest of the time." —Jack, 8

"Camden is mean to everyone, that's why he's popular."
—Kristen, 9

"I have a photographic memory so it feels like I'm cheating on spelling tests." —Jack, 9

"Boys are either happy or mad. But girls are difficult. It's hard to know them. They have a lot of different feelings."
—Ben, 10

"People should sue the guy who invented homework."
—Neil, 10

"Boys like to do things that make them sweat. Like sports."
—Keely, 10

"You know how you can make boys follow you? Just ignore them and walk away. Then they will run after you."
—Emma, 10

"Every boy is different. I like to play with boys if they're nice. Boys can be nice but some get mad too fast."
—Miguel, 10

"I don't like reading because I do understand the words but I can't make a movie of it in my head." —Chris, 10

"It's better being a girl because boys are not allowed to bully girls." —Ben, 10

"ADHD isn't real. It's just that the work's so boring and easy that kids don't care." —Ben, 10

"Being distracted helps me learn. It makes me rush which makes me have to do it." —Ben, 10

"The way to keep your new year's resolution is by having your mom and dad make you." —Ben, 10

On when boys become men: "Boys become men when they can drive, smoke and drink. Well, I forgot one thing, and that is when they are civilized." What is being civilized? "Being civilized means to make the right choices." —Jack, 10

On why it takes him a long time to fall asleep: "It takes a long time to choose a nice thing to dream about." What are you going to dream about tonight? "I don't know. My brain chooses it. It's always a surprise." —Jack, 10

On pink camouflage clothes: "These clothes are for fighting in tulip gardens." —Jack, 10

"I'll never be able to sing like Bob Dylan. He creates so much excitement. I could never do that." —Jack, 10

"When you're born you're like an engine: *vroom, vroom, vrooooom*... Then when you're bullied you're turned into a damaged engine: *vrom, vrom, vr...* And when you're bullied all your life you're a broken engine: *vre... vre... er...*"—Jack, 11

"The past is an ox driver that is beating the future." —Leo, 11

To mom: "Everybody creates their own individual God who is out to get them. You are my God." —Jack, 12

"Bullies create 'common enemies' so that people will unite with them against these 'enemies.' That's why they seem to have so many friends so often." —Tyler, 19

The Launch: Why Boys, Why Bad, Why Mothers?

Here is the first editorial I wrote, introducing the site.

Why this site?

This site grew out of one mother's efforts to raise a boy semi decently. I will talk about my personal story in the blog *Clara's Clearing*. But here are some general reasons why I started Mothers of Bad Boys.

Why "Boys"?

There is a great deal of statistics that show boys are not having an easy time growing up. Any quick research will reveal this. Boys are lagging behind in schools, getting punished more, dropping out, getting diagnosed or labeled with outlandish disorders, and generally "getting into trouble."

What I find difficult is to distinguish between real problems affecting boys and our frustration at boys for not fulfilling our expectations. Clearly a number of disorders are on the rise. Autism, for instance, is alarmingly prevalent, and more so in boys. The growing instances of extreme forms of what is called ADD or ADHD cannot be denied. Getting to the bottom of what is causing these "disorders" is certainly crucial. But it is equally important for us "normal" adults to take a look at ourselves. I especially think it is important to look at what we expect of boys.

It has become increasingly difficult to separate the reasonable and unreasonable expectations we have come to have of boys. The confusion of parents, educators, and society at large over what is "normal" and "healthy" for boys, has certainly transferred itself to boys. But instead of labeling ourselves, we are labeling them. My first hope for this site is to help us understand boys a little better.

Why "Bad"?

When I first mention the name of this website to people they either chuckle and say "Yes!" or they are a little shocked. "Boys are not bad," they say.

Exactly.

It has been my experience that while it is unusual for anyone to openly use the word "bad" to describe boys, we do not hesitate to treat them as such. It is by actually using this word that we can clearly see how absurd it is to call any child "bad." Sometimes a little plain speaking can do wonders. For one thing, it might save us from well-intentioned hypocrisy.

Bad is a perfectly good word. It has been around for a long time and it cannot be willed away by replacing it with euphemisms. If we think our kids don't see right through substitute words like "inappropriate" or "different" (wink wink, nudge nudge) we're kidding ourselves. All we need to do is to listen to the words the kids use themselves. Recently my son blamed something bad he had done on another boy because the other kid "is a bad boy." I am sure my son had not heard anyone actually calling the other boy bad; he had just picked up on the unspoken consensus.

Some euphemisms are actually dangerous. I increasingly hear the words "at risk" applied to boys. Most of the time, if you ask the person who uses this phrase, "At risk of what?" they don't have an answer. Their "knowledge" ends right there. But there are those who do have an answer and the answer is yet another label: starting with learning disability, ADD, ADHD, defiance disorder, etc., and leading up to more criminally charged labels as boys grow older.

Now, I am not denying that all kinds of physiological disorders are affecting children in general, and boys in particular. I really don't know. The question is, are we absolutely sure that we are not attributing "disorder" today to what in the past was simply called "bad behavior"?

Another reason that we should look at the word "bad" closely is because boys are quite obsessed with it themselves. Aren't they always either fighting "bad guys" or impersonating them? Isn't the battle of good versus evil an almost constant motif in the stories that most appeal to boys? Just look at the billions of dollars that entertainment industries are making packaging and repackaging "bad": Darth Vader, Voldemort, the Joker, the Shredder, and on and on. If children could articulate it they would probably point out how ridiculous our effort to banish the word "bad" is—how, shall we say, *childish* it is.

(If you think about it, facing the word "bad" makes us face our own worst fears, both rational and irrational. But let our boys start their own Sons of Bad Mothers website and explore that one!)

The most interesting thing about using the word "bad" is that it seems to have a very good outcome. It evokes contrariness in people: "Boys are NOT bad," they retort indignantly. And then all the good things they have to say of boys flow out of them: Boys are funny, imaginative, and affectionate. Their energy is electrifying and awesome. They are hypersensitive to fairness, courage, and honor. They are very smart.

Aha... mission accomplished!

Could it be that we have slowly become accustomed to attributing negative things to boys? (I don't need to remind you that automatically attributing negative qualities to any population group is called prejudice.) So let's try to remember all the good qualities that boys have as we look into what makes life difficult for them—and for us.

Why "Mothers"?

Let's face it, in the overwhelming majority of cases mothers are the ones who are held responsible for their children. We are the ones who field complaints from kids and adults alike. We get calls from schools. We are required to discipline kids at home. We are even expected to somehow, miraculously, control our kids' behavior when we're not present. We are offered "training"—which inevitably requires that we never get upset, behave with utmost equanimity at all times, and know exactly what to do. And, of course, we are the ones who get blamed—not the least by our own kids when they grow up and find themselves psychotherapists who indulge the very self-centeredness that society blames mother for not curbing in them. Multiple whammies is our lot.

The truth is that our boys push our limits as they experiment with pushing their own and, later, others' limits. We don't like our patience tested so often. We do get tired of dealing with the consequences of our boys' transgressions. We are frequently embarrassed by them. But worst of all, we worry. We worry that our boys will be mistreated and labeled. We worry that funny childhood pranks will develop into unfunny juvenile delinquency, or will be pushed in that direction by our reactions. We see how much depends on the resources of individual boys' families and the privileges of their communities. We tremble at the thought of the brutality that may someday claim our boys as victims, perpetrators, or both.

And what exactly do mothers want?

We want our boys to be free spirits and civilized people. We want them to be bold and kind. We want them to know their potential and learn what to do with it. We want them to appreciate good things, get serious, and have fun. We want to be good mothers to our sons—and we want to have a life too.

Apart from the above, on a practical level, it makes sense to perceive mothers as a sort of coordinator between the various influences at work on kids, a kind of relationship/information hub. Whether or not we think this is good or fair or politically correct, I think it would be productive to assume that this is how it is for now, and see how we can work with it to the best advantage for our kids and for ourselves.

Where do fathers fit in the picture?

That is the question!

I will not attempt to answer this question. I will invite—no, *challenge*—men to use this site to voice their thoughts, qualms, and insights. They are the ones who have firsthand experience of being boys, if not bad boys. I suspect it is ultimately up to them to snatch boyhood from the clutches of its present crisis mode.

I would invite—no, *challenge*—men to do one thing here: Speak as men. Don't worry about what you *ought* to be saying or what you think women want to hear. I know very well how overpoweringly and, yes, oppressively women can behave toward men. I think we might be the more verbal of the species (and we use this as our only weapon of domination) but that's no reason for you to pout.

Please speak up, gentlemen. It is for your boys' sakes—and it is liberating (believe me, we've been there done that!).

The Main Blog: Clara's Clearing

It is a truth universally acknowledged that boys
behave badly.

Observations, thoughts, encounters, happenstance...

I called my own regular blog *Clara's Clearing* because I wanted
to have a space, a clearing, to look at what was happening
day by day and to keep a record of what was happening with
Jack. What I didn't anticipate is how much I would radically
change over the course of the blogs!

I wrote the first parts of the blogs (from second through
fourth grade) when Jack was in fifth grade. From fifth grade
on I wrote as things developed, somewhat in real-time.

The Making of a Bad Boy, Part I: The second grade nightmare

This website grew out of a very bad year we had in second grade. It was that year that I learned that typical boy
behavior can gain the unspoken label of Bad Boy for many
boys. As I write Jack is in fifth grade and I have the benefit
of hindsight in relating these stories.

Our second grade nightmare started early in the school
year. It was still September when my son's teacher told me
that she was worried that he would not make it to third
grade.

This relatively young teacher was new to our school but
in the couple of years that she had been there she was well
liked. I had heard many good things about her and looked
forward to a year with her. I did my usual duty of offering to volunteer in the classroom and was happy to follow
her lead on that. In short, I started the year well-disposed
toward this teacher and quite upbeat, so when she commented that Jack might not make it to third grade I was a

little confused. Make it to third grade...?! This is a public school; practically everybody goes up to the next grade. What does this mean? I wondered—but I attributed the comment to her lack of experience and did my best to keep my attitude positive.

But this September comment was just the beginning and things only got worse as the year went on. By Halloween I was getting alarmed. On that day there was pumpkin carving during class and I volunteered to help. The teacher, let's call her Ann, had divided the children into groups of five or six with a parent volunteer at each table. My son and another girl, however, were put at one table by themselves, with me as the adult supervisor. Now, this girl, we all knew, was from a very difficult background and was consequently not an easy child. When my son was assigned at the same table alone with her I suspected that the two of them were now officially the "untouchables" of the class. And putting me in charge of them seemed to be giving me the message, "Nobody wants these children. You deal with them."

Shortly after that day the calls home started. Practically every day there would be a call from Ann, often a message on the answering machine. It looked like there was nothing that my son was doing that was not objectionable. There were frequently vague comments like "Jack made the wrong choices today" or "Jack was disrespectful to his classmates today." One that I found particularly ridiculous was: "Jack took his classmates' learning away today." There were minor infractions such as "Jack made faces at his friends" and more serious-sounding ones such as "Jack stole money today."

The messages started to feel like a kind of harassment. I felt that Ann was harassing me so that I would harass Jack, so after a while I stopped asking him what had happened. At any rate, the accusations were silly and the worst of them, about stealing money, turned out not to be entirely accurate. As Jack and the boy whose money was "stolen" explained to me, Jack had found a dollar bill on the floor and instead of turning it in to the teacher he had pocketed it.

At a meeting that Ann requested to have with me she told me that Jack had used inappropriate language. "I'm concerned about the values he's learning at home," she said. "Do you use sexually explicit language with him at home?" I wonder if she really thought that according to our family values it was OK for our kid to use profanity and steal. (Later I heard through the grapevine that a more experienced teacher had given Ann the advice that it was not her place to make comments about people's "values.")

By Christmas I was told that my son was "disrespectful to girls" and had called two girls names. I made him write apology cards to the children and buy them little presents from his allowance. But when I asked the mothers of the girls about the incident they knew nothing about it and said that their daughters liked Jack and kept his presents as favorite keepsakes.

Sexism was not the only charge against Jack. He was also accused of being racist when he spat at another child. "I'm very sensitive about civil rights issues," Ann said, reporting the incident to me. When I checked with the yard staff they told me that there was a lot of random spitting going on during recess and nobody was singled out for spitting or being spat at. The most outrageously ignorant comment, however, was when Ann suggested that I have Jack tested for Asperger's Syndrome. Now, anybody with the most elementary familiarity with autism spectrum disorders would be very hesitant to throw such diagnoses around. I mean, I have seen people calling kids "hyper" or even "ADD" but Asperger's? I figured that to Ann that was just another label accusing Jack and our family of something—anything: we were sexist, racist, defensive about developmental "issues," and had bad family values. These all seemed pretty much of the same order to her.

Meanwhile I was volunteering in the classroom as a reader. Ann's rule was for the reader to bring in her own reading material and read to the children in a circle. As it turns out, if there's one thing I'm good at it is reading. I know about books and read with a bit of drama to make it interesting to children. I brought in interesting stories from different countries and discussed them with the children. Kids love to express their thoughts and opinions so I gave them plenty of opportunity to do that. In fact that's why I like to read to kids. I love to hear what they have to say. They can be pretty insightful and are often very funny.

The highlight of my reading sessions was when I brought in T. S. Eliot's "Old Possum's Book of Practical Cats." The kids did some grumbling at first—they were not accustomed to being challenged—but with some explanation and a little gentle persistence on my part they soon got into it. I explained the character of each cat and the general plot and made sure they understood each line. Yelling out the refrain together was especially fun: *"Macavity's not there...!"*

I noticed that during my reading Ann sat far away from the circle and shot me poisonous glances. I ignored them. The kids were enjoying the readings and I believed that what I was doing was good education for them. The teacher's aide often commented on how much she enjoyed my reading too. The last book I brought in was "People" by Peter Spier. This is a sensitively written and wonderfully illustrated classic about all kinds of people: not just people from different cultures, but rich and poor people, people with different interests, professions, attitudes, etc. I never got to finish this book. Ann started making excuses to put off my reading sessions and finally cancelled them altogether. She said the librarian was going to read to the class from then on. After that, the time I spent in the classroom was practically eliminated.

Ann made a lot of mistakes—I won't really get into that. But one of her most basic ones was that she seemed oblivious to the fact that people talk to each other. She should have known that I would of course try to verify her accusations against Jack with others, the way I did with the mothers of the two girls and the yard staff. She should have guessed that perhaps sometimes people would report things to me on their own. She just seemed strangely unaware that others were observing her. Here are some of the things that other teachers and staff told me about her.

At one point Ann told me that one of the other teachers had said that Jack was aggressive and had behavior problems. When I talked to that teacher she did not know what I was talking about. In fact she was shocked and said she would look into it. A few days later she called me to say that she was concerned that Ann had difficulty handling kids and that Jack was not the only child she was having problems with. This was confirmed by another teacher.

Another time, one of Jack's extracurricular teachers told me that after an inappropriate touching incident during her period Ann had called her to find out if Jack had been the culprit. This teacher was disturbed by Ann's call and felt alarmed enough to report it to me. She said the incident had not even occurred during the period of Jack's class.

All through the year Ann insisted on, as she put it, putting things "on record." She said of our interim principal that year—someone she vigorously fought not to have permanently hired—that the good thing about him was that he liked to put things on record. "But don't worry," she said to me, "in elementary school all these records get thrown away." Rather bizarre, I thought!

There were other incidents that are too elaborate to include here; maybe I'll blog about them in the future. But to make a long story short, Ann had certainly taken a dislike to Jack and our family and she harangued and harassed us the entire year.

The Making of a Bad Boy, Part II: A background

So what kind of a kid is Jack?

Let's go back to first grade, the first year that he was in a real classroom setting. Jack did not take to the structure of the classroom. He talked, he sang, he did not sit still, he pushed boundaries with other kids, he did not stick to rules—in short, he engaged in a lot of typical boy behavior. What didn't help was the fact that he was almost the youngest in the class and could easily have started first grade the following year. We decided to put him in first grade not just because he was ready academically but because he was physically big for his age and holding him back would have made him a head taller than the rest of the kids. So we took a deep breath and sent him to first grade. To sum it up I'd say his social skills were not as developed as his intellectual skills and his physique, which, again, is a typical developmental pattern with boys.

At home too Jack liked to push limits. He was always testing to see how far he could go and what he could get away with. As a baby he liked to push against me to reach for things. Later, his toddler contrariness did not entirely go away. By four it turned into resistance. He resisted bath time, resisted getting dressed, resisted going out and resisted staying home, even at times resisted doing what he himself wanted to do, just for good measure. He was also very independent-minded and liked to take matters into his own hands. If he felt wronged, for instance, he would take on an older, bigger kid himself instead of going to an adult for help. He was attracted to butting heads and testing his strength with other boys. He wrestled, threw karate chops, fought with light sabers, and fired imaginary guns. Once I saw a T-shirt on a little boy that read "Too many bad guys. Too little time." That's just what Jack was up to.

Another personality trait of Jack is that that he does not like to repeat things. Even when he was very young he lost interest in games and puzzles after he figured them out once. Making him repeat things is still like pulling teeth. When he learns to do something he considers it done and does not like to repeat it or demonstrate his knowledge or ability. So in first grade, once he copied a word or learned an addition or subtraction, he was done with it. He resisted doing it again tooth and nail. Being in a classroom environment of "practice, practice, practice" was frustrating for him and consequently for the teacher.

The mother of one of the best-behaved girls in first grade told me that her daughter complained about the teacher screaming at kids. As the mother of one of the kids who drove the teacher to yell I had sympathy for both the nice, quiet children and the teacher. Teaching a classroom full of quirky, fidgety kids is certainly not easy. Goodness knows that my own patience was frequently tried with only one kid. I could only imagine how disruptive and annoying it must have been when my son, for instance, poked his neighbor or burst into song while the teacher was trying to get everyone to work. I was certainly sympathetic to the teacher and the parents of the exemplary kids in the classroom but I can't say I ever encountered any bitter complaints from anyone.

So in first grade I was aware that Jack was not adjusting to the rigors of the classroom quickly enough but I did not have serious concerns. The advice of the first grade teacher at the end of the year was for Jack to take music and drama lessons since he seemed to have an aptitude for those. The afterschool teacher suggested team sports to improve his attitude about rules and to develop more team spirit. Nevertheless, when second grade started I thought it was time for Jack to make faster progress on classroom adjustment.

During my first talk with the second grade teacher I was fully supportive of demanding more progress from Jack. I thought it was time for him to "grow up."

That was my mistake—on two accounts. First, at age six and seven a kid still has an awfully long way to go before "growing up." Growing up does not happen on demand or from one moment, or one year, to the next—how did I make such a stupid presumption? I have also learned the truth of the assertion that the challenges that kids encounter—and create—grow with them. There is no such thing as a parenting-made-easy blueprint and it is just wishful silliness to expect that one happy day you can just put parenting on cruise-control and be done with it.

Second, I probably gave the wrong impression to the teacher. I come from a family of educators and grew up with a great deal of respect for the teaching profession and teachers themselves. But I think it was a mistake to give my full support to the second grade teacher before I knew her. I think I inadvertently made Ann feel righteous in adopting a "nip it in the bud" approach to what she saw as Jack's "bad" classroom behavior. I will never know what she really thought but perhaps to Jack I gave the message that I was "on the teacher's side." And when for whatever reason the teacher singled Jack out for blame or "discipline," he felt wronged not just by the teacher but also by me. Undoubtedly this made him act out more.

At any rate, I think Ann took my support of her as a kind of weakness in me. Perhaps she thought it was time for someone to exercise some authority and deal with Jack with an iron grip—and she took it upon herself to do that. Or perhaps it was my mistake to have cut her too much slack on account of being young and inexperienced. Given that she was not exactly unintelligent and uneducated I thought with some guidance she might learn to see what she was doing wrong. But whatever her shortcomings and my mistakes, I knew that there would be no quick and easy way of protecting Jack and coping with the situation.

The Making of a Bad Boy, Part III: What I did

Looking back on second grade one thing particularly stands out in my mind: While Jack hardly ever said anything bad about his teacher, *she* never had nothing good to say about him. It was very difficult for me to find out from Jack how he was being treated. I think that was partly because of the independent streak in him that made him want to take matters in his own hands and partly because he probably saw me as taking the teacher's side too much. I was definitely guilty of that; now I think I should have taken any even slight complaint that he made more seriously.

There was also the possibility that for all her negative comments to me Ann was not overtly nasty to Jack. She did have a degree of professionalism. In fact, many parents liked her very much (although I have gathered over the years that her popularity has diminished). The mother of a very bright and well-behaved classmate of Jack—the kind of kid who is the dream of every teacher—could hardly believe what I was telling her about Ann. My experience was so different from hers. So the fact that Ann had two very different sides contributed to the complications.

As any honest mother would admit, it is very difficult to know exactly what to do at all time. It is especially hard when you have to react on a daily basis to confused and confusing allegations against a seven-year old. My first reaction was to find out what was going on between Jack and Ann—and when Jack did not seem particularly unhappy or angry, what was I supposed to conclude? Furthermore, our principal that year was an interim one who by virtue of his temporary status was not equipped to give any real assistance. The teachers never accepted him and I knew that they would not have cooperated with him even if he had wanted to help. (Ann led the faction against his permanent hiring.) I felt that I was left to my own devices and resources. I will never be sure that my way of dealing with the situation was the right one, but this is how I went about it.

My first concern, of course, was Jack. To get a seasoned perspective I started talking to a family therapist who had experience with public schools. She and I discussed every incident in detail before she met with Jack. When she met him she found him to be a typical seven year-old and grounded enough not to be terribly vulnerable. Another therapist who saw Jack more extensively also found him a "resilient" little boy. She told me that even if he was being a little extra unruly in class it was probably his way of fighting back against the teacher's dislike of him.

I talked to everyone I knew who had experience with children. One teacher said that kids tend to misbehave when they sense themselves trapped in a "hostile environment." A high school counselor said that he thought it was actually better in the long run for children to feel a sense of control by "fighting back" when they feel unfairly treated. A therapist friend told me that surrendering to a "whipped dog" attitude is the onset of depression.

As I looked more closely at what was going on and talked with others at school I became somewhat reassured that there were people who were looking out for Jack. There is only so much damage a teacher can do when a lot of people are watching her. I also began to see that I was more the object of Ann's dislike than Jack and that a lot of her attacks were directed at me. So I thought that the best coping strategy was to turn the situation into an opportunity for Jack to learn to cope with adversity and for me to inform and prepare myself to protect him in the long run.

My family therapist guided me in the direction of some excellent work about children in educational settings: Alfred Adler[1], Rudolf Dreikurs, Jane Nelsen. At her suggestion I brought Ann a copy of Nelsen's "Positive Discipline," which offers an excellent guideline for classroom

---

1   Adler's work is brilliant in analyzing the power struggles that children are part of and engage in both at home and in school. This is an overlooked aspect of relationship dynamics.

management. "I don't read these kinds of things," she said. At home we tried Nelsen's "positive approach" and started having family meetings based on her model to find solutions to classroom problems. These meetings eventually became a regular means for us to address all kinds of issues that have come up over the years.

As for coping with the school situation I had to think of ways that suited who I am and what our family is like. We are not generally the kind of people who respond in kind to hostile and ignorant behavior—that kind of response is not in keeping with our "values," the ones that Ann was so concerned about! After hearing what others had to say about Ann we had enough material to "fight" her. She said she was fond of "putting things on record"; well, we certainly had things to "put on record" on her. But what was the point of adding to the poisoned environment and creating adversarial relationships at our school? I have enough experience to know that in public school battles can become grotesquely bureaucratic and in the end accomplish very little. You can easily waste an awful lot of time and energy fighting those battles. I felt I had to find solutions that are best for Jack in the long run and reflect what I believe in as a parent.

That's when I started talking to other mothers. And, lo and behold, I learned that a lot of boys were facing similar situations. I learned that having a hard time sitting still is not unique to Jack. I learned that he is not the only boy who is always testing limits and what he can get away with. I learned that he is far from the only one to be punished by losing recess every other day. In fact, Jack's pediatrician (herself the mother of two boys) told me that she was thinking of starting a group for mothers of boys who were having a hard time in school. I took detailed notes of what was going on at school, and with a little bit of research I came across what is called "the boy crisis." I realized that boys are being punished and labeled and diagnosed with disorders at an alarming rate.

The more I looked into the "crisis" the more I thought that a lot of the psychobabble and politically-correct nonsense that is thrown around against boys just translates into calling them "bad" without actually using that word. I started joking with other mothers about our "bad boys" and came up with the idea that we should start a support group: Mothers of Bad Boys.

One day while my friend Doris and I were chatting in my kitchen Ann called. That was the call about Jack spitting at another child and her comment about "civil rights issues." As chance would have it, Doris was a public school teacher in New York City for many years and is African-American. She is from a very politically engaged family and has first-hand memories of the civil rights movement. As I reported Ann's comment to her and explained the situation, her eyes got wider and wider. "You've got to advocate for Jack," she said.

The more I learned about what was happening to boys, however, the more I felt that advocating for my son alone was not enough. My experience is that individuals usually don't get away with an attitude unless there is a greater trend supporting it. I suspected that the problem was larger than Jack's teacher and realized that to advocate most effectively I would have to look at the bigger picture. I thought the best place to start was to raise consciousness about the difficulties boys are facing. So instead of fighting Ann I decided to channel my efforts in a more positive and effective direction. Instead of creating an angry and adversarial environment at our school I decided to create a forum to promote understanding, compassion, and positive action for boys.

One lazy afternoon over a nice glass of tea at an Indian restaurant I was venting my frustrations at Jack's school situation to a friend of mine. I mentioned my joke about starting a Mothers of Bad Boys support group. The eyes of my friend JJ, the publisher of a successful interactive website, suddenly flashed. "You must start a website," he said.

And so this website came into being.

The Making of a Bad Boy, Part IV: How second grade ended

Academically speaking, the year ended well for Jack. He scored high enough on his tests that he qualified to be part of the GATE (gifted and talented education) program—although I did not find out about that until fourth grade, but more on that later. A month before school ended my father died, and though it was a very sad occasion for my son I was glad to see that he coped very well with his own sadness and the sadness of everyone around him. He was even philosophical about it. "Don't cry, mom," he consoled me, "that's how the generation of life goes."

So there was an element of "all's well that ends well" to the year and Jack himself must have noticed that life goes on above and beyond what goes on at school. But things do have repercussions. I noticed the first negative repercussion of his second grade experience when at the end of the year Jack said, "I don't think I'm ready for third grade." And there was definitely anxiety in the comment. I assured him that he was ready and he was further reassured when the test results came in. Having scored advanced in math, the subject in which he takes most pride, was especially gratifying to him. But I knew that the idea of being or not being "ready" for third grade was not coming from us. There was only one place where that self-doubt could have come from. His teacher had a whole year to plant the idea in his head since that first time she mentioned it to me in September. I can just picture her sneakily feeding the insecurity, day after day.

A second repercussion of the year was that other children noticed that Jack was somehow looked at differently by the teacher. They of course internalized it. A certain pattern was established in the way other children viewed and treated Jack. To put it in the language of the children themselves, it somehow became okay to "pick on" Jack— the teacher did it, didn't she? Just last week one of Jack's classmates came up to me and said, "It's sad that Jack got so picked on." This is three years after second grade and not only the "picking on" still goes on but the kids have a very good memory of when it started.

The third negative repercussion has everything to do with why the negative singling-out of Jack has lasted this long. By being put in a situation to have to defend himself against unclear and unfair attacks Jack developed bad habits in response to being "picked on." These knee-jerk defensive responses did not ingratiate him with his subsequent teachers, or the kids. It is not hard to see how when any small transgression of a child is met with an over-reaction of blame and punishment, he quickly learns to fight back by intensifying the transgressions. It's not hard to see that when a child sees that what he is doing is annoying someone who doesn't like him he figures that he can torment them more by doing more of it. Kids do this all the time and they often admit it too.

We can and of course do try to teach our children not to fall into a "tit for tat" habitual response to being mistreated. But who can deny that "tit for tat" is the logic that is most easily understood by children? Boys, in particular, are drawn to that simple and primitive response. It takes a lifetime to learn that there are better ways of fighting off attacks.

I will write more about subsequent years later, but before I end this blog let me make one important thing clear. I am not at all into turning my child into some poor helpless victim. First of all, Jack has a strong character and he long ago determined that he would rather fight back than be browbeaten or made to feel bad about himself. But you can't expect a seven year-old to know how best to do this. He ends up experimenting with different strategies and hopefully eventually finds out for himself that "tit for tat" only makes things worse.

Second, I don't at all encourage Jack to think that others are to blame all the time. I have always insisted on him seeing the consequences of his own reactions and to take responsibility for them. In fact, sometimes I wonder if I went too far with this. Sometimes I wonder if I should have been less tough on making him take responsibility for his actions. I think my strictness may have backfired a bit—at least for now. But I do have hopes that in the long run he will learn that the best way for never becoming a victim or a victimizer is to see your own behavior clearly and take responsibility for it.

Endnote on Ann

In later years I learned this about Ann: While the first few years that she worked at our school she was seen as a sweet-natured and dedicated teacher, she was increasingly seen as angry and always at war with one imaginary enemy or another. People noticed that she walked around with a dark cloud hanging over her head and a sour expression on her face. I think the main problem was that she did not derive any pleasure from being with children. I know that ultimately the reward of teaching is being with children and watching them grow, hopefully with some assistance from you. There are no other rewards in teaching, everyone knows that. No amount of activism is a substitute for the reward of happy and successful children. Ann must learn this, or quit teaching. The year after we left I heard that she left our school.

The lessons I learned

Difficult and painful as second grade was the experience opened my eyes to a few things and taught me some valuable lessons. Here are a few of them.

First, sooner or later...

The more I looked into the "boy crisis" the more I realized that most of us will sooner or later encounter it. Most boys, at one time or another, are either perceived as "bad" themselves or have to deal with other "bad" boys. Frequently they end up experiencing both sides. I became aware that raising a boy is a lot more complicated than solving some immediate classroom problems. I looked at the second-grade teacher, for instance, not so much as an individual but as a type that we will all encounter at one time or another. To me she personified some of the ambivalent and ignorant attitudes of society towards boys—and children in general. I saw in her many of the shortcomings that are all too prevalent in our schools. These shortcomings affect all children, boys and girls.

Second, privilege makes a big difference

I also learned of the enormously significant role privilege plays in the creation of "bad boys." In fact, the reason I was more or less successful in protecting Jack against the worst of his second grade experience was because I had the benefit of certain privileges.

1. I worked at home. This allowed me to be present and involved in my son's school and to have the time to dedicate to solving problems.

2. I had a lot of education to draw on. I have a background in developmental psychology and have been an

educator myself so I don't easily get intimidated by "professionals" or any kind of jargon they might use. Furthermore I have training in research and advocacy and I can write.

3. I had the resources to afford therapists. Their insights and experience not only supported us through bad experiences but also helped me put things in a broader context than I would have been able to alone.

4. Our school community is for the most part smart and supportive. It is a diverse environment that promotes tolerance and by and large looks out for the best interests of the children.

Ultimately what these privileges translate into is protection. The children of people like me are a lot more likely to be protected against attitudes and treatments that could easily push other kids over a certain edge.

Third, kids always pay a price

One of the most painful lessons to learn is that kids always pay a price for the stupidity of adults. I saw that even in the case of my privileged and protected son damage was done. I saw how the incompetence (and God knows what else) of his teacher did manage to plant seeds of self-doubt in my son and seeds of dislike and even prejudice in other kids and perhaps other teachers. I saw how stubbornly these seeds get embedded in people's consciousness, young and old. This is a very difficult thing for a mother to see. What makes it especially painful is to feel ourselves standing helplessly by and watching it happen.

My hope is that this website makes other mothers feel a little less helpless.

What came next in third grade

The first thing I want to say is that I am not a teacher basher. My son is in fifth grade now and has had three more teachers since Ann in second grade. While each teacher has had her own strengths and weaknesses none of them have singled Jack out for mistreatment. This had been my expectation—that even though an excellent teacher is as hard to find as an excellent anything else, teachers as a rule are not in the business of picking on students and tormenting their families.

In fact, I have learned that it is the children who pick on and torment each other. This started happening to my son in third grade, peaked in fourth grade, and, thanks to his sharp and diligent fourth grade teacher, it considerably diminished by the end of the year. Our current principal, also an observant and dedicated professional, took a serious part in curbing ganging-up and bullying trends at our school. He is the one who told me that apparently fourth grade is when this kind of behavior peaks in schools.

(This morning a fellow mother from our school, a good friend, called and described to me what was beginning to happen to her third-grade son. Oh my God! It sounded exactly like how it started with Jack.)

As for attitude of teachers, I can't help thinking that Ann—the sweet, soft-spoken, politically correct one whom everybody thought they knew—had passed on some incriminating innuendo about Jack to other teachers. It's natural. Teachers talk to each other. So I would bet that the third grade teacher already expected a "problem" in Jack. Now, most boys are already eyed with suspicion as having some kind of problem so when one comes to you already established as a "bad boy" I suppose you can't help but to over react to every deviation from absolute exemplary behavior.

Jack's third grade teacher at some point—to make it easier for him to concentrate, she said—put him at a single desk away from everybody. (The rest of the kids sat at groups of four desks.) One of the mothers who volunteered in the classroom as a reader was horrified by that and told me about it. When I talked to Jack about it he said that he liked having his own desk, especially because the desk was in a sunny spot by the window. The teacher even put a little plant on his desk to make it more pleasant. So I figured if Jack likes being alone and it doesn't look like the teacher is punishing him, there's no harm in it.

But... here we were again with Jack being singled out! This time it was not necessarily in the eyes of the teacher that he was singled out but in the eyes of the other children. He started being picked on in the yard. And of course it spread to the classroom. (This is what the mother who alerted me foresaw and I didn't.) Needless to say, Jack's reactions did not help matters. He vacillated between rejecting the kids by annoying them more and more, and trying desperately to buy their friendship by bribing them. He would even sneak his allowance money (I didn't let him take money to school) and his toys to buy temporary friendship and even protection against other kids.

Who's the bad boy now?

The bullying troubles in third grade got really bad toward the end of the year. I had written a letter to the principal about it and talked to the teacher, hoping that things would improve. A couple of mothers told me that they had had to intervene on Jack's behalf when they heard the bullies persuading other kids to join them in ganging up against him. The teachers and the principal were silent on this.

I really didn't know what to do. It was close to the end of the year, I was terribly busy finishing a book, and I was just putting band-aids on things and hoping summer vacation would save us. And I hoped for the best in fourth grade.

When fourth grade started, however, my hopes for improvement were quickly dashed. The bullying started all over again: fresh, aggressive, and spreading like wild fire.

My son was going berserk trying to defend himself. He would say things like "I'm afraid I'm going to be murdered at school." I am not exaggerating. In his 9-year old experience he feared for his life.

So what exactly was the bullying that was going on?

In our neck of the woods where physical aggression is a no-no, bullying is mostly psychological. It starts with ridicule and insult. It includes threats of violence—to the victim as well as to the children who are reluctant to join the bullying gang. In involves giving and withdrawing allegiance: "You are my friend," "You are not my friend." And of course the question of who is "cool" and who is not.

Being bullied at school is being immersed in a very nasty, poisoned, and scary environment at least six hours a day. The adults—mainly teachers and parents—are inept, absent, or part of the problem. The bullied child is bewildered and afraid. Some withdraw into themselves and become depressed and some fight back. My son is the fighting back kind. Being physically big he had no trouble taking on the boys if he had a chance (not the girls of course, even though a couple of them were instrumental in creating the gang behavior). Of course physical aggression is not tolerated but when we're not looking, kicks in the shin are indeed answered with kicks in the shin. "Taking him down" is still practiced with full primitive meaning. It's definitely much easier to defend oneself physically—if you're big enough, that is.

But psychological aggression is much harder to fight off. The main reason for this is because this kind of aggression is a social one. It involves relationships. You build relationships by hurting others and you hurt others by building relationships. And if you're picked on and turned into a victim, nobody wants to build a relationship with you—or nobody dares. You're completely alone, while the aggressors are not. If a whole group of kids attacked you physically someone would notice. But if a group of kids attacked you psychologically, it very well could completely go unnoticed by people in authority. And I suspect even if it does not go unnoticed, as most adults don't have the skills—or the backbone—to stand up to gang behavior, they would just as soon just look away.

I quickly realized how bad the situation was. I pulled Jack out of the afterschool program where things got particularly out of control. I looked into changing schools. I was not only worried about the abuse he was subjected to but the habits he was picking up. Since he couldn't take out his anger physically he had gotten into fighting back by annoying children. This is something that had started in third grade.

The more the kids isolated and rejected Jack, the more he insisted on behavior that would make him very unattractive to them. He became unruly and disruptive in class, especially whenever he had to work in a group with the kids whom he knew despised him. He distracted them when they tried to work. He did not cooperate on projects. He did not follow rules in games. The class lost a couple of recesses because of his unruliness in the classroom. The collective punishment of course made the kids dislike Jack even more. I understand why he would act up in class especially: it was safer to do so. After all, the teacher would not allow the other kids to "murder" him.

While I was frantically searching for another school— having no hope for things to change—Jack's fourth grade teacher stepped in. She made it very clear that she was NOT going to look away.

Fourth grade teacher to the rescue

My son's fourth grade teacher, Sara, was a young and energetic woman who took her work seriously. One of the first assignments she gave her students was an "I Am" composition. This was a sheet with partial sentences for the children to complete with their own thoughts and feelings. Here is my son's, his comments in italics:

> I am *Jack*
> I wonder *if I have any friends*
> I hear *people*
> I see *truth*
> I want *friends*
> I am *Jack*
> I pretend *nothing*
> I feel *gloomy*
> I touch my *throat*
> I worry *about nothing*
> I cry *about my shame*
> I am *Jack*
> I understand *nothing*
> I say *nothing*
> I dream *about murder*
> I try *to make friends*
> I hope *for a friend*
> I am *Jack*

I will leave it to your imagination how this made me feel. I will only say that I started searching for another school. Maybe I'm a bit too skeptical by nature but I just didn't have much hope for improvement at our school any more so I was not even going to start talking to the teacher, principal, etc. We had been at this school for three years and there had not been a single happy year. My son was miserable and afraid, though his already well-formed male ego would not easily admit to being afraid.

Then we had a meeting with the fourth grade teacher. Quite unlike most other school staff we had talked to over the years, Sara openly expressed her alarm and displeasure with what was going on. She was open, forthcoming, and did not speak in ambiguous generalities. She did not just "talk to the children"—she took matters in her own hands. She of course talked to the kids repeatedly, but she also talked to the parents. Most effectively, she was right on top of the kids as she saw ganging up behavior. She did not turn a deaf ear to the insults and ridicule Jack was subjected to. She caught the kids red-handed in the exclusion games they played and confronted them. And she did this over and over again—until the kids started to get the idea.

She also talked to Jack repeatedly. She pointed out to him how some of his behavior reinforced the other kids' dislike of him and how he had gotten into the habit of even provoking them. She was both kind and strict with him. She is by nature a warm-hearted person and Jack being an affectionate kid responded very well to that. He also started to get some of the ideas he needed to get—the main one being that at least some teachers cared.

I know that the principal also played a role. I will never know exactly how or what he did—confidentiality issues sometimes prevent us from knowing the best efforts of school staff. But at some point my son received an apology letter from a girl who according to her own confession "started it in third grade." This girl was not in Sara's class so I assume that it was the principal who had talked to her and her parents. Incidentally, this girl was wrong to think she had started the whole thing so the next afternoon on the playground I let her know that it was not all her fault and a lot of other kids were involved. I also had my son write a letter to her thanking her for her letter and expressing his hope that she would now stay his friend.

My instinctive first impulse for gauging how things are going with my son is to watch him closely and ask about his version of things. While I was continuing my search for a new school I started to get the feeling that he was being less miserable. Observing Sara I was also reassured that she was not loosening her grip on the situation. She really took those kids on.

I ended up abandoning the idea of leaving the school. There were many different reasons for this. First of all, as you well know, one is not able to just go and sign up for one's favorite school, public or private. Second, my natural skepticism kept me from believing that this sort of thing happened only in our school. Third, here was my kid being excluded from the group of kids he had been with a number of years already, why would I put him in a situation with a group where he was automatically an outsider? Fourth, I was seeing that a teacher who takes bullying seriously can make a difference.

But there was also another point that I felt very strongly about. I did not want my son to learn the lesson that one runs away from difficulties. My maternal instinct was telling me that while Jack was certainly suffering, he was also in a weird way engaged in taking on a whole group of kids. There was a part of him that was contributing to creating a challenge for himself. I did not want him to walk away from this challenge in a defeated retreat. I wanted him to stay and learn the lessons he needed to learn. Once I was reassured of Sara's compassion and commitment I felt he was in a safe enough situation to learn the lessons he had partially set himself up to learn.

One afternoon toward the end of the year I miraculously succeeded in getting Jack and a school friend of his to sit around the kitchen table and write an essay about themselves. This is what Jack wrote:

> I was born in 1999. I have had a very hard life. I was bullied a lot at school. I was treated like I was a soccer ball as in meaning that I was kicked around a lot but now I can relax!
>
> I think I was treated unfairly at school so I was even scared to go to school. I was scared because I thought I would be killed at school, so I put up a fuss in the morning!
>
> I wish I had a million $$! I love my life! Ya!

I immediately made copies of this essay, one for Sara and one for the principal. I figure they always hear from us when things are not going well, they should also hear it when things improve—especially when they have worked hard for it.

It's the attitude, stupid

Forgive me for being blunt but sometimes you've just got to say it the way it is.

I will never know the exact course that Sara took in turning things around for Jack—confidentiality issues again. Having been a teacher myself I can imagine that she tried many different things, was successful at some and not at others. She probably talked to other experienced folks (her mother is a teacher too so she probably gave some good advice) and she very likely improvised a good deal. I'm sure our principal supported her efforts and was active on his end too. But as I look back on this experience I think what really did the trick was Sara's unwavering attitude, her resounding NO: *Not in my classroom.*

The other day a friend, another mom at our school, called me to say that there was going to be an anti-bullying meeting the next morning. I showed up but to my frustration missed the meeting because I could not find the room where it was being held. My friend told me later that the meeting was about whether our school would qualify for district-supported anti-bullying programs. We did not qualify. It is up to our PTA to fund the program if we want it and I bet we don't have that kind of money.

On the way to this meeting I ran into another friend, father of another boy at our school, and from what he told me I realized that his son Ryan is now being targeted by bullying. I had known that over the years Ryan had been tormented by a couple of boys, one in particular. This year I heard that Ryan is going around giving money to kids to "be his friend." I had noticed him lately playing with much younger kids. Now I recognize these signs—it means that kids his own age are not playing with him. It means that the tormenting of the original couple of boys has now spread much wider.

As this man and I were talking our former PTA president walked by and joined our conversation. She told me that the school had looked into anti-bullying programs during her tenure as PTA president. They had found that these programs not only cost an arm and a leg but they are hard to choose between. Each one has an angle: gender or race or sexual orientation or God knows what else. You open up that debate and there's no end to personal agendas and competing political correctnesses—she didn't say this; it's what I surmise.

So what are we supposed to do?

What I honestly think is that spending big money for anti-bullying programs is a waste of resources. And any program—no matter how attractive it might be for adults—is completely useless if it does not engage the children themselves every step of the way: talking about what's going on, brainstorming, discussing solutions, planning, and engaging the kids themselves in carrying out the solutions. And all of this on an ongoing basis: airing of grievances, regular evaluations, tweaking of methods, and public recognition of good effort and good results. In other words, we don't need yet another top-down, authoritarian "program" to beat right and wrong into our kids' heads. In fact, could it be that children see that sort of rule-setting as a form of bullying by adults?

So what is at the heart of putting a real anti-bullying effort in practice?

Attitude.

We need to give not just the kids but our whole community—teachers, staff, families—the message that bullying is not acceptable. We don't need to specify individually every group of people against whom violence of any kind is not permitted—neither younger kids, nor girls, nor different ethnicities, nor gays, etc. etc. I think what we need is the message that whatever bullying is and whomever it is against it just simply has to stop.

Not in my classroom, not in my school, not under my watch, not among my friends, not anywhere, not anytime...

I truly believe that people of any age are quick in snapping to when they sense a very serious attitude. I think ninety-nine percent of the people, young and old, have a lot more self-control than they let on.

But we adults have to ask ourselves, how serious are *we* about this?

Zooming in on the main bully

I unfortunately don't have a lot of time these days to spend at my son's school. But every once in a while I try to hang around and listen to the kids and exchange a few words with them. One of those days while I was talking to some younger boys, one of my son's classmates of many years came up and sat with us. I was not talking about Jack but this friend suddenly turned to me with this comment: "Jack gets picked on—it's really sad. It was Terry who started it." The kids are finally talking about it.

I am not going to analyze Terry. I will just give some sketches of what he and his family were like.

We met Terry in first grade. He had been at the school the year before (the kindergarten year that Jack missed) and was already in a sort of domination struggle with another boy, Jason. My first real encounter with Terry and his family was when at Jack's birthday party Terry's father referred to Jason as "that wild beast." Over the years I got to know the "wild beast," who is indeed rambunctious and more than a little given to bullying (physically and verbally) but Terry's father's comment alarmed me. There is hope for improvement in children but adults are a different story. I learned over time not to even try to talk to Terry's family about their son's bullying. I had a feeling the school administration did not have much success in their attempts either.

In second grade, while I was still trying to improve relations between the kids, I invited Terry to go ice skating with us. He did not skate so I spent a lot of time with him on the ice, trying to make him feel comfortable and enjoy himself. While I was trying to teach him some basics, twice he wrapped his ankle around mine and pulled me down. Each time he said with a smirk, "Not much of an ice skater, are you?" I'm a perfectly adequate ice skater and not usually at a loss for words, but I just didn't know how to respond to a seven year-old deliberately tripping me and then making snide remarks. I let it pass but learned my lesson to stay clear of him.

Jack had a troubled relationship with both Terry and Jason. There were a lot of power struggles and inclusion/exclusion games that were played between them. Jack was routinely snubbed as the "new kid" even long after many newer kids joined the group. All three boys had strong personalities and Jack was both attracted and repelled by the other two. Jason's mother and I tried all we could think of to improve the situation between the two of them. But I think the only thing that we succeeded in doing was give them the message that even if they chose to engage in "alpha male" power struggles, their families were out of it.

Terry's family—his father, really—was beyond communication. Jack often reported to me how nasty his father was to Terry and that Terry was terrified of his dad. The dad was also nasty to Jack at any opportunity. School staff also discreetly expressed their frustration over this man's attitude. "Disrespect" was a word that often came up regarding both Terry and his father. His mother was sweet and submissive beyond approach.

So what is to be done in a situation like this?

In public schools, not much. If you're lucky you'll have a teacher or two who care, a principal who is supportive and not easily intimidated, understanding parents with whom you can communicate and who are a good influence on their kids, and a group of kids who are not abnormally vicious. Kids have to be guilty of almost criminal behavior before they are expelled from public schools.

And frankly, I don't believe expelling kids left and right is the answer either. What does that teach children—to "eliminate" undesirable elements? My own instinct all along has been to help my son find real solutions—and indeed, *decent* solutions—to bullies and other ignorant and hostile individuals (like teachers!) one encounters in life. That requires looking at ourselves with honesty as well. Children can be taught to do that. At any rate, I do know and believe solutions for dealing with bullies can be found. We need to have resolve.

As for us, we did have some luck with our school community. But, sad to say, you know what our greatest stroke of luck was? At the beginning of this year Terry left our school to join his brother at a private school. Things have now finally improved.

So much for solutions!

More zooming in on the bully

The fact is that when you're dealing with a real bullying situation (not just individual and sporadic bad behavior) chances are good that your child is not the only victim. The trick is to talk to the kids. I have always been successful in getting answers from kids. They do speak the truth—and they can be much wiser than we give them credit, and possibly much wiser than us.

One day, talking to a group of kids about Terry's treatment of Jack, one of the girls said, "Everyone says Terry will grow up to go to jail." When I asked why the kids think so she wasn't able to give me a coherent explanation—which is natural. She just expressed a vague feeling among the kids.

Over the years I have listened to a lot of back-seat conversations between kids as I drive them places. One of those times my son and two friends were discussing Terry. Again, they could not quite put their fingers on what was wrong with the things that Terry did. They did not feel comfortable calling him a "criminal"—which is what they said someone has to be to go to jail. One of the kids finally blurted out, "Well, he'll definitely be a frat boy." "What's a frat boy?" I asked. "Mean. Obnoxious. Drunk. Does drugs. Hurts people..." they threw in.

Now, the strange thing is that Terry had a certain allure among these same kids. When I asked about this one girl said to me, "Terry is mean to everyone; that's why he's popular." Other kids came to her help and explained that if you're not on Terry's good side then he'll really be mean to you. I believe that. But I have a feeling there is more to it than just the threat a bully poses. I think there is something attractive in being part of a strong force—for good or for bad.

I wrote in a previous blog about the "I Am" assignment that the fourth grade teacher gave her students at the beginning of the year. She posted many of the kids' responses on the bulletin board outside the classroom. She didn't post Jack's—understandably. But saddened and alarmed by Jack's responses I made a point of reading all the other kids' responses. I wrote down all the posted answers to the "I hope..." part of the assignment. Here they are:

I hope...
—to get 100% on spelling test
—to get a dog
—to get a horse
—to help the poor

—to be big
—to get an iPhone
—to rule the world
—people learn
—that tomorrow is better than today
—to be a bounty hunter
—I get good grades
—to stay a child
—my friends come to my party
—to live forever
—that I'm smart

I also noted Terry's response to "I hope": *for the US to win the war.*

Sure enough. It is attractive to be part of a strong force. Terry had learned that—but then again, so had all the other nicer kids who made him popular despite his meanness.

This is why I think we need to find better solutions for getting rid of bullying than expelling bullies. Everyone is a potential bully.

Forgive me for saying it again, but... *it's the attitude, stupid.*

A very curious thing

The more I looked into the bullying going on against my son the more complications I discovered. For one thing, I found out that many children were affected by Terry's bullying. He bullied and intimidated many. But one story I heard was particularly troubling.

Sam, the son of an Iranian woman at school, had also had problems with Terry. Sam's mother, Leila, told me that one of Sam's friends told her that Terry teased Sam by making disparaging comments about Iran. This friend said that Terry says "Iran sucks" and makes "I-ran" jokes to provoke Sam. The interesting thing is that Sam had never mentioned this to his mother. When Leila talked to him about it he said that he sometimes laughs at the "I-ran" jokes but when Terry makes fun of his mother for being Iranian he feels he has to defend her.

This was a shocking revelation to Leila who had never felt discriminated against at the school. One day as she climbed the stairs toward Sam's classroom one of his classmates spotted her, ran into the classroom and announced to a group of kids, "The bitch is here." Terry was not among this group but it was clear that the teasing of Sam and disrespect toward his mother had spread. At any rate, after a talk with the principal and the classroom teacher the Iran-related abuse seemed to cease. But we will never know what was said to whom and what steps were taken.

I could not help putting Terry's anti-Iran sentiments in the context of his "I hope the US wins the war" context. Leila and I still wonder how the kids reconcile the politics of this country with having classmates who have connections to countries with whom the US is at actual or potential war. But clearly there is unreported tension among the kids.

Another incident shed more light for me on this tension. I had volunteered to drive kids from Jack's class on a field trip. I had my son and two classmates of his in the backseat of the car. On the way back to school we drove by a Chinese immersion school where the majority of kids are of Chinese background. Kids from our school occasionally go to this school because we share an afterschool program. Passing by this school Jessica in the backseat said: "Not that I don't like Chinese kids but I don't like to go to schools where there are no American children to play with." In the rear view mirror I shot a glance at the other kid in the back seat, Carlos, a Mexican American boy, to see his reaction to this comment. He was looking straight ahead of him and his face was completely blank.

I of course objected to Jessica's comment with "They're as American as anybody," but I'm afraid Carlos learned what was to relevant him, which was the world of children in which he lived. Adults can believe whatever they want or be as politically correct as they must (and we are very politically correct in San Francisco) but kids learn their own lessons from observing the actual reality before their eyes. But I won't go into that...

In my first blog about the bullying against Jack I mentioned that there were a couple of girls who were also part of the original bullying campaign. Jessica was the main girl involved. Again, I had heard about her bullying tendencies from other mothers as well.

So here we have two kids—Terry and Jessica—who are bullies and who make comments that can only be called racist. Is this surprising?

What I think, though, is not that some kids are racist and that's why they are bullies. I think racism is a socially acceptable outlet for channeling violence, and feeling superior by seeing yourself as part of the "winning" team. It is not just that racism creates bullies. It is also that it is bullies who create racism.

This is not surprising either, is it?

So, am I sorry?

I'd say that altogether we did not have a great public school experience. In fact, if I were not by nature on the understated and stoic side I could really complain. My son is now in fifth grade and when all is said and done kids do grow up and mature. I think he's getting much better at staying out of trouble. I think he's starting to get the idea that if you are the kind of person who thrives on challenge you can choose from a whole range of challenges. Some challenges are idiotic and create problems for yourself and your family, and some challenges can make you very cool and accomplished. I think—I hope—Jack is starting to see this.

Let me give you a little more background information so I can explain myself better as to why I'm asking myself whether I'm sorry about taking Jack out of private school.

When Jack was barely four he started out at the pre-school of one of the most popular private schools in San Francisco. That was in 2003, when everybody thought their incomes and property prices were going to double every year. There was a big scramble to get into private schools and the schools were getting more arrogant and selective by the minute. I, like most first-time parents, wanted the very best for my kid at any price. So when Jack actually was accepted into the private school of our choice we were very happy.

But being an inexperienced mother was only one part of me. The other part of me, however, had other ideas. Being an older mother (I had my son in my early forties) I was rather on the margins of the culture of the other parents. Not only was I generationally different but being older and more accomplished I had a much more developed sense of self. The experienced side of me clashed with my inexperience and indeed lack of confidence as a mother. So to make a long story short, I sent my son to a private school despite my own understanding of myself. And my understanding of myself told me that I didn't like private schools.

I remember talking to a neighbor at the time and at one point she referred to herself as a "public school parent." I was envious! I wanted to call myself a public school parent too. I say all this so you get a feeling for the conflict in me and how that definitely did not give me a "good" attitude about my son's private school.

That said, though, I think my confident self was the one who was right. It wasn't just that we and the school were not "a good match." The more I have thought about it over the years the more I have come to believe that that school in particular and private schools in general—at least at that point in time—were deeply flawed. My problem with my son's school, first and foremost, was that it was a joyless and deeply conformist environment. Second, it was basically a gated community.

I'm not going to go on and on describing the oppressive atmosphere of the preschool and kindergarten where my son spent his days. Suffice it to say that at the very first Halloween party at the school I was shocked at how unspirited the event was. It really was heartbreaking to see such a hushed and brow-beaten parade of goblins and Batmans and witches and what not. I had never seen such a pathetic bunch of dressed up kids, beaten into well-behaved submission at such a young age. That event was early in the school year and I noted this lack of high spirits more and more. Later in the year one of the parents made a film about the kids for a fundraising event. From that film I got a glimpse of how lost and somber my son looked in that environment and I really did not like it.

Equally disturbing, however, were things that are more social and political in nature. From what I saw at that school I learned how deeply discriminatory private schools have become. Doing my share of volunteer work at the school and sitting on various committees I became more and more bothered by the "screening" that goes on in private school admissions.

First of all, the exorbitant tuitions—between $15,000 and $20,000 in our area in the early 2000's—conveniently weeded out all kinds of "undesirable" people. I mean, if you can't swallow that kind of tuition, you automatically don't belong to "us" kinds of folks. Of course all these schools claim that financial ability does not enter into the admission decision—but I wonder if there's anybody out there who actually believes this. So... poor and even middle class people (and certainly anybody with more than one kid) are already weeded out.

Then comes the question of "diversity." You look at any public school brochure and they make sure they casually put in some dark faces in the pictures. First of all, as if any dark face—African American, Latino, or even Indian—proves that the school does not discriminate on the basis of financial need. There are lots of darker-skinned people with money and lots of poor white families. What really bothered me, however, was listening to all the talk about "recruiting" diversity students. I really disliked the use of the word "recruit" while talking about admission policy. I mean, we never talked about "recruiting" rich white kids, did we? And anyway, why would we need to "recruit" minorities (who are not strictly speaking necessarily minority in numbers where we live!)? If our doors were really open to minorities we wouldn't be talking about "recruiting" them, would we?

The reason we talked about "recruiting" and not "accepting" was the question of screening. We didn't want just any kind of "diversity"—we wanted certain kind of "diversity" people. So exactly how "diverse" were we?

The point is that, ultimately, what makes people diverse is not skin color or income. It's the kind of people they are. My problem with the way most private schools operate is that they screen for particular *kinds* of people. They are discriminatory based on personal and cultural traits that go much deeper than skin color. They pick people who can be molded in a particular way. They value pliability and ability to conform. They like people who don't challenge and don't make trouble.

Conformity and docility are certainly not my values. And as I found out, the natural diversity in public schools has no choice but to make room for people with my kind of values. I of course also found out that battling the troubles in public schools is not pretty or easy. Even when they don't destroy you they leave their scars. Yes, if my son's public school had more money to have better yard supervision a lot of the bullying that he was subjected to would not have happened. If the school was really able to demand

better teaching from its teachers the kids would have ben-
efitted enormously. Of course this is true. And of course it
is true that private schools do have better yard supervision,
are free to kick the butt of repeat bullies, and do attract
better teachers. (I do wonder why about the latter, though.
Public school teachers are better paid and have more job
security. Could it be that teachers are also attracted to the
winning—i.e. moneyed—side?!)

So I ask myself, Am I sorry I took my kid out of private
school and put him in public?

No, I'm not!

There was something about the influence of private
schools that I just did not want on my son. And I myself
couldn't take the scene.

One balmy evening last summer I was having a chat
with the mother of one of my son's friends. We were talking about choosing middle schools. This very well-intentioned woman was trying to convince me that I should
consider sending Jack to a private school. "It's not about
you," she said, "it's about what is best for him." I didn't really feel like arguing with her at that moment—warm summer evenings are too rare for us San Franciscans for me to
want to waste it arguing a point. So I nodded as I nursed a
cold beer. But I think she was wrong on two accounts: It *is*
about me too, first. And second, I'm not sure what is "best"
for my son is what is easiest.

The decision of where my kid goes to school is about
me in a number of ways. The most important one has to
do with the question of values. There's no question that we
transmit our values to our kids—who can deny that? We
can't put who we are on hold when we have kids. I *don't*
value people based on their income, skin color, or their
sense of entitlement. What I value is openness and toleration and a certain degree of humility. What I especially

value is people feeling free to be who they are, instead of being cowed into submission or uncomfortable in their skins trying to live by others' standards. I find this sense of freedom more among public school people than private school.

And the question of what's best for my kid... The funny thing is that a few years ago the husband of this very woman had said something that I often quoted. When they had taken their kids out of public school to put them in private he was not overjoyed about it. "I want them to grow up with some street smarts," he grumbled. I identified with this comment. I definitely want my son to pick up street smarts too. I don't want him to grow up in an insulated and protected environment that not only shuts out anybody who is not privileged enough to afford it but never challenges you with facing the not-so-pretty sides of society.

What do I mean by street smarts? I mean being able to think fast on your feet and rely on your own resources—and not social privileges—to survive and prosper. I think functioning in a democratic society requires street smarts. And like all aspects of a democratic society this requirement can either encourage personal merit or teach you to hustle unscrupulously. The choice is yours—and, again, it's a question of values. A dog-eat-dog mentality certainly has its own rewards, but how important are those rewards to *you*?

In other words, it's up to you to teach your kid to become self-reliant and develop personal merit—or sic him, as it were, on to other dogs in pursuit of bones succulent with fresh flesh and blood? (I suppose you can detect my own values here!) Forgive me for getting a little cynical, but I sensed that private schools engage in dog-eat-dog mechanisms through their screening. Then they leave their children and "communities" to pretend there's an even playing field out there and hustling is beneath them. (And of course this service costs some money.)

I think you're not a swimmer until you can swim in choppy waters.

Then there is the question of what's interesting. I find diversity—real diversity—far more interesting than homogeneity with some color thrown in. In public school you encounter lots of people who not are only different from each other, but different from you. To the extent that children get socialized in school, there's a lot more to discover and learn—and maybe, possibly, appreciate and enjoy?

This is the long explanation. The shorter one is this:

Early on I got the hunch that my kid was not going to much like school. So I figured, if school is going to be an unhappy experience why pay tens of thousands of dollars for it?!

The OMM (One Mad Mom) Club

I interrupt *Clara's Clearing* to bring you relevant pieces from other blogs on the website. Most of the contributors to the OMM Club blogs were readers and I can't get their permission to publish their writing because they wrote anonymously. Here I will print the ones that I wrote.

OMM: What are they teaching girls—and boys about girls?

I don't have a daughter and raising a son has been far from a piece of cake, but lately I've been getting chills about what some mothers of girls must be going through. My son is ten years old and starting to get interested in "preteen" stuff. God help us.

We don't have a TV at home but when we visit my mother I let Jack watch TV. I let him pick his own shows and keep an eye on his choices. It used to be that he was only interested in cartoons—Cartoon Channel, Sponge Bob,

Teenage Mutant Ninja Turtles, Ben Ten, that sort of thing. I've watched plenty of this stuff with him and aside from the loud and rapid-fire action that I think promotes ADD I didn't really mind them. I found their content for the most part inoffensive and often quite funny. They are action-packed, full of blasting gadgets and high speed vehicles, and kind of gross—the way boys like it. In fact, most of the cartoons that are on TV seem to me more geared to-wards boys than girls. I don't even recall coming across any "girlie" cartoons.

Lately, however, I've caught my son starting to watch non-animation, relationship-oriented, *preteen* shows that seem to me more geared toward girls than boys. I don't care about that part. What has disgusted me is the way girls are portrayed on these shows. First of all, their attire.

What the boys (generally between twelve and four-teen) wear on these shows is standard stuff: t-shirts, polos, jeans, khakis, sneakers, etc. They all have unremarkable hairstyles, mostly neither too long nor too short. Girls, on the other hand, are always dressed to the hilt, complete with hairdo, makeup, jewelry, fancy shoes—the works. This already is bad enough. But the shocking part is how body-revealing their attire is. The clothes are often skimpy and curve-huggingly tight and frequently reveal skin. And of course the girls are all super skinny and "gorgeous" where-as the boys are quite average in their looks and sometimes even overweight.

A friend of mine was recently telling me that her close friend's teenage daughter and her friends have been doing self mutilation. They cut themselves. This friend's girl has a little extra weight on her and is full of self hatred about it. A girl in her group of friends had recently attempted suicide and all the families were duly freaked out. They were des-perately trying every resource and remedy they could find. This sort of thing doesn't seem so common with boys.

Another thing I have noticed in these preteen shows is

that the girls all have attitude. While the boys talk and behave normally, the girls have very unnatural mannerisms:
they giggle unnecessarily, they prance around showcas-
ing their nubile bodies, they do pranks on boys (stuff you
would never see boys getting away with), and, boy, do they
roll their eyes an awful lot. They do not have a thought in
their heads except for dates and clothes and catfights. Not
that the boys have a lot going on for them in the brain department either, but at least they're not so showy about it.

As I watch these shows I am appalled and thoroughly
disgusted. If I had a daughter I would be worried out of
my mind. What kinds of things are girls learning from this
culture? How to be vapid? How to be a sex object at an increasingly young age? How to have no aspirations but to fit
age-old female stereotypes?

And what indeed are boys learning from this culture?

The other day I was shopping with Jack and I asked him
to go look for some dates for the dessert I was making.
He came back with a sly look on his face and said: "I didn't
find dates but I found *a* date." And he pointed out to me
a young girl, about twelve or thirteen, dressed in skimpy
shorts and a slinky tank top, belly button and cleavage exposed. I appreciated my son's pun but I was flabbergasted
to see what his idea of a "date" was. Oh my God! At age
ten he has already gotten the message that you date girls
like that.

It is really depressing. Now, I'm not too worried about
my son's taste. I think by the time he's of dating age he
will know better. At least I'm going to make sure he learns
better, though who knows whether people act on the better things they learn in life. I know that I generally lose no
opportunity to point out to him all the different kinds of
falseness that the media is constantly bombarding us with
about girls and women. But still I do worry about what he
is learning about them.

If I had a girl, however, I would be a great deal more

worried. I would be worried not just about the ideas in her head but also about her physical and mental health. This particular falseness that is relentlessly propagated by the media—that is, what is expected of girls to be considered beautiful and attractive—is positively dangerous for girls.

As I look at the spunky, free-spirited girls dangling from the play structure at my son's elementary school I shudder to think how they might change in a couple of years. Will their natural glow be covered up by makeup and their lithe bodies enslaved and exposed by dictates of fashion? Will their free movements be replaced with self-conscious awkwardness or provocative mannerism? Will their natural self confidence be replaced by "attitude"? And will the unnatural, insecure, full of mannerism, little sex kittens with attitude be what boys find attractive?

OMM: This constant battle with junk

Well, we all know raising children is hard work. Even in the most ideal circumstances—happy family, supportive community, peace and prosperity, etc.—it is still hard work. We can't really complain about that because the idea is that we should not have kids until we really know what we're getting into. But there are parts about being a mother that are not just hard work but unnecessary hardship. Those, I absolutely hate and cannot get used to.

One completely unnecessary torment I feel subjected to daily is this constant battle I have to wage against junk: junk food, junk stuff, junk ideas—stuff that are nothing but garbage and, at best, end up in garbage dumps (I say "at best" because I wish there was a garbage dump for junk ideas too).

Now, I am no purist. I occasionally let my kid have junk food—candy, fast food, soda, sugary cereals, etc. (I don't want to raise a "hungry ghost.") I do my best to feed my kid good food and never stock junk items at home but I have a hard time spending my days around planning and preparing food (may the Lord have mercy on me for neglecting to feed my kid organic vegetables and brown rice every day). I am especially not good at banning things—I really do have an issue with issuing bans.

Also, my kid has his share of stacks and stacks of *stuff*: toys, knickknacks, whatever it all is that is piled up in every corner of the house. Again, I try to exercise some restraint in adding to these piles of stuff. But you have birthdays and Christmas and grandma coming back from a trip—not to mention, "It's my allowance, I can do whatever I want with it"—and pretty soon you have heaps of useless and half-broken stuff that nobody knows what to do with. The trouble is that this stuff is attached to the fresh and sharp memory of a kid who knows the history and function of each item in minute detail: "But this piece goes with that and Freddy gave it to me when..." So don't you dare touch that junk.

Sometimes I just want to scream, buried underneath heaps of crap: candy wrappers, broken plastic, disposable entertainment, and duplicates and triplicates of them. But that's nothing compared to how I feel assaulted and barraged by advertising. "Buy this, eat this, play with this... and torment your parents until you do." I feel I have been turned into some kind of drill sergeant who has to constantly be laying down the law for my kids. "No," I say, "No. No. No." No to this and No to that. No, I won't buy this. No, you won't eat that. No, that's enough. No, put that back. No, we're leaving.

And please don't start moralizing for me about how I should "explain" things to my kid. My kid at the age of five had all the explanation he needed for the rest of his life. Lecture on the environment? Check. Effect on cute little animals in nature? Check. Effect on their own bodies and "growing up healthy"? Check. Trip to the garbage dump? Check. Recycling and composting? Check. My husband even once put a match to a $20 bill to demonstrate what buying junk does to money. What else are we supposed to do? And are our "explanations" adequate defense against pining after Mac's gadgets and what Lulu was wearing the other night? Is there *any kind of defense* against billboards and sides of buses and grocery store check-out stand displays?

I won't even mention television. We don't watch television. When I say we don't I mean we don't even have television reception at our house. But again, I am not a purist. I don't try to ban television exposure. There are always grandparents' and friends' houses. There is TV-watching on the computer everywhere. My kid knows as much about what's on TV as anybody and he knows all the commercials, complete with jingles, as well as anybody. He repeats crap to me like "But it's made with whole grains," "It's got natural sugar in it," or "If we order now we will save ten bucks."

No, I have to say. No, that's junk food full of chemicals. No, buying junk is not saving money. No, that's just advertising. And then I yell: Advertising is bullshit, don't repeat that bullshit to me (may the Lord have mercy on me for resorting to profanity with my kid; we are all sinners).

And let me tell you, all this is that much harder when you are dealing with "bad boys." I know it first hand and I've observed a lot of mothers in action. These guys are programmed to push buttons (so to speak). I mean, they keep pushing and pushing till they get a reaction. And even after you have completely lost your parental equanimity and made a total fool of yourself (and pulled a muscle) turning half-way around and yelling at them in the back seat of the car, they are not finished with you: "Why?" they say, "I just want to know why."

Of course they damn well know why. They know it backwards and forwards and can even quote from the most recent PBS show on the topic. But they are way smarter than that. They know that PBS documentaries don't stand a chance against the onslaught of advertising that comes at you no matter where you turn your head. They catch that twitch in the corner of your mouth when you see the new "health food" offered by Burger King. They register your scowl and grumble at the new and improved iPod. And they just can't resist giving you that little flick that makes your composure crumble. "I'm just asking, Mom," they say. "You never explain your reasons."

I am so sick of this. I feel I have been turned into a policeman who is always on the job to enforce the law. Wield power and authority. Threaten punishment. Drag off to jail.

And to add insult to injury, I don't feel like one of these modern policemen with shaved heads and menacing dark glasses who have unknowable objects in black leather casing attached at their waists. I feel like one of those feeble policemen in old French or Italian movies who are more the objects of ridicule than fear, the ones who bands of little boys play pranks on and laugh at.

Raising kids is already hard work—sometimes extreme manual labor and sometimes pure psychological torture. But I am sure I never signed up with the police academy.

OMM: Mad... but also disappointed

I just returned from my son's school where I was supposed to drive a carload of kids camping. This is a fifth grade expedition to a local farm where the kids spend the night and experience farm life. It should be a great trip— but I'm afraid not a good beginning of the year for us.

I arrived at the school with my allotted share of supplies for the trip a few minutes late. I had waited for the school bus traffic to subside so I could pull up to the door and load up the kids and their backpacks and sleeping bags. By the time I got there, however, it turned out I was not needed. The teacher apologized, saying that she miscalculated how many drivers were needed. What really happened, though, I have a feeling, was that the kids who were assigned to me opted to ride with another driver. Or more specifically, they chose to ride with another kid than mine.

We've had some bad years at school, as I've written. What happened this morning, though, made me realize it's not over. My son still is the untouchable of the class. I'm mad on many different accounts but let me concentrate on one right now.

There is a core group of kids who have systematically excluded Jack from the first day he arrived at this school in first grade. As late as last year one of the girls was still saying: "Jack suddenly shows up in first grade and wants to be part of our group..." That was fourth grade, mind you, and Jack was still excluded ostensibly because he was not there in kindergarten. Never mind that every year there are new students...

There is one boy in this group, Dylan, with whom Jack is particularly good friends. They really enjoy each other's company and spend a lot of time together outside school. The problem is that the dominant member of the group I mentioned uses Dylan to exclude Jack. In fact, before Jack and Dylan became close, Dylan was the odd-man-out of the group. Suddenly in fourth grade Dylan became the darling of the dominant boy, Jason, I suspect just to spite Jack. In Jason's presence Dylan completely loses a sense of himself. He becomes powerless and almost mesmerized by Jason.

Dylan's parents are not happy about this situation either. We have had a few talks together with the kids to try to make Dylan see that it is Jack who is his real friend, not someone who is just using him to hurt Jack. But as Dylan put it most plainly and eloquently: "Jason is just too much." I take Jack and Dylan out of the afterschool program once every week to strengthen their friendship and give them a chance to enjoy being with each other outside the realm of

Jason's influence. Over the years I have also tried, with Jason's mother's help, to strengthen the friendship between Jack and Jason, but that just hasn't worked. I gave up on that a while ago.

So here we are, the beginning of fifth grade, and this nasty behavior toward Jack is starting all over. I'm mad of course. I'm not mad at specific individuals really—that's useless. I'm mad at the ignorant and vicious culture in which our kids are growing up. I'm mad that educators are unwilling and/or unable to create an environment in which intelligence and dignity are really valued. I am not mad at other parents because I don't expect much of parents. We have no control over bad parents and good parents have no more control over their kids than I have over mine. That's exactly why we need schools and educators; we need them to provide sound and decent environments for children, whatever their situation at home.

But I'm also disappointed. Again, it's useless to be disappointed in others, kids or adults. They are who they are and it's out of my control. I am disappointed in my son. I am disappointed that instead of shunning the group that excludes and hurts him he seeks them out. I am disappointed that he wants to belong to a group that doesn't want him. I know that the only solution to his problems is for him to say, "To hell with you all." He will probably become quite an object of desire then, but I say to hell with that too. There are many other kids who are quite wonderful at the school. Why doesn't he choose to play with them?

This morning when it looked like I was not needed to drive, Jack immediately ran to see if he could get a ride in Jason's mother's car with the kids who were riding in it. Thank goodness that car was full. He ended up riding with two other boys who are splendid kids. In fact, they loosely belong to a group—I say loosely because they don't exactly have a "group"—who usually hang out together after school. These kids are wonderful—bright, kind, interesting, you name it—and Jack likes them very much and finds them "cool." These boys never excluded Jack or joined others ganging up on him or anyone else. They are simply outside the realm of that certain sick and vicious culture. Now why in the world won't Jack just drop Jason's group when he has this alternative?

When I tell Jack that he should have nothing to do with Jason's gang he says: "I want to prove to them that they are wrong." I just don't know what to make of this answer. I don't know if it's good or bad that Jack wants to "prove" that he is worthy of friendship. I don't know whether it's better to fight certain battles or just retreat. And try as I might, I have no say in it either. Jack has been going along with the ugly games that this group plays with him. He has established bad habits reacting to these kids and I feel an utter failure in my attempts to change these habits. He is angry and frustrated and so am I. It makes me angry to see my kid basically abused (and myself into the bargain)—and it makes me disappointed in Jack that he makes the choice of bringing it upon himself (and upon me, always frantically trying to fix things).

This morning I left Jack in the care of the parents of one of the wonderful boys and he was happy to ride with them. But I can't help worrying about what happens when they reach their destination. I don't have a good feeling about it.

OMM: Not enough

When I wrote my previous piece ("Mad... but also disappointed") I wasn't intending to make it a serial. But as I wrote I saw that I needed to expand on some things.

I mentioned that there are two groups of kids that Jack has the option to play with. In the spirit of being plain-spoken, let's call Jason's group the "bad kids" and the other group the "good kids." I wrote that it makes me angry that we have to contend with bringing up children in an environment that does not really nurture respect, and I am disappointed that my son is more attracted to the cruel kids even when he has other options—but that's not all. This whole thing makes me feel guilty too. I feel I am simply not doing enough.

Let me give you the situation more elaborately. At my son's school the "bad kids" are in the afterschool program while the "good kids" are not. One reason that Jack does not get away from Jason's gang is because he stays in the afterschool program while the good kids go home. The mother of one of the good kids told me back in first grade that even though she would love to have her daughter in afterschool she thinks the program does not provide adequate supervision. Sure enough, the kids who are under family supervision in the afternoons are much nicer kids. They not only don't join gangs but are not even aware (at least not yet) of those kinds of dynamics.

But I also know that the kids who are not in afterschool have at least one parent who devotes him or herself to the kids every day after 1:10 p.m. (which is when our school lets out). Our situation is this: Right now I don't have to earn money, my husband makes enough. So I don't technically "need" afterschool programs for my son. But that's not all there is to it. First, I have to think about the future. If I don't work now that will jeopardize our future survival. To put it simply, my husband is fast burning out as sole bread-winner and if I don't keep my own professional life alive we could soon be in trouble. Second, I like to work. I enjoy what I do and I really dislike being financially dependent. In short, I work because I need to and I want to.

That means I cannot devote every afternoon to entertaining a lonely and bored child or arranging playdates and extracurricular schlepping. As it is, I have Jack and Dylan one afternoon a week and only twice a week Jack stays at afterschool until 5. That's the best I can do—and clearly, that is not enough. In fact, there is that nagging voice repeating inside my head at all times: "Not enough, not enough, not enough..." I am not doing enough to make my son happy. I am not doing enough for his education. Heck, I am not even doing enough to save him from bullies.

And so the anger is turned inward: "You selfish, inadequate mother... You are uncaring and irresponsible. Look at so-and-so: no wonder her son/daughter is such a sweetheart. You don't spend enough time with your kid and the time you do spend with him is not quality. You get mad at him because you would rather be working on your own project. You even have the temerity to be disappointed in him... Be disappointed in yourself, you wretched wench. You bad, bad mother..."

But I'm also the kind who resents being made to feel guilty. So I get a double whammy: I feel guilty because I get angry and I get angry because I feel guilty. I walk around a bundle of conflicted emotions and frustrated energy. And guess who is on the frontline of suffering the consequences? My poor kid, who is also a bundle of conflicted emotions and frustrated energy.

So for the past five years I have struggled with the question of whether or not I am doing the right thing by putting my kid in afterschool. Am I heartlessly exposing him to gangs and bullies? Am I indirectly teaching him how to be a bully himself? Am I neglecting him? Is he being emotionally scarred for life? Will he blame me in the future for not devoting myself to him and him alone? Suffering the anger I feel toward those who are hurting him now and myself for failing to stop it is not enough—will I in the future have to suffer his anger too?

And I just can't stop wondering: Is this what motherhood has always been about? Or is this our new and improved version?

Back to *Clara's Clearing*

How unreasonable can you get?

I will now take a break from recounting school woes and talk about something I enjoy almost more than anything else in life: dance.

Now, I'm not a professional dancer, never even got close to being one. But I've been a serious student of dance for decades. The dance world being rather open to non-professionals, I have had the luck to study with some of the best teachers in New York City and San Francisco. I have also gotten to know many professional dancers for whom I have great affection and respect. I think very few people know how much dancers have to offer not just as artists but as educators.

I still take ballet class a couple of times a week. The other day my usual teacher was away and we had a substitute. As the whole class of mostly over-thirty people waited patiently at the *barre* or sprawled on the floor, stretching, the studio door opened and in walked the substitute teacher with sure steps and a confident smile. "Oh my God..." I bet the thought went through all our minds simultaneously, "she's twelve."

The substitute teacher was a very small young woman with a heavy Japanese accent. "Class is going to be different," she announced. "Do your own thing if you need— with no distracting others." She demonstrated with deliberate and articulate movements and she counted the music with total assurance. She would occasionally lapse into very thick Japanese accent, but even when it was hard to understand her words the clarity of her thinking came through. Wow—I thought—wouldn't you like to have a daughter like that?

I could just imagine her as a small child: focused, disciplined, and with glittering intelligence. Every parent's dream child. Every teacher's dream student. I felt a pang: *My poor bang-bang-shoot-shoot boy can't hold a candle to her.* As I watched this spectacular specimen with awe I caught myself feeling very disappointed in my son. He would infinitely rather spend an afternoon driving remote-control cars up the wall than focus for a minute on learning a step, let alone doing a *tendu* with proper technique. Looking at that little Japanese firecracker with her unwavering command of authority, I faced one of my most secret disappointments: *My kid will never be like that.*

Sounds familiar?!

But it also got me thinking. What do we expect of our children? What do *I* expect?

I for one—though I bet this is true of the majority of parents—want my son to be better than me. In everything. Whatever I do, he should be able to do better. And whatever I can't do, he should learn to do. In effect, I have to admit, he should compensate for all my inadequacies. As I watched the little Japanese teacher with her unflinching air of authority, I thought my son in fact might have to *overcompensate* for me in a lot of things.

Unreasonable? Certainly. But if you listen to your inner parent you'll have to admit it's not that unusual. How willing are you to admit that your kid is not, nor ever going to be, the absolute best in everything? And, horror of horrors, how willing are you to admit that he might in fact not even get as good as you are in some things?

Not only isn't your kid a driven, accomplished youngster like this teacher—I was secretly telling myself—*he doesn't even have enough discipline to stand at the barre like his middle-aged mother, still trying to learn, still in pursuit...*

If you think parents' sense of inadequacy is bad wait till you feel that guilty sense of superiority...!

And, oh, by the way, by the end of the class I noticed our substitute teacher wasn't that young. In fact, she was in her late twenties—which in dance years, is rather mature.

I told you it was going to be about being unreasonable!

The best advice I ever got

Years ago, while I was studying for my PhD oral exams, I would take afternoon breaks and go to ballet class. I was pretty freaked out about my exams and I didn't really know how to study for them. I went out and bought hundreds of index cards and sat with the stack of books on my reading list that I had not yet read. Never in my life had I taken notes while I read but this being the biggest exam of my life I thought I should do what I saw others do.

At that time I had a ballet teacher, Don Farnworth, who had rehabilitated himself twice: once from polio and once from sliding off the roof of his house and smashing both hip joints. He was tough. Occasionally he would make people cry. He would limp over to you and stare you in the face. "Be still," he would command. "Stop fidgeting." (Have you ever noticed how much unnecessary fidgeting we do?) Or he would say to an injured dancer: "Don't keep looking for the pain. It's still there. Don't go there." (Have you ever noticed how when we hurt, physically or emotionally, we keep going to it as if to check if it's still there?!)

Anyway, Don gave me one of the best pieces of advice anybody ever gave me. It was especially useful at that particular time, studying for my orals. "Use what you know," he would say, standing over me and squinting his eyes in a challenge. "Use it." The day he said that to me for the first time a light bulb went on in my head. I went home from the studio and threw away all my index cards. There was no way I was going to learn anything new for my exams. It wasn't a question of cramming. It was a question of doing what Don was telling me: use what I already knew.

And it worked. I passed my orals and can now confess from the safety of my degree that I never even got to the bottom of my reading list.

Bullying is back

It sure was nice to take a break from chronicling the egregious crap that goes on in our school and write about dance. But, very sad to say, now I have to go back to it. This time, however, I am not talking about what happened in the past grades. Now it's halfway through fifth grade and I will be reporting on the situation as it develops. This time I'm very angry. This time I feel the compassion and understanding of our family is finally betrayed.

My son's been missing a lot of days at school. He pretends to be sick and knowing that things are getting bad again for him I let him stay home. About ten days ago his afterschool teacher, a lovely young person, told me that she had to intervene and ask the guy who was bullying him to leave the project they were working on. I was happy to hear that. And when I talked to my son he had some suggestions for her. I made him write a letter to her. Then I wrote a letter—a very decent one—to the director and staff of the afterschool program and attached a brief and useful article on preventing bullying (which I got from the National Association of School Psychologists' website). I will post all of this correspondence here. Meanwhile, I got Jack out of afterschool as much as I could.

Last Friday Ken, the father of a friend of Jack's, called and said that he was alarmed by "the email" and wanted to help make things better for Jack. "What email?" I asked. I hadn't received it, so he forwarded it to me. Our sons' teacher had sent an email to a group of kids' parents about how they should talk to their kids about group-bullying Jack. She had given some details. I will post this email later. What was interesting is that Jack and his family were excluded even from the acknowledgement of the problem, let alone any attempt at a solution.

I am very grateful that Ken had the kindness and intelligence to let me know what was going on. My husband and I discussed what we should do and decided to wait for now. I am waiting to see if any of the emailed parents, the children, or teachers will talk to us about what's going on. Last year even though we had the good teacher, Sara, who really helped with the situation, we only heard from one family, and their daughter was the only one who wrote a letter of apology to my son.

I will post things as they develop. First, here is Jack's letter to his afterschool teacher:

Dear Teacher:
   I would like it if you would interfere and punish XX or anyone else who bullies me the first time. Because the second and third times are hurting me. It doesn't hurt you but it hurts me. When you give them a second and third time it just gives them more chances to hurt me. They know they have three chances to hurt me and they take those chances. This hurts and harms me. They know what they can do, which is to harm me.
   When they hurt me the second and third time it makes me mad and that gets me into trouble. When I get mad I get into trouble. What that does is that it hurts me not them. Because what they want is for me to get into trouble. But if you jump in the first time they'll learn their lesson not to bully me. If you give them chances they will take them.
   It's not fair that I can't stay at Afterschool as long as I want because of bullying. I am a good kid. If you think I'm a bad kid because I get into trouble it's not my fault. If bullying keeps on happening I'll have to leave and that's just not fair. It's not fair that I have to go when they are the ones bullying me all my life.
   I like it that you throw in a lot of effort to stop them. I'm glad that you care about me getting bullied and you're so nice to do something about it. I hope I can stay at Afterschool as long as I want because I love Afterschool and I want to stay.

A very unexpected thing

Jack quit school last week.

And today I formed a "private school" for homeschooling him. That's California law. I named my "school" after the wonderful elementary school I went to as a kid. I don't call my school homeschool; I call it freeschool. This is what happened.

The last blog I posted was my son's letter to his afterschool teacher. I attached that to a letter I wrote to the afterschool director and teacher. What I said in that letter was that I had lost hope in the school doing much about the bullying but was hoping the afterschool staff would be more responsive. I thought the worst bullying was happening at afterschool. I was completely disappointed in the afterschool director's response. She was cold both to Jack and me and blamed us more than showing concern. After years of being very supportive of her I felt completely betrayed.

It was while I was dealing with the afterschool situation that Jack's friend's father had called. It turned out that Jack's teacher had sent an email to a bunch of kids' parents who had been involved in a nasty situation with my son. The teacher had not said anything to me or copied me on the email. I was grateful that this friend's father forwarded me the email.

According to the email the kids had been nasty to Jack for some time. The latest was that one of the kids had asked for a vote to have Jack kicked out of the class and many kids had raised their hands. I guess this was even too much for the teacher. I suppose everything else up to that point was OK with her. This is what she said in her email:

> I fully understand individual frustrations, but this behavior falls in the category of bullying. Would you please talk to your child about not participating in the group behavior.

She then enumerated "strategies I have implemented to move away from people who annoy you," such as moving away from the annoying person, speaking directly to him, etc.

This is a letter I wrote addressed to her and the principal:

> This is the second day this week that Jack has chosen to stay home. He has missed many days this year because of waking up in the morning with "stomachache," "headache," or wanting to "throw up." I have not been outspoken about this in the past and I believe that has been a mistake.
>
> That Jack is bullied and ridiculed by any number of children, we all know by now. What I would like to point out in this letter is the context in which this behavior appears.
>
> Last Friday an email went to the parents of certain kids in Room 10 who had participated in a particularly nasty episode: "voting" Jack out of class. One of the parents was so concerned about the event as well as the email that he called me immediately. When he realized I had not been included in the email he forwarded it to me.
>
> There are a number of things wrong with this approach. San Francisco Unified School District informs me that it is my right to be informed when my child's name is mentioned in any correspondence. Transparency is absolutely necessary. But I'm less concerned about the legality of the matter than the humanity of it.
>
> Ms. Teacher, when you exclude me from such correspondence these are some of the messages that are conveyed to both those who do and those who don't receive the correspondence:
>
> The hurtful gravity of the situation need not be acknowledged to Jack or his family by the school.

The participation of Jack and his family in finding a solution to a situation that is hurting Jack is not
needed.

The open acknowledgement of other parents and
their children that Jack has been hurt are also not
needed.

This lack of open acknowledgement and lack of
transparency in finding solutions gives the impression
that things are just being swept under the rug. It fosters
the kind of closed-door and secretive environment in
which all abuse, including school bullying, takes place.

Let me point out another aspect of the context in
which this bullying is taking place. Let me draw your attention to two sentences in Ms. Teacher's email:

"I fully understand individual frustrations, but this
behavior [i.e. the taking of a vote against Jack] falls in
the category of bullying."

"Strategies I have implemented to move away from
people who annoy you are..."

What these two sentences imply is that you "fully
understand" that Jack "annoys" other children, but,
still, people should not bully him. Not only do you not
make any mention of "fully understanding" how Jack
might be feeling, but you are implicitly acknowledging
that children are right in not liking him. In other words,
you understand and acknowledge that Jack is an annoying child but you don't understand and acknowledge
that something might be precipitating "annoying" behavior in him—or that perhaps, just perhaps, Jack might
be a hurt child more than an annoying one?

Do you not think that children pick up on this implicit siding with their feeling of annoyance? Do you
not think this implicit "understanding" of the impulse
to behave badly toward someone is subtle permissive-
ness of that behavior? And do you not think that this
quiet, under-the-rug communication with parents gives

permission to the parents to deal with this situation in an off-hand, don't-ask-don't-tell kind of way?

I fully grant that this bullying did not start in your classroom. Last year the fourth grade teacher went through an awful lot of trouble trying to eliminate this behavior in her classroom and under her watch. But it was not in her power to completely stamp out the behavior, hence its recurrence this year. Part of the reason her efforts did not fully succeed is because of this lack of acknowledgment on the community level, including the families of bullying children. Consequently, with the exception of the parent who called me last week, after close to three years of widespread bullying against Jack, we have to this date received only one open acknowledgement from a family. What I have received from other parents since your email went out are guilty but averted eye-contact and never a mention of the ugly behavior of their children, of which they are quite ashamed, I'm sure.

These are some general ideas about the context in which bullying occurs, is tolerated, and gets perpetrated. If you were a child, would you wake up happily in the morning and go to a school like that?

Endnote on fifth grade teacher

A year after we left I heard this teacher also left the school. I don't know if it was a coincidence that both the second and fifth grade teachers we had problems with soon left the school. Maybe one reason they were so uninterested while Jack had them as teachers was because they already knew they were leaving, or maybe the district had something to do with it.

It really was over

After the situation at the afterschool program and the classroom teacher's email I reached the point of having lost all hope for any changes at school. At this point I just wanted to know what our rights were.

I called the office of the San Francisco School Superintendent. At the mention of bullying problems they asked me the name of our school. The purpose of my call was not to declare war on anyone so I did not reveal the name of the school just yet. I said that I just wanted to talk to someone to clear my own mind. They referred me to the "family voice" office where I talked to a superb professional, Mr. Martinez. He talked to me for a long time, asked many questions, and was quite alarmed by what I told him. He too asked the name of our school. I said that I did not want to stab anyone in the back, to which he replied: "You're stabbing your son in the back."

As I was speaking to Mr. Martinez I realized that the time for me to try to work with the school was over. The last thing on my mind at that point was to take my son out of school but I realized that I had been pushed in a certain direction from which there was no return. I did not yet know where that direction led but I knew it was time to have it all out. I told Mr. Martinez that I would reveal the name of our school after I told the principal that I was going to do that.

I hung up the phone and went directly to the school. I asked for an emergency meeting with the principal and walked straight into his office. I told him what was happening with the children, what the teacher had done, and whom I was talking to at the district. He said that he would call up Mr. Martinez himself, for which I was grateful— I hated having to "snitch" on the school. He also told me that he was in the process of introducing strategies for dealing with the bullying. I knew he had been working on that for a long time so I believed him, but I knew that for us it was too little too late. When I left his office I still didn't know what I was going to do. By the time I got home the principal had called and already spoken to Jack who had stayed home that day. That made Jack feel a lot better.

I waited a couple of days to see if I would hear anything from the school or Jack's teacher. Hearing nothing, I called Mr. Martinez again, and this time we talked much more openly. I forwarded to him some of the letters I had written to various teachers and principals over the years (in five years we had had three different principals) and sent him the link to my blogs on this site (in the following days there were long and frequent hits from a cluster of San Francisco IP addresses on my blogs!). That was on a Friday. I made an appointment to go see him in person the following Wednesday. Again, I had no idea what I wanted to do. I just wanted to discuss things with someone and hoped that that would help me figure out what to do. That same day I wrote the letter that I posted on my previous blog and made sure the teacher and the principal got it the same day.

That weekend I suddenly realized school was over for us. I felt completely devastated that a bunch of kids—many of them not bullies at all—had voted my son out of their class. Jack had been putting up with this for a long time. And I, with my best intentions, had indeed, as Mr. Martinez pointed out, stabbed him the back. I realized the reason I did not know how bad things were for Jack was because he had stopped telling me. He had rightly figured that neither the school nor his family was going to do anything about it, so why bother. That weekend I told Jack that if he did not want to go back to school he did not have to.

He took some time to think about it. That Monday was a holiday and by Tuesday Jack decided that he wanted to go back to school and finish fifth grade. He especially wanted to be there on graduation day. When he came back from school on Tuesday he reported that his classroom teacher had spent a long time that day confronting the bullying at every opportunity, talking to the kids, having discussions, mediating, and what not. Jack was very happy about that—somebody was finally acknowledging what was going on. But he also understood that the teacher would not be able to keep this up indefinitely—which is what I had said to the principal about his ideas for addressing the bullying. This kind of time- and labor-intensive effort is not sustainable. Things might improve for a little while—just as they had in the past—but they would eventually go back to the way they had been. Plus, as Jack himself observed, suppose the teacher monitored the situation in the classroom, what about recess? What about in the hallway? What about at afterschool?

Wednesday morning Jack woke up and said that he had decided to quit school. It was a lucky coincidence that I had my meeting with Martinez that morning, so I took him along. It was a very good meeting and Jack had a chance to speak for himself. I was very proud of him. He was articulate, strong, and perceptive. Mr. Martinez spoke to him with understanding and respect for his intelligence, and I know that it meant a great deal to Jack to be taken seriously and treated with such respect. Since he had by that point decided not to return to school we really just talked about the bullying problem in schools and not about solving any problems for Jack. It was a very good meeting and ended up being a closure to Jack's elementary school experience.

The next step was to write an official letter to the school and inform them that Jack was not coming back. The day I delivered that letter the principal called Jack again and had a very nice and long talk with him. He told Jack that he was sorry to have lost him and invited him to join his class on graduation day. The phone call and the invitation made Jack very happy—but watching his face beam with happiness made me realize how sad this whole thing really has been.

The apologies come in

When we went to pick up Jack's books from his classroom the teacher told us that she has asked students to write apology letters to him. A few had come in already so she gave them to us. Interestingly, they were mostly from the kids who had nothing to do with the bullying. I wonder if there will be others!

These letters are so wonderful I want to share some with you. First, the kids who had nothing to do with the bullying.

Sadie:

Dear Jack, Hi! How are you? I'm sorry you had to leave. Even though I didn't do much teasing I feel like I did a lot. I wish you would come back because you were so nice to me. Everybody feels sorry especially me. I am very sorry that everybody was teasing you.

Citalli:

Dear Jack, How are you? I know what it feels like to be bullied. I just can't believe you leaving school. I guess there won't be any other person in class to sing. I just can't believe it and you're my friend. Please come back.

Dana:

Dear Jack, I'm sorry the way we treated you here. I also want to tell you it was fun being in your table group. I wish this never happens to you in middle school.

Clare:

Hi Jack, I'm so sorry you won't be coming to school with us any more. We will miss you! In school, we're learning poems. I hope you're doing well in school and having fun too!

Here are a few notes from kids who had participated in the bullying:

Sean:
    Dear Jack, I'm sorry I've been super mean to you. I really wanted to say sorry so I wrote this note. I'm really sorry. Please forgive me Jack, and I hope you won't be teased any more.

Henry:
    Sorry Jack for teasing you and being mean to you but we all learn from mistakes. And we made a mistake. Sorry Jack and good luck.

Matthew:
    Dear Jack, We are so sorry that we were mean to you. We just wanted to have a little fun. I hope you realize that soon and decide to come back. No more mean stuff.

Would you call it karma?!

    I can't help but notice a kind of irony in what happened to Jack at school.
    The story behind this website is that I became alarmed at the way boys are silently labeled as "bad boys" and treated as such. I decided to advocate for boys. My response to the various accusations against boys was: Boys are not sick, they are not budding criminals, they are not in need of "correction" all the time. *Boys are not bad,* I wanted to scream all over the internet.
    That was in second grade and my son was the one receiving the label of bad boy. After third grade, however, while Jack still carried the suspicion of the authorities on his back, he actually became the victim of some really bad behavior. Neither Jack's academic achievements nor the

fact that he was not the one targeting other kids with physical or verbal nastiness did away with the negative judgment he received in second grade. While he was the one
absorbing the bad behavior of other kids he was nevertheless considered problematic. Nobody said that to my face,
but let's just say I'm not stupid.

At this point I really don't care what the teachers
thought about Jack, me, or anything else. I am so relieved
not to have to give that more thought. What is interesting
to me is how the tables sort of turned on us over the years.
I mean, here I am, advocating how good boys are and next
thing I know my own son is subjected to some really bad-
boy (and −girl) behavior. Isn't that ironic?

And here I was writing about how happy I was to leave
the "gated community" of private school for the "real
world" of public school... How the values I held in raising
my son in an open and more democratic environment were
so important to me... How I wanted my son to learn to rely
on his own resources rather than social advantages... And
next thing I know, the very public school that I extolled
over any private school basically spits him out as an undesirable element: His classmates literally voted him out of
class and the teacher barely batted an eye. Isn't that ironic?

So what do I make of this irony? Shall we call it a bizarre
kind of karma?

I don't know. I'm still thinking about it. Maybe this is
a test of my beliefs and my commitment—in which case
let the gods hear that this was not at all necessary. I don't
budge from my beliefs and commitments.

Not even the boys—and girls—who behaved with a
rather strong demonstration of the ignorance and cruelty
of childhood are "bad." Ignorance and cruelty in children is
just raw material. It is a kind of exploration: We encourage
children to explore, don't we? Why shouldn't we expect
that they will take us at our word and do some real exploration in every human direction? Why would we think that

the curiosity of kids only extends to pretty, sunny land-
scapes, strewn with sweet tempers and kindly motives?
Kids are just as curious about the darker side of life.

What I have learned from this experience is that yes,
kids will be kids, which means that yes, they will reflect all
aspects of their homo sapiens genes. Of course kids are like
us—that's because they're human. They are who we are.
That seems obvious enough. And yet, we hardly think twice
about finding faults with them that we don't find in adults.
We pathologize and criminalize them. It would be so easy
for me to say the kids who bullied my kid are sick and violent. They sure behaved in a sick and violent way. They see
plenty of sickness and violence everywhere and they *will*
go there. It's all too obvious how they reflect back the exact nature of their environment.

So is there a solution?

Ain't *that* the question?! I'm sure if you bring it up everybody will have all kinds of theories and prescriptions
to offer. Me, I actually don't flatter myself with coming up
with solutions. I don't know about theories and prescriptions. I can only come up with observations. And my observation is that it won't do to call children sick and violent.
It also won't do to make them lists of do's and don'ts. My
only suggestion is to share this observation with children:
Cruelty has its attractions and ignorance its conveniences.
Let's look at what those attractions and conveniences are...

But then again, do we have the courage to look at the
attraction of cruelty and the convenience of ignorance in
ourselves? Will any of Jack's teachers give this a moment's
thought? Will any shadow of sadness even pass their consciousness? Will they look this simple fact in the face: Under their watch a group of perfectly nice kids "voted" a
classmate out of class. And the result? The voted-out classmate did indeed leave while the teachers and kids continued on with their ways, after the little bump of a particular
incident.

I think this shows that the convenience of ignorance is stronger and even uglier than the attraction of cruelty. Banality of evil, anyone?

I'm not the first one to make that observation. Nor am I the first whose beliefs and commitments encounter the force of a certain cruel banality. Perhaps not much of a karmic message there... Just life as it ever was.

In unabashed praise of my son

Over the years, trying to be fair to the utmost, seeing things from many different perspectives, and, not least, not wanting to spoil my son or make him feel the center of the universe, I have been very held-back in saying good things about Jack. Now, I'm going to indulge in that a little.

I have great confidence in Jack. He is not just smart—I think an *unsmart* child either doesn't exist or is an extreme rarity. He is observant and insightful. He is capable of behaving with a kind of maturity that you would never expect from someone his age or goofy rambunctious disposition. He is talented in a number of things and I think he's going to do some interesting and perhaps even impressive things as an adult. I'm not worried about that.

What I want to write here is why as I look back over the past five years that he's been in school I am so proud of him. From grade one to five, Jack has basically been tormented every day in school. As a classmate of his put it to me last year, "Jack suddenly showed up in first grade and expected to be our friend." Geez. And when this particular girl complained to me of this unreasonable expectation of Jack's, they were in fourth grade. Continue on to fifth grade and the picture emerges that the kids never accepted Jack. I had thought it was a question of maturity and that over time the kids would forget that Jack was a newcomer in first grade. I was wrong. But it's not my intention to analyze what's wrong with a certain kind of kid culture. What

I want to give you an idea of is the context of Jack's every-day school life: his constant effort to fit in and the group's constant rejection of him.

Here's another crude aspect of Jack's place in the group: He was one of the youngest and one of the biggest. He was bigger than all the boys, except for one major bully who was a year and half older. Of the girl bullies two were older and bigger than him. I always wondered if there was a size competition among the boys. The boys did not wres-tle or play-fight with girls but among themselves there was always talk about who can take whom "down." I imagine Jack had ample opportunity to demonstrate that he was stronger than most.

But—and this is my point one—even though he was taunted and tormented and even though he was not a "wimp" by bully standards, he never initiated aggres-sion. And point two is perhaps even more important: Even though he was rejected by the group and even though many joined the group by making alliances with the bullies by turning against him, Jack never joined the tormenting of other kids in order to be on the bullies' good side. In other words, Jack did not become a gang member. He never stooped to being the lackey or side-kick of a bully.

If anything, Jack stood up to the bullies. He took them on. We can say this is wrong all we want, but it is a fact of life—and has been as long as there is recorded human his-tory—that there is a certain male tendency to fight. And there has certainly always been a certain social and cultur-al tendency to expect that males *should* fight—they cer-tainly should fight *back*. Now, older and wiser as we are, we counsel our kids that they should avoid confrontation. "Walk away," we advise. "Make others friends." This is so much easier said than done.

My favorite piece on this website is the contributions of Tyler, whose article "How I Became This" I have been posting the past couple of weeks. Tyler is 19 and a very intelligent and articulate guy. And as a lot of people have been commenting, he is also right in what he says. But of course he could not express himself as well he does now when he was a little kid. And as I read his pieces I realize how I've failed Jack in the past years. He could not explain to me what he faced every day and I could not imagine the cruelty and stupidity of the school environment. I don't say the "cruelty and stupidity of children" not because I don't think kids can be cruel and stupid. They certainly can. The reason I don't like to blame children is because I really, from the bottom of my heart, believe that children merely reflect the cruelty and stupidity of their environment. And ultimately, just like adults, kids act in stupid and cruel ways when they know they can get away with it. They are not blind, they see that those in higher authority are guilty of it and get away with it.

This is the dynamic that Jack did not join. He fought back in his childish ways. I am confident that he will learn to be more clever and effective in the way he fights this as he grows older. Heck, he might even learn that avoiding pointless confrontation is not a bad strategy after all. But I am proud of him for not giving in to the temptation to join stupidity and cruelty in order to belong. I am not really worried about him seeking out power struggles, or turning into a Don Quixote for that matter, but there is one thing I do worry about. I worry that he has gotten the wrong message about friendship. I think he needs to relearn the meaning of "friend."

The Easter egg hunt

Yesterday we were at an Easter egg hunt picnic. Jack brought over some slips of paper that were placed inside eggs that were thrown at him by a group of girls—two sisters and a toady. They said: "you are a loser. Peace out!," "ur ugly," "crybaby."

I talked to Jack, the girls, and other kids who had seen what had happened. The story as I gathered was this: The girls had had a head start and collected almost all the eggs, about thirty of them. Most other kids had shrugged their shoulders and just walked away without any eggs. But Jack had insisted on collecting his share and had found only five. He had objected to the girls and they had taunted and made fun of him. He in turn had gotten angry and chased them, telling them that he would give them a black eye if he caught them. They had gotten away, taunting him some more from a distance. He had cried out of frustration and said that they should apologize to him. Then the girls had placed the hate notes inside empty eggs and thrown them at him. "Here's your apology," they had said.

To update this site I look at a great deal of news items about children. Because of my son's situation I have also been doing research on bullying. What I have found is that verbal bullying—cyber bullying when it is done online—is a very serious and widespread violence that younger and younger children are inflicting on each other. This violence is driving kids and teenagers to suicide. This is terribly serious. The messages that were put inside the eggs for Jack are exactly the kind of things kids say to each other to inflict utmost hurt. And just like it had happened with Jack, there is usually a group of kids who band together and attack one kid.

When I talked to the group of very nice kids who had happened to witness what went on between Jack and the girls I pointed out to them that this exact wording is what some kids use to hurt others. They said they knew. One little girl, about eight years old, said that it had happened to her and that she's "learning to handle it." These very kind and wonderful kids ended up calming Jack down and he later said that they had helped him "handle it" too. He said that having these nice kids stand by him, talk to him, and be his friends really helped him.

But this is frightening. I keep thinking if this sort of thing can go on right under the noses of a bunch of picnicking adults, what do kids do to each other when we're not there? And what happens when, unlike what happened on this day, the group of bullies is bigger than the group of nice kids? What happens if the good kids, or at least the ones who are not part of the bullies' gang, don't come to the aid of the bullied kid?

I shudder to think.

What has become of friendship?

A few weeks ago I linked to a news item about the sharp rise in the number of children calling a UK national helpline because they feel lonely. Many of the kids who called said that they had no friends. This got me thinking about friendship. Actually it didn't start me thinking (I'm always thinking about friendship) but it got me to create a "tag" for friendship. (Tags are ways of organizing contents on this site according to topic so, say, you go to the "Health" tag and find all the pieces and news items that have appeared on this site on the subject of health.)

When I registered my "private school" to comply with California homeschooling laws I gave it the name of the elementary school that I went to. The minute I got the electronic confirmation for creating my school I emailed two of my friends from that school to give them the news. My friendship with these two goes back to when we were four years old, in preschool. We are still friends with many of our schoolmates from those times and thanks to the internet we still manage to stay in touch, although most of us are now scattered around the world. And this is the circle just from that school. I have close circles of friends from high school, college, and graduate school, not to mention family friends whose parents were friends of my parents. To me, friendship is what makes life tolerable.

As I am writing this my son walks over and takes a peek at what I'm writing. "Remember what I told you about friendship?" he asks me. I can't recall it so he repeats it for me: "Friendship is a way of hatred."

Say what...? I don't remember hearing that. What does he mean by that?

"Friends get jealous of each other and start making fun or hurting each other because they get jealous of them hanging out with some other friends," he explains. "Unless they are true friends... If you are true friends even if you have a fight you usually forget about it and become friends again."

This is interesting. I started this blog to write about my own ideas—and really, nostalgia—about friendship and my son comes over and punctures my writerly bubble. (Aren't they good at that?!) I was not going to write about jealousy. But now I've got to explore it with Jack. I ask him if he has true friends. "Yes," he says, "Dylan, Chris, and Evan." What makes them true friends? "They don't get mad at me if I play with other kids. They don't get jealous."

There was one boy who wanted to be Jack's friend really badly a few years ago. "You're my best friend, right? Right, Jack?" he would endlessly repeat. Then this same kid became one of Jack's tormentors (not part of the bullying gang but equally hurtful). Jack said that this boy became jealous when Jack played with other kids and avenged himself by saying nasty things to Jack. I knew of this story and I asked Jack if he got the idea of friendship creating jealousy from this experience. "No," he said. "I already knew that. Everyone knows that."

I wish I could hear more about this but Jack says this and walks away. I call him back. He doesn't want to talk any more. "I told you," he says. "Friends get jealous and hurt each other." But I insist. I want to hear about how to be "true friends." This is his final words of wisdom:

"You hang out with them until you're sure they're your true friends. If you're not true friends just hang out, but not too frequently—just hang out without being friends so they won't get jealous."

This is as much as I can get out of him. He just derails my blog and walks away!

So where was I...? I was going to wax eloquent about my own wonderful friendships. And it's true. I do have many deep and deeply satisfying friendships. Were there no jealousies? Yes there were. Two of my friends especially come to my mind and some of that jealousy friction still exists between them. There is a long history of hurt between them and although a sort of competition over their friendship with me has at times been caught up in it, their troubled relationship does not really have to do with me.

What's confusing about Jack's comments is that jealousy is the last thing that comes to my mind when I think about friendship. Yes, it was an element that did creep into my friendships at times but it did not play such an important part in the making and breaking of friendships for me. Is there a major difference in mindset between me and my son?

What I remember doing as a child—and what I hear my son expressing as a desire—is playing with many kids, having many friends. So there's no difference between us there. Could the difference be in the expectations of our milieu? Could it be that back in my childhood non-exclusive friendships were more accepted than they are now? Could it be that *including* and *excluding* individuals in and from groups are more part of this generation of kids than they were of mine?

I think perhaps the culture of friendship has changed. Perhaps friendship is now modeling itself after romantic relationships—where else is the concept of jealousy coming from? And perhaps, worse than that, being part of "groups"—belonging to gangs, in a way—is what's defining friendship.

Could that be it?

Here's to Jean, Theo, and John Steinbeck!

When a couple of months ago I told a friend of mine, Monda, that I was going to homeschool Jack she was not at all surprised. "I was expecting it," she said. I myself had not expected it, how could she?! Monda said that she sensed I was going in that direction. I swear I was not aware of it myself. But, there's an old friend for you... I guess when you know someone since seventh grade you sometimes see things about them that they don't see themselves!

I had been running a homeschooling series by Denny Mather, a contributor on this site. Apart from my professional interest in children's education, though, I had a personal interest in homeschooling because of my nephew Theo who was homeschooled since sixth grade. My sister-in-law, Jean, decided to homeschool her son when she moved to a small town with a culture her family was not at all used to. Theo was more than miserable. He was getting sick.

When Jean decided to pull him out of school and pretty much single-handedly teach him I was kind of shocked—not shocked in disapproval but shocked because I had never seriously thought about homeschooling. I remember thinking smugly to myself, "Poor Jean, I guess that's what happens when you move to Hicksville: no liberal folks, no decent education." I thought we privileged people in politically correct, upscale San Francisco had nothing to worry about! Really, I thought exactly that: Nothing to worry about.

Jack was two when Theo was taken out of school. By the time Jack was four I had already started worrying. First the frigid and hypocritical private school we sent him to disappointed me deeply and shortly after that our public school problems began. Still, I never thought about homeschooling. We watched as Jean slowly navigated her way through books and curricula and built a network of like-minded folks in her small town. We watched as every year Theo grew into a more interesting and accomplished kid. We watched as their whole family got more and more involved in Theo's education and—we could hardly believe our eyes—really enjoyed the process. And this was while we were working harder and harder to make things work and feeling more and more wretched in our beautiful, liberal San Francisco.

But I have to be honest that no matter how miserable we all were in our school experience I still would not have had the faintest notion about homeschooling had it not been for Jean. She had no teaching experience and I had— she had not been a developmental psych major and I had— she was not a third generation educator and I was—still, I had nowhere near the courage that she had! It took her bold example to give me the confidence to do it.

And the interesting thing is that Jack has always been particularly enamored of his cousin Theo. He's always looked up to him and found him the epitome of coolness. He even imitates the way he talks and his mannerisms. Theo has always been very gracious and obliging to Jack and has humored him. Robert and I have been pleased that Jack finds Theo a role model because we also think very highly of Theo.

When I decided to homeschool Jack the first book that came to my mind to study with him was the old classic, Jules Verne's *Around the World in 80 Days*. We sat with a world atlas and a world map, on which Jack traced the journey of the characters in the novel. As we followed the journey from Europe to Asia and to America we studied a good deal of geography and history. What we noticed, however, was that the American part of the journey was not as full of history as the Asian and European parts, and it certainly did not do justice to the great and varied American landscape. I was thinking about how to augment our coverage of America when I remembered something about Jean and

Theo's early homeschooling days.

When Jean had just taken Theo out of school she asked friends and family for book recommendations. I remember that my husband suggested John Steinbeck's *Travels with Charley*. Toward the end of his life Steinbeck travelled across the country with his dog Charley where he encountered many interesting places and characters. My husband thought since Theo and family had just moved across a few states that might be an interesting book to read. So one of the first books that Jean and Theo read when they began their homeschooling journey was Steinbeck's *Travels with Charley*.

And bingo... I found our next book! We are going to the library to check out that book next.

So here's to Jean, Theo, and John Steinbeck: Couldn't have done it without you!

So what do I do with this site now?!

My first motivation in starting this site was a selfish one. I wanted to help myself cope with the difficult time Jack and we, the family, were having with school. As I investigated the problems boys were having, however, I realized that the problem is bigger than us and I thought that I might as well raise some awareness and advocate for boys as well as helping myself cope. I figured what helps my son and me survive must be of some use to others as well. Since Jack was going to be in school for many more years I figured I was in this for the long haul.

But then things happened and now I find myself homeschooling him. That's splendid—but what do I do with this site now that I don't have a "bad boy" problem? I don't have a school problem therefore I don't have a bad boy problem. (Isn't this interesting?) But the more this site grows and the more feedback I get, the more I realize that even if my own "bad boy" problem is over for now (let's not be too optimistic!) the situation of boys is not at all improving in schools. I can't drop the ball now.

It grieves and worries me that so many boys are having a miserable time being a child. It also terribly saddens me that so many families, mothers in particular, are so stressed, harassed and worried that they don't enjoy raising their sons. It should not be like this. Children are supposed to enjoy being children and parents are supposed to enjoy raising children.

Clearly lots of things are going wrong. And lots of people are looking into what is going wrong and what can be done about it—see the works of Peter Gray and Lawrence Diller for starters. The regular contributing mothers on this site—Denny Mather, Aurore B. Realis, Sedona, for example—also have a great deal to say about how they see what's wrong and how they have coped. And lots of people around the world are reading what all these folks are saying. Just today the site had hits from 23 countries in five continents.

So you see why I can't drop the ball now? I will certainly continue to pursue my goals in raising awareness and supporting advocacy for making life happier not just for boys, but for all kids and their families. But my question is, what do I, Clara Middleton, blog about now?

Am I still officially the mother of a bad boy?!

I have a sneaking suspicion that I am, even if it doesn't feel that bad anymore! I still have a boy who pushes limits (and buttons galore) and has a wild and unruly streak in him. Now I don't just live with him, I also teach him. (I think "So help me God" was invented just for such occasions!) My situation vis-à-vis my son has completely changed. While in the past I was in a reactive mode now I am in a proactive one. Best of all, however, I am in a *creative* mode: I have to make things as I go along. I suppose I can call this making—*building*—something, giving my son an education.

So I am thinking of starting a blog series called

Educating My Boy. I will try to chronicle my efforts as well as the trials and tribulations of giving my boy an education. Now it's me and the "bad boy" face to face.

So help me God!

CHAPTER 3

Homeschooling

In February of fifth grade Jack quit school and we started homeschooling. He was homeschooled through middle school. I describe the "academic" part of homeschooling in Chapter Four. The blogs in this chapter describe the day-to-day experience of homeschooling.

While Jack was in public school Robert and I started our own publishing house. We published a number of authors whose works we admired, creating a "brand" that would serve as a calling card for our business. Good books seldom make money, so the idea was that we would expand into offering editing services to authors who wanted to submit their work to other publishers, and publishing consultancy to would-be publishers. When Jack quit school I knew that I would not be able to follow up with our expansion ideas. This translated into quitting my job (although when you are self-employed somehow your job is not considered a real "job"). I also had to put my own writing projects on hold. Books of all sorts had to be postponed. In short, my career and our fledgling company suffered a setback.

While I had a working and writing life (the period when Jack was in school) I contributed blogs to a popular site, not my own. Anticipating my inability to continue, I wrote the following farewell blog on that site.

A Great Vanishing Act

I like to flatter myself that some of my readers on this site are wondering where the hell I disappeared to. I used to have a pretty regular presence here and dug a lot of the people and stuff on the site. Not anymore. Nowadays unless a friend sends me a link to something, I have no idea what's on this site. Heck, last time JJ was in town we didn't even manage to have lunch.

I'll tell you what happened to me. I had to take my kid out of school. I'm "homeschooling" him now—*freeschooling,* I call it. By California law if you want to homeschool you have to establish a "private school" which is nothing but filling out a form online and every October report that you are still in operation. Technically the state can at any point show up at your door and demand to see what you're teaching your kid. That's all right with me.

The first thing I did after establishing my school is that I emailed two of my friends from my old favorite elementary school (we've been friends since preschool) and told them about my Free School. One of them asked if I was now planning on joining "tea parties." No my dears. It's not just Christian fundamentalists and radical right-wingers who homeschool. There's a lot more of us out there than that.

Let me tell you what made me pull my fifth-grade son out of school in the middle of the year: bullying and ganging. My son had become the object of attack of a couple of bullies and one of them had organized an ever-growing gang against him. One of the main bullies, Jason, was a big, powerful dude (older than most kids because he had been held back, I suspect because of his behavior) who threatened and intimidated other kids into joining his gang and not playing with my kid. Although almost two years younger than Jason, Jack would not be browbeaten to join his or anybody's gang. He's just not the sort. Being a big guy for his age and a bit of a tough guy himself Jack is not the type to walk away from challenges and give bullies free reign over the school yard. He fought back. "I couldn't resist getting extremely mad at the gang leaders, so I would fight them," he said, "because if the leader goes down the whole gang goes down." I did everything in my power to convince him that it is best to walk away from provocation and conflict, but I'm afraid that's a lesson that people have to learn for themselves.

I won't get into the details. Suffice it to say that it got so ugly, with teachers behaving so callously and incompetently, that the school district got involved. Boy, were they mad at our school! I could have given the school a lot of grief but I didn't. I documented everything, wrote about it, and just left with my kid. I'm not one to attempt to reform American public schools. And now, actually, I'm very glad that things got as bad as they did so that we had no choice but to leave. In fact, I don't want to write about the disaster that American schools—public and private—and the educational system have become. I want to write about what a great thing it is to *free school* my son—and what a toll it takes. But first hear me out on another aspect of the education my kid was getting (or not getting).

You see, for years now I've been trying to make the best of my son's school experience. I was very active with the PTA. I ran afterschool clubs, I created clubs and hired professionals for them, I funded many, I volunteered, made donations, supported the school, teachers, other parents, you name it... On top of that, my husband and I tried to actually give Jack an education outside of school: read good books with him, exposed him to real art, science, life, the world... I kept thinking to myself, it's OK, my son will be educated despite the daily six hours that get absolutely wasted in school. He'll get educated despite even the lack of textbooks in school. Yup. Public schools can't even afford textbooks any more. Kids come home with random sheets of photocopied study sheets and assignments that have no meaning and no connection to anything else. Worse than that, they come home with *Time for Kids*. This is a publication of Time Magazine that has pretty much replaced books in American public schools.

I won't go into *Time for Kids*. I'll only say that every time I saw it come home with my son my entire being went into revulsion. We don't have TV at home. Every time I catch a glimpse of network kid shows, especially Disney Channel, I feel that a vile and vulgar subhumanity is staring me in the eyes. Then here is my kid being "educated" on one of the most insidious, despicable, and stupefying products of American media: The Time/Life Corporation, or whatever the conglomerate is called now. The last *Time for Kids* that came into our home was right after the Haiti earthquake and had on the cover a picture of a couple of black kids carrying boxes of disaster relief supplies as benevolent American military personnel looked on in the background. It gave me political and moral creeps.

And I swear, it is not just political. Here's a sample of the level of the prose in that publication: "I love that hockey is a team sport. Your teammates become your friends. They are like your sisters. You have to work together in order to win." Let the English language and every even semi-literate English speaker who ever put pen to paper be damned. In fact, from the face of it the English language doesn't even exist in schools any more. Kids are not taught English; they are taught Language Arts. Those photocopied sheets of paper containing random lists of baby words are Language Arts. How I wish I could tell the inventor of the phrase that their "language art" is neither.

And math... that killed me. What they call math is really arithmetic. And basic addition and subtraction and the multiplication table are now called "math facts." My son who is quite average in his "math" and other subjects was routinely designated by annual state-administered exams as "gifted and talented." I mean, thank you, I am flattered,

but who are you kidding? My son is learning next to nothing in school and I'm supposed to feel all goody inside?
What's infinitely worse, my son is supposed to think that
this is what is required to be considered "gifted and talented"? He's supposed to think he is doing just fabulously and
getting educated to boot.

Expose my son to daily violence and work my own butt
off for this? Forget it. We're out of here.

A few years ago Jack told me that his ideal form of education is "learning a couple of hard things a week and being
free the rest of the time." Now that's a smart comment. He
knew that the education he was getting was what I call a
mind-numbing waste of time. He also confirmed something
that I suspected all along: you can teach kids the same way
you teach college students. So I decided to put my ideas
into practice.

My first step? Reading *Around the World in 80 Days*
with him. Remember the Jules Verne classic? It's such great
reading. We sit with an old and illustrated edition of the
novel, a hefty world atlas, a large world map, and a pen.
On the world map Jack draws a line tracing the journey of
Phileas Fogg, Passepartout, Aouda, and detective Fix. On
the atlas we look at the places they pass through in more
detail. Starting with the Suez Canal I started adding history to geography. My favorite part so far has been India
where I gave Jack a good introduction to British colonial-
ism, looking at a fabulous little map that showed all the
different Indian provinces under maharaja vs. British rule.
We discussed the East India Company and the Parsis in India, which of course touched on the history of Islam and
pre-Islamic religions. The Dutch in Indonesia, the French
in Vietnam, the opium dens in Shanghai—we talked about
all these. Right now the Fogg party has just landed in San
Francisco and we have the US ahead of us...

And you know what? The kid remembers everything.
It's so interesting to him. The other day I overheard him
say to someone that history is his favorite subject. Before

I took him out of school he didn't even know what history was. And this is only a little over a month after leaving school.

In addition to this, he's a teacher's assistant in a science lab where they have afterschool programs for school kids. He also joined a rock band, sat behind a professional drum set for the first time and took to it like duck to water. In the summer I'm not going to make him do any "school" work but perhaps we'll read Agatha Christie. And next year, forget about "math fact" kind of crap, I'm going to start algebra with him. What game or puzzle is better than algebra? What is a better introduction to design than geometry?

For "social studies" next year we're going to read Mark Twain's *The Prince and the Pauper*. What better introduction to sociology? I'll also borrow some comic book versions of the Ramayana and Mahabharata from my Indian friend and that will be my kid's intro to Indian mythology. He's become interested in Greek mythology from the recent Percy Jackson books and of course we've read some Shahnameh stories—the treachery of Afrasiyab in the Rostam and Sohrab story had him spellbound when he was five.

Now please, I really am not trying to tell you that my kid is "gifted and talented." He's quite a regular kid. The whole point is that regular kids are perfectly capable of being educated on the best books in the best way. Heck, you and I read Jules Verne and Mark Twain for fun, didn't we? And we learned. We listened to stories and memorized a poem or two in school, and we learned. A lot of us even grew up liking calculus and trigonometry, never having heard about "math anxiety."

Why can't our kids get educated this way?

They can, of course. But that means at least one parent can hardly have a life of her own. Yup, I used the feminine pronoun on purpose. It's usually the mother who gives her life over to the kid. The same old same old—but an updated, post-postmodern version of it. I'm back to being a traditional mother, devoting myself to my kid. (I guess my friend wasn't that wrong in thinking I might be joining the tea party thing now!) Though in the *traditional* traditional days the mother was not giving a ten-year old a college education while at the same time keeping him fed and in clean clothes.

And that's not even all. What's a killer is that my new "traditional" mode is superimposed on a rather nontraditional role I'm also playing. I'm working as co-publisher and editor with my husband, developing a business so that he can quit the drudgery of his day job. We're simultaneously working on our third and fourth books while I'm also the editor/publisher of a growing website. As principal blogger I've written about my son's school experience on that site and now I'm also blogging about our "freeschooling" experience. It's a lucky thing that my traditional and nontraditional roles at least overlap on the intellectual level.

And that's why I'm not blogging here anymore. I work (raise a kid), I work (educate him), and I work (write, edit, publish, market).

I haven't just vanished from this site; I'm vanishing period.

Who'da Thunk?

As it happened, a couple of weeks after taking Jack out of school we went on a skiing trip. My husband would wake up early, go into the dining room of the hotel where we were staying, and work on his computer. One morning when I came down I saw Jack sitting next to his dad with his computer in front of him. "What are you doing?" I asked. "I'm writing a novel," Jack replied.

This was as much as a surprise as anything could have been. This was a kid who hated writing with a passion. In fact, we were often called to parent-teacher conferences to discuss his refusal to write. Often we would get his in-class writing assignment home, a blank piece of paper with half a sentence on it, with the teacher note: "This is what Jack produced in forty minutes. I am concerned."

His last writing assignment in fifth grade was to complete a story by the title of "The Garbage Monster's Biological Wish," which was a collaboration with a local organization, 826 Valencia, that partnered with public schools to promote reading and writing. It was a little booklet with an unfinished story for the children to finish. This is how the booklet began:

> The garbage monster, Muscle, was covered in all kinds of trash, from half eaten apples and brown banana peels to stinky diapers. The more garbage he ate, the bigger he became. He was afraid of soap because it would dissolve him...

After many a twist and turn Jack finished the story thus:

> Muscle laughed and said, "Good luck with that!" Then Fred said "Let's help them!" "Nah!" said the monster. Then they all got turned into monsters! THE END

On the back cover of the booklet kids were to write an "Early Review" of their own writing. Jack wrote: "I'm thinking they'll think it sucks." Students were also asked to complete an "About the Author" section. Jack wrote: "I hate writing. I like pork buns! I like sports!"

The first thing I want to say about kids, especially boys, hating to write is that I suspect it has first and foremost to do with the physical act of writing. For kids, writing involves grasping a pencil and making fine-motor movements upon a page. I know for a fact that most of the boys I have met hate writing as a physical activity. Most of them put up less resistance writing on a computer.

The mental-activity part of writing is an act of communication. As a teacher of writing I know that's where you begin. There are tried-and-true tricks for getting people to produce a piece of writing: first you help them generate thoughts, then you help them sculpt it into writing. A few years back I tried this method with a friend's daughter in fifth grade, and it worked just as surely as it did with my college students and in writing classes for office workers who needed to write decent reports and memos. Becoming a writer is a different story, and most decidedly not everyone who needs to be able to write wants to be a writer.

At any rate, I never worried that Jack couldn't write so for the most part I ignored the teachers. But to see him *wanting* to write a novel was a total surprise. A truly great writer of the twentieth century, the Chilean Roberto Bolaño, has a deceptively simply observation that should guide any attempt at writing, from children to professional writers: *Reading is more important than writing.* Jack proved the truth of this statement.

We had always read good books to Jack but he had never voluntarily written a word—until he suddenly decided to write a novel. I hate to be vulgar but I think that was his way of giving the finger to his school and the teachers. Here is the abandoned novel (in "journal" form, he explained) that did actually get worked on after that initial enthusiasm, even if it was never completed! I am reproducing it in the font in which Jack wrote because I think that was part of the excitement for him.

James Smith   *March 16, 1746*

By command of my king, I shall set forth on a voyage to explore the New World and I shall document my findings for his majesty. The voyage, I am told, shall take place tomorrow at dawn, but now I must rest, for tomorrow will be quite long.

James Smith   *March 17, 1746*

My night was quite disturbing. I saw my father (who is dead) in an insane asylum screeching and calling my name. I wanted to call out to him, but I just couldn't speak! I finally woke drenched in perspiration.

I got to the docks at 6 o'clock and saw a crowd of people huddled around something with horrible sense of sadness in the air and depression on their faces. As I came forth I saw why there was depression in their faces. They were all huddled around a motionless body with a note stuck to the hand. The note said, "Watch out aboard your ship. There is a dangerous killer among the crew."

Despite the frightening message, I went aboard. It was a dreadful place, strewed across the deck were buckets, rope, and some things I cannot name. Unfortunately (since I haven't room to put you down to write) I must go.

James Smith   *March 18, 1746*

I have (after many hours of trying!) found a table to write upon. We have started to sail and I am starting to feel sad and miss my mother, because I saw, as we left the port, many children aboard waving to their mothers and crying. Unknowingly I started to cry as well, not because I was leaving my mother, but because she left me! She died when I was very young and my father was a drunkard and he ran off and himself killed. I never knew how, but I do know that I'm glad he died, because he was merciless, cruel, and would regularly box my ears! But enough personal thought and back to the present.

While I was crying a booming voice said, "Why are you crying mate?!" I twirled around to find myself staring up at a tall, burly man with a frightening scar across his left cheek. All the words I could form were, "You are Vur Horston, a vampire!" He started to laugh so hard that I could not hear the orders the captain yelled to the crew! I guess he found it amusing that I found him out but then he said, "I always get that from children!" But the reason I thought that was because I have always had an interest in vampires so I thought it was him. He told me his name was Helf Gret. "What type of name is Helf Gret?" I asked. He said he didn't know. I was a little surprised at that. You would think a person would know what his own name means! He told me he needed to talk to me so now I must go.

James Smith   June 16, 1746
　　　The seas are might jagged today! I have tried my hardest to help upon the deck but the sailors are quite rude! I wish that I had more time to inform you of what is happening, but the captain requires me.

Clara's Clearing, continued

Decompression, the first stage

The important fact about our homeschooling situation is that we're not starting from scratch. The positive part of it is that I have a ten-year-old who can read and write and has basic arithmetic. This small little detail makes a world of difference. It makes life a lot easier on me. The negative aspect of not starting from scratch is that we have a lot of things to overcome. We have a lot of bad memories to leave behind and a lot of bad habits to unlearn. Some homeschoolers call this "de-schooling."

The Home School Association of California, a non-profit organization that gives information and support to home-schoolers in California, has an excellent little publication, "Starting the Homeschool Journey." One little piece I particularly like is "Making the Most of Decompression Time," by Lillian Jones. This is how it begins:

> One fairly universal dynamic is the need for a de-compression period after leaving school. The intensity of the need for decompression time is usually in direct proportion to the time that was spent in school and to whether or not (or to what degree) it was a difficult experience.

It was very important for me to read this. Indeed a "de-compression" time is absolutely necessary and inevitable. Let's face it, most people who leave school have not had a good experience of it. Leaving school, as my husband put it, is not like stepping off the downtown bus. You don't just hop on down and it's all over. It takes time to process what you have left behind. This is the first stage of undoing some of the damage.

I have to be very honest about something. I wish I could describe exactly how my son has been affected by his school experience and pinpoint exactly what bad habits he needs to unlearn. I can't, because I don't know. All I know is that I have to help create a happier and more interesting life for him and develop new and better habits. Hopefully in time he will be the one to tell me about his school experience. He can be surprisingly incisive and articulate, so I have a feeling he will someday tell some interesting stories and offer a valuable evaluation of his school experience.

Meanwhile, I can only speak for myself. I know "educating my boy" should be more about my son than me, but I am also smack dab in the middle. So forgive me if I talk about myself.

The decompression time has kicked up a lot of feelings in me. First and foremost, now that there is no need for my defenses to be up, I am realizing what a beating we all took in the past nearly seven years. I am realizing how hard I worked trying to see the best in things and making things work. I am exhausted. Swimming against the current, dodging random punches, winding up a broken toy... these are the images that come to my mind. It is a relief to stop and walk away, but you also feel the lingering effects of sore and tense muscles and frustrated hopes.

The decompression has also kicked up confusion. I can't help wondering why in the world we had such a hard time of it. OK, my son is not a quiet, easy child. He likes to challenge and be challenged. He can be loud and rambunctious. He needs to be free and outdoors, etc. etc. But there is hardly anything unusual about any of this. So why did he have such an unpleasant time in school? I don't say a "hard" time because the academic part—the "school" part of school—was not hard for him at all. He did quite well in that. I can only conclude that the social aspect of school— namely the kids and the teachers—are what made school life so unpleasant for him.

When you narrow down the problem to "social" causes a lot of insecurities kick in. I am basically a confident person with a solid sense of myself and my abilities. But I have to confess that my son's school experience has really confused me. Over the years I have often wondered whether there was something wrong with us. Are we weird people? Are we perceived as weird people? Is there something wrong with us or the way we live? Why in the world would my son be so rejected by other kids and disliked by teachers? I cannot forget that last episode in my son's classroom: the kids *voted* my son out and the teacher let it happen. What does this mean?

There is no use asking these kinds of questions. There are no answers. Who knows, and indeed who cares, what people think of my son or our family. I know that the only way to deal with these insecurities is to let them come out of their hiding places and wait until they dissipate in thin air. Decompression indeed. Let loose the pent up steam and watch it evaporate. So my advice to my son, after letting him express pent up bad feelings when he chooses to share them, is that we have to put all that behind us. "That's all over," I tell him, "and from now on it's going to be great."

It really is going to be great from now on. I'm not just saying this, I really feel it. We may be going through a difficult time right now, or rather, we may *sometimes* be having a hard time now, but the future is bright. I feel a kind of freedom and independence now that I have not felt since my son started school. In fact, I feel like I have my son back again. I feel that over the years he was slipping though my fingers but I finally caught him before he was washed away by some current. He is too young for me to "let go" of him. I will, when the time comes, let go of him to his own more mature self but I will not let go of him to unknown forces at the age of ten.

It is now nearly three months since my son left school.

I don't think the decompression period is over yet but I am beginning to see that the fog from the still gushing steam is starting to break up, with patches of clear sky showing through. Could it be that the "de-schooling" that home-schoolers talk about is the returning of this clarity? Would it follow then that "schooling" does indeed propel kids into a kind of fog or some kind of murky waters?

I don't know. And I can tell you this, that I have no time now to think about that sort of thing. All I know—and have time for now—is to start some new things and new ways of doing things. This requires some serious reorganization. And we have already started to reorganize our life.

The honeymoon

The first couple of months of homeschooling are definitely sweet. It's the honeymoon stage and decompression feels like a million bucks.

In our case, the first relief was from daily torment. For the first time after years, Jack did not have to face his tormentors every day. He was not constantly on the defensive or being punished for his attempts to get even. He was calmer and more relaxed. He also enjoyed the fact that his unhappiness was finally being acknowledged—and he even felt a little vindicated. The day he came with me to meet with the school district's family liaison officer he especially felt validated.

Occasionally, however, I noticed a look of confusion on his face. He wasn't quite sure what was happening. I got a sense that the acknowledgement and validation he was receiving actually made him a little worried, as if this was also somehow going to have negative consequences for him. I also got a sense that he felt a little guilty too. After all, he had behaved "badly" too. Even though everyone was reassuring him that his "bad" behavior was a reaction to being bullied there was a part of him that kept feeling guilty no matter what we said to him. Kids have an enormous capacity for guilt. It's really sad.

Still... relief prevailed. Jack felt free and special to be homeschooled. And as we met other homeschoolers in our area he started to get a sense of the new friendships and new activities that were in store for him.

The second relief we felt was freedom from the tyranny of the clock. Nobody was rushing Jack out the door in the morning. He did not have to stop in the middle of doing something interesting because time was up. He stayed up later at night and read in bed at leisure. There were no school curfews—and no tense parents trying to impose curfews.

I have to say I really enjoyed the freedom from the tyranny of the clock too. I could stay in bed longer in the morning—no more getting up early to make it to school for the 7:50 a.m. school assembly. Not being rushed in the morning really improves my mood. Also, I too could stay up as late as I wanted. I am very happy to be able to stay up late and enjoy the quiet. Sometimes I am very productive late at night—and as it has turned out, losing a lot of working time during the day I actually need those quiet productive hours at night.

We also enjoyed the freedom to do what we wanted during the day. The first couple of months we went out to breakfast and lunch a lot. We walked around a lot. We lazed an awful lot. We allowed ourselves all kinds of luxuries we had no time for during school.

Third, something I particularly enjoyed, was the relief from trying so hard. I had not noticed how hard I was constantly trying the past years. I was trying singlehandedly to improve things on all fronts: helping Jack, supporting the teachers in whatever decent effort they were making, defending Jack against bullies, trying desperately to create good friendships for him, and through it all being an active PTA member: organizing this, coordinating that, volunteering in the classroom, making contributions left and right.

What for...?! I really am not being vain saying this but I believe that while I did a good deal to improve school life for a lot of people I received very little in return. In fact, looking back I wonder if all the work I put in was seen in the wrong light. I wonder if my generosity was really seen as some kind of overcompensation for having a problematic kid, a "bad boy." But no matter, enough of that, whatever it was...

And now we interrupt our program to bring you this:

As I am writing this I am hearing my son practicing with his music teacher in the living room. They are working on *California Dreaming* together, singing and playing the guitar. This is one of my most favorite songs. Now I hear them moving to the piano learning the chords...

This makes life worth living. Even when the honeymoon is over.

Yes folks, as you probably know already, honeymoons are not permanent things!

After the honeymoon, the crash

Well, it was bound to happen, wasn't it?!

A couple of months into our liberation from school all kinds of things fell apart. First of all, the emotional crash... Being forced to do something that is mostly torment for six out of your ten years of life leaves not just scars but some open wounds as well. On a deep level Jack was—still is— quite confused. He is glad to be out of school but he still carries a lot of unhappiness and anger in him. He is given to meltdowns.

One day, at the homeschooler's park day (our homeschoolers' group gets together in a park every Monday), Jack came over to me, put his head down on my lap, and bawled. I had watched from the corner of my eyes how he

had tried to play with different kids and join various activities all afternoon but had not been quite able to connect.

I asked if the kids had been unkind to him. "No," he
said, "they're nice kids." Then what's wrong? He buried
his head in my lap. "Mom, it's like I miss being bullied," he
cried. "I'm so used to being bullied that being happy makes
me unhappy."

What do you do with a revelation like that? You of
course say all the things you can think of: "That's behind
you. It still hurts but it will get better. It's OK to cry. It's confusing. Things will get better"—that sort of thing. Really,
what do you say to anyone, child or adult, who says happiness makes them unhappy? You just mumble something
and muddle through some response while your heart aches
for them.

It is also true that in addition to unhappiness Jack has
developed all kinds of bad habits. With other kids he is
pushy and defensive at the same time. He is pushy in the
way he wants to make them like him and is defensive in
their reactions to him. Any small disagreement or resistance upsets him. He overreacts. To sum it up in simple
words, he feels insecure. And as you know, other children
do not react well to insecurity. They either go on the offen-
sive or they reject the insecure child. This response from
other kids not only hurts Jack but it reinforces whatever
bad feelings he has about himself. The vicious circle is very
hard to break out of. It is going to take many new experiences—and many new kids—for Jack to relearn making
friends.

This is the emotional backdrop. Against this backdrop
you have long hours of being alone in the house with nothing to do. We live in an apartment. We have a tiny useless
backyard and not many places where Jack can be outside. I
have to go with him if he goes out.

Tell me, how many times a week can you, or your work
schedule, handle hours spent sitting in a park? How many

hours a week can you handle playing games that you suck at or just plain don't like? I am, after all, not a ten year-old boy. I cannot be a playmate to a ten year-old boy. I cannot be a mother, teacher, coach, friend, emotional counselor, playmate, etc.—and I won't even mention other pressing family obligations—all at the same time or one after another, all day, every day. And that was part of my emotional breakdown. I felt angry and resentful at the school and the kids and their families who had put me in this position.

On top of that, I try to work. My work is flexible and at home, but still, there are projects I have to keep up with and/or finish. I had not anticipated pulling my kid out of school so I was not prepared. I was in the middle of things.

So what happens when you have a bored child, nowhere to go, and a mother who must spend hours every day at her work...? Television! Computer! Video games!

We don't have cable and get no TV reception but Jack found a way around that. He watched TV shows online. When he got bored of that he played video games. When he got bored of that there was always "checking my emails" and "meeting my friends" on computer games. Hours and hours of screen time. I growled, I cringed, I felt really really bad, but I had work to do.

This went on for a while. I desperately tried to keep up with my work the way I did while Jack was in school—until I had a breakdown. One morning I woke up sobbing. I was in such bad shape that my husband had to stay home from work and take Jack out just so I could have a couple of hours to myself.

You take any two people, both emotionally on edge, and throw them together 24/7, and you do NOT have two happy people. Jack and I simply overdosed on each other. We got on each other's nerves an awful lot. We both needed time away from each other. We felt like two rats in a cage. In fact, I should not put all this in past tense. This continues to be my main homeschooling challenge.

I still have not found a real solution to our need for "independent time" (I don't know what else to call it!) but emerging from my meltdown I realized I had to do some things differently. I realized I had to reorganize my life and even make some major changes in all of our lives.

Uncertainty, improvisation, approximation

While going through emotional breakdowns and making life changes I don't expect myself to be "teaching" or my son "studying" an awful lot. Math has completely slipped but we do keep on plodding through my version of a liberal arts "curriculum." As I pick books and read and discuss them with Jack I give education more thought than I probably ever did. I am determined to give my son an excellent education. (Maybe not today, maybe not tomorrow, but soon, and hopefully for the rest of his life.)

The more I think about my educational philosophy the more I realize I don't really have one. I have strong feelings about what I like or think is important but I can't even begin to formulate some kind of theory, or subscribe to anybody else's. Uncertainty, improvisation, approximation: this is the closest I come to describing my approach to education.

First and foremost: Uncertainty. I have no idea what I'm doing. Yes I've studied Adler and Piaget. Yes I've read Rudolph Steiner and John Holt. Yes I have even worked in preschools and taught college. In fact, as a result of doing all this I have come to the conclusion that the human brain is so complex and the human experience so varied that nobody can be all that sure about how children learn and why.

John Holt sums it up nicely: Fish swim, birds fly, and children learn. Obsessing over ways of teaching children is like trying to break down swimming technique for a fish or flying technique for a bird. Waste of time—so I'm not going to bother about teaching method or curriculum. But neither do I have the personality to just let my kid loose in a green meadow or the library stacks and put my faith in his chance development. So I try to provide some kind of direction.

Which brings us to: Improvisation.

Pick a book, any book—especially when it's a tried and true good one—and you can improvise lessons in all kinds of subjects: history, geography, psychology, sociology, art, science, you name it. When I was reading *Around the World in Eighty Days* with Jack I put an atlas in front of us and traced the journey that is described in the book. Now I myself have a much better idea of exactly where the Red Sea is and how close Shanghai is to Tokyo. I know that Jack is not going to learn all the places we looked at on the map but world geography is probably not going to change in any significant way any time soon. Each time he encounters one of these places he'll likely to remember a little more about it.

And all kinds of other impromptu lessons also popped up while reading *Around the World*: the invention of steamboats, castes in India and butler-master relationships in Britain, cultural traits and the idea of stereotypes, the tricks of creating suspense while telling a story, the perils of building railroads in the American wild west, and so on.

The same process goes on with other books we read. I have no idea what I'm going to "teach." In fact, more often than not I don't even have anything to teach. We look up things, we guess, we admit we don't know—and we even often admit we're too lazy to look something up. We move on, we go back, we lose interest, we persist, we fight... The process is very much like improvising a dance sequence. In the end we have made something—however invisible it may be after the moment has passed—and ended up somewhere different from where we started.

Which brings us to: Approximation.

This is one of those things that I feel very strongly about. I think it is completely absurd to have in mind some kind of absolute learning destination: You have arrived at point A and now you know: Physics. You have made it to point B and now you are: A Musician. Congratulations! Now you are Cook and you can Doctor... You have arrived. You can now stop.

That's not how it works, is it? I think it is much more accurate to think of learning as achieving approximations. In fact, I think of learning as a kind of spiral. You sort of hover around the same point in larger and larger circles covering more space, or in smaller and smaller circles approaching a center. There's no beginning and there's no end. There definitely is no concrete, absolute chunk of learning called Knowledge. Everything is in degrees and approximations.

So as for us right now, I am going to improvise teaching and Jack is going to get approximately educated. That's the best we can do.

Running into "truancy laws"

In San Francisco a project called Pavement to Parks has been initiated to turn under-used street space into little parks. One of these parks has been built—entirely of recycled and reclaimed materials—close to our house. We and all the neighbors we know love it. After years of being enclosed by buildings, now the neighborhood kids have a place, even if very small, to run to and let off some steam. One neighbor family wheeled their portable basketball hoop over there for everyone to enjoy.

As a homeschooler's mother I am especially delighted in our new park. It is half a block from our house and I let my son go there by himself and shoot some hoops. Yesterday, a few minutes after Jack left for the park he came running back. "A guy there told me I was not allowed to play in the park," he reported. "He said it is against truancy laws."

I had not come across that one before! So I walked back to the park with Jack to see what the deal was. The guy was still there. He was a nasty looking older guy with a scraggly gray beard and a black leather jacket, fiddling with a Harley Davidson. I told him that my son is not "truant" and it is his right to play in a public park. I don't remember exactly what he said but he hissed in my face and behaved intimidatingly toward us. He said something to the effect that the park is for people to quietly sit and drink coffee and not for playing basketball. He said that the basketball hoop had already been removed by him and other like-minded neighbors but others keep bringing it back. He told us to go away.

Like hell we were going to go away. I told him we would call the police to come and settle the dispute. He finished fiddling with his bike and drove away with an ear-splitting roar from his muffler, or lack thereof. Quite a bit of noise pollution from a guy who likes others to sit quietly in the park and drink coffee!

Jack and I went to the basketball hoop. Someone had put a piece of plywood over the basket, drilled holes on each side, and put a lock through the holes. One of the locks was unlocked so we pushed the plywood to the side and played.

When we came back home I called our local police department to see what they think. The police woman I talked to did not like it at all. She told me that next time someone objects to us using a public park we should tell him that if he would like it the police will come over and explain things to him. I put the number of the police department in my cell phone memory and have every intention of ringing them up next time this guy or his friends approach us.

The story of this guy and others like him on the block is something like this. The "underused" piece of pavement that the city has turned into a park used to be their private parking lot. One guy, I found out, has six cars that he used to park on the street where the park is now. But there's almost a whole row of shady characters on that block who hate the park for their own reasons. I have bad memories of these people.

Years ago when my son was little I was passing by with a stroller when a group of jeering men backed up their car as I was passing. Their idea of a joke was to threaten to run over a baby in a stroller. These are the kind of people who are opposed to turning unused pavement into park. From what I hear there is a lot of objection to building these parks in other neighborhoods as well. I wonder if they are all like these neighbors of ours?

At any rate, it was funny to me how a definitely up-to-no-good character was threatening us with "truancy laws." He and his friends must have done some brainstorming to come up with some "law" that they could use to beat children over the head with. They probably have intimidated a lot of kids not just with their law talk but with their ugly and nasty selves.

Now, as for us, we are of course going to be back there again, playing basketball. But, I would be lying if I said the motorcycle dude has not managed to inject some poison and anxiety into our enjoyment of the park. What really pisses me off is that now I do not feel it is safe for my son to go and play by himself. That means not even a free five minutes for me.

So this is the continuing story of a city homeschooling family. Children can hardly have any freedom of movement and have to be accompanied by adults at all times. No wonder kids are basically locked up inside schools all day. And I thought we had liberated ourselves from the "cage" of schools…!

A different kind of city encounter

After I wrote the previous blog about the creeps one

meets on city streets, I started taking mental notes about the different kinds of people one meets day to day. This is certainly part of a kid's education. A week after my encounter with the neighbor who tried to intimidate my son to not play in the park we had an exactly opposite encounter.

We live a few blocks from a branch of the San Francisco public library. I allow my son to ride his bike to the library by himself. The street he rides on is a busy one. Although the traffic does make me nervous I think that at ten kids are generally capable of crossing streets safely. I'm also pretty confident about Jack being savvy enough not to engage with potentially dangerous people. I do breathe a sigh of relief whenever he comes back safe and sound but I think a little "free range" activity is good for kids.

The library opens at ten. Jack leaves around 9:30 and I give him some money to stop at Muddy's, a local café, and have breakfast by himself. He really enjoys that. The other day he and I walked to the library together and stopped at Muddy's to have coffee. As I was ordering at the counter the café owner, Hisham, asked if Jack was my son. When I said yes he proceeded to tell me what a fine kid he thinks Jack is. He said that he was very impressed with how politely and responsibly Jack behaves when he goes to the café by himself. He even paid Jack the ultimate compliment any father can pay a boy. "If you were a few years older," he said, "I would introduce you to my daughter."

The whole time Jack was listening to us, a little shy but also flushed with pride. I thanked Hisham and felt proud of Jack but I kept thinking about exactly why Hisham's words made me feel so good. There were reasons other than the gratification of hearing someone complimenting your son.

First, hearing Hisham made me feel safe for my kid. When you realize there are people in your neighborhood who take notice of kids in a kind and positive way you feel that the environment in which you live is not so hostile. This was so unlike the neighbor last week who snarled at

Jack to get him to leave the park. Not only did I feel that Jack was safe while he was at Muddy's but that knowing Hisham he could always run into the café if he felt unsafe on the street. This trust is what builds communities.

Second, hearing someone say something good about my son I realized how little we do that these days. Back when Jack was in second grade (I wrote about it in an old blog) I noticed that while he never had anything bad to say about his teacher, his teacher never had anything good to say about him. Over the years, in fact, I hardly heard any teacher say something good about any kid—with exceptions in the case of a couple of absolutely perfect little girls. In fact, even when there was something good that a kid had accomplished—say, good test scores or a nice piece of writing—the teacher would gloss over that to get to some shortcoming, "problem," or just negative comment. In my experience the teachers were more interested in making "diagnoses" than in teaching or the learning process. I think taking on the role of diagnosis-maker makes them feel more elevated professionally. Or maybe they think they are not doing their job well if they don't work hard at finding all kinds of things "wrong" with kids.

What was particularly interesting to me was that our school was supposedly a "Tribes" school. The primary precepts of a Tribes school are these: Attentive Listening, Appreciation/No Put-downs, Mutual Respect, and the Right to Pass. I always thought of these precepts as a way of introducing a useful vocabulary to children. Beyond that I hardly saw any effects. I particularly noticed the way the second precept was talked about. In our school, in contrast to "put down" the kids were encouraged to give each other "put ups"—that is, to praise and compliment each other.

It's certainly good to teach children to find and express good things about each other. The trouble is, I never encountered any "put ups" coming from the teachers. And when the teachers don't acknowledge good things in kids how are the kids going to learn to do it to each other?

It was very clear that the instruction to give "put ups" to each other felt completely false to the kids. And sure enough, they made a mockery of the whole Tribes idea by giving each other such deliberately fake praise that made the recipient feel more insulted than complimented. As far as I could see the kids hardly ever saw kind words and appreciations expressed in a natural and spontaneous way by the adults. In other words, the Tribes formula became yet another "do as I say not as I do" instruction.

Which brings me back to Hisham. In many cultures—in our neighborhood the Latino and Arab cultures—people are much more forthcoming about praising children. Adults are openly kind and generous to children. They always have a sweet gesture, gentle pat, or kind word for them. At the core of it is taking notice: *I see you, child, and you are good.* The kind words that are expressed to children or about them, make parents and kids feel good. But more importantly, they teach a valuable lesson to kids: Not only a "do as I do" lesson but something like an "I practice what I preach" lesson. It's called honesty.

Honesty, generosity, trust, feeling noticed, protected, safe… Isn't this what community is all about?

Help! We're regressing

Make no mistake. Taking your kid out of school is a big decision. It's going on six months that I took Jack out of fifth grade and I'm just beginning to get an idea of what it really means.

I don't know any adult who has been homeschooled. All the parents of the homeschoolers I know went to school themselves. I myself went to school for as long as there was school to go to. The only schooling experience I did not have was a post-doc! And I went to some of the best schools, in name and in actuality. The greatest school

I went to was my elementary school whose principal is still a source of awe and inspiration for me. And taking my own teaching experience into account, we have three generations of educators in my family. So how does such a seriously schooled person adjust to not sending her own kid to school?

It's not as easy as it may seem. It throws your entire life out of whack.

I was thinking the other day that not since age two when my son went to a day care three days a week have I had so little time to myself. Back then I used the few hours I had to just do chores and some resting. When preschool started and I had more time I went back to my work. Not full time, but I slowly started easing back into it. By first grade I was in full swing of things. I not only worked but occasionally had lunch with a friend or just sat and looked out the window for a while.

But it's not just that I don't have time to myself or for work anymore. I am now doing things that I thought I was done with. Now, wherever my son is I have to be too. At ten a kid is not old enough to do a lot of things on his own. When your kid is in school or in a structured program like afterschool, you are away from each other. Not the case when he has no other environment to be part of. You and the kid are attached at the hips. You end up doing things you used to do a long time ago.

Take parks, for instance. That's the first place it occurs to me to go to when we have nothing else to do. And where do you go in a park when your kid is alone? The play park! Luckily Jack has no problem playing with kids younger than himself so he often finds someone to run around with. And I? I sit on the bench and watch like I used to do when he was a toddler. I might return some calls (bad reception, uncomfortable seat, noisy background) or play solitaire on my iPhone (bad light, glare in the eyes, boring, boring, boring). For hours. You want the kid to be outside, right?

Or, I take him to this or that class or lesson: Sit in the car, feed the meter, be on the lookout for closer parking spot, make phone calls (at least the seat is more comfortable), play solitaire, or even read a little. Like in the days I sat on the bleacher while he took trampoline class, oh, how many years ago...?!

I know, I know, you're thinking it's not so bad. I am lucky to have the flexibility to be able to change my life for the good of my child. In fact I keep thinking about my poor husband working long stressful hours and I admonish myself for not feeling lucky. More importantly, I am old enough to know how short life is. I hear the minutes and hours tick away and remind myself that the next (very) few years that are left of my son's childhood will go by so fast that I will regret not having enjoyed these days. Guilt, regret, self-censure... I make sure I don't leave out any of it!

But make no mistake, regression is not fun. You just don't want to go back and do all over again something you are done with. I don't want to go back to second grade, do you?

And that's just me. What about the kid himself?

It's a confusing time for Jack. Imagine this: you're in fifth grade, the "senior" class in your elementary school, kindergarteners only up to your waist, fourth-graders a head shorter than you, king of the school yard, getting lectured on puberty, hurriedly combing your hair when the new girl shows up, going through chapter books in a day... and then, bam, you're back climbing on the play structure, watching out for the toddlers toddling in your way, and your mommy sitting on the bench, watching.

Poor kid! He's being so good about it. As good as he can, of course. There are times that he is not good at all. He clings to me and does his best to annoy and infuriate me. He is loud and disruptive and hogs attention. He resists everything. He doesn't want to go anywhere, doesn't want to do anything. He is LONELY. Going to the park with his mom is BORING. He kicks and screams—not literally, but in spirit.

And that's how we've both regressed. We are traveling the road of many years ago—and kicking and screaming the whole way. It is not pretty. Though we certainly try to hide it as well as we can.

Am I trying too hard?

A comment by a reader to my previous blog really hit home with me. The comment was: "This is a little crazy to change your entire life for school. You are a very concerned mom and maybe you try too hard." Since I read that comment I keep asking myself, Am I trying too hard?

One thing is for sure. I would have never in a million years pictured myself having to change my entire life because of having a kid. Having a kid as a center of my existence goes against who I am and what my values are. I do not consider my kid as the center of the universe and I am very anxious that he should not consider himself the center of the universe either.

In my blogs here I try to be very measured, and as calm as I can be. It's for my own sanity, really. If I were to give in to all my negative thoughts and feelings it would not be good for anyone. I think the biggest challenge of being a parent is keeping your own feelings and reactions in check. I try to do my best but I frequently—very frequently—fail. I do have strong feelings, and strong feelings can only be kept in check up to a point.

One of the strong feelings that I don't express much here is how angry I am. We have all heard that "It takes a village to raise a child"—well, I feel the "village" has abandoned me. Having to leave school feels to me like being kicked out of the "village." My kid was abused, my hard work was taken advantage of, and then we were spat out like a sucked-dry pit of a fruit.

Talk about trying hard. I tried so hard to help build a happy and good environment, not just for my kid but for all kids in my son's school. I tried so hard to see the best in the school and the teachers. I tried my best with the PTA. I tried so hard to nurture friendships for my son... Listen, my son was "voted" out of his class. And the teacher allowed this to happen. How can I not feel that my entire family was "voted" out of the school? How much more literally can you be kicked out of the village?

So what was the result? I was thrown back on my own resources. When you can't change the environment—no matter how much it is the environment that is at fault—you end up having to change yourself. Believe me; I don't want to "change." I really don't think I should be the one doing the changing. And Jack, even though he lacks the experience and language to tell me in words, communicates to me in his frustration and anger that he does not understand why it should be him to be subjected to so much change.

So what is our option? We have been kicked out and the best thing to do is to go somewhere else and start something new. And starting something new takes a lot of effort. And uncertainty. And self doubt. And more effort... So you will inevitably appear like you're trying too hard. And perhaps you are trying too hard. It's just because you don't know what to do and you certainly don't know how best to do it.

But I also want to add here that even though I do at times feel abandoned and lonely I know that I am not alone. There are a lot of homeschoolers around and the numbers are growing, all over the world, in fact. I will soon get around to blog about my exploration of that world, something I really look forward to doing. But even as little as I am now connected to homeschooling communities, what has been confirmed in my mind just by hanging out with them a little is that the "village" from which I feel kicked out wasn't much of a community to begin with. It's certainly a big consolation to know that what you think you have lost was not much to have in the first place.

So am I trying too hard?

I don't know. I'm just doing some things that appear to me to be the right things to do: work less; concentrate more on the kid for now to see what new patterns we can establish; move out of the city to make life a little easier on all of us; and experiment, experiment, experiment.

Have you seen the old Fred and Ginger movie, *Swing Time?* It's a great movie and has a terrific song by Jerome Kern, "Pick Yourself Up." When I feel really down I imagine myself as the glorious Ginger Rogers with those knock-out legs of hers, sprawled on the floor singing: *Pick yourself up, dust yourself off, and start all over again...*

So there. That's my revenge. I'm trying hard—too hard, not hard enough, or just right, I don't know. We'll have to ask Goldilocks about that. What I do know is that Fred and Ginger worked very hard. Those gorgeous legs were only the byproduct of how hard they worked. Fred Astaire was such a perfectionist that not too many dancers could keep up with him. That sublime effortlessness in him was the result of endless sweat and labor. He made Ginger into a star. (I have heard people say Ginger did everything Fred did, only backwards. No, my dears. In ballroom dancing the man leads. And if he can lead he will lift the woman's technique a notch or two.)

Now, I know I'm not such a one-of-a-kind gift to humanity as Fred Astaire. Compared to his dancing I'm just straining and stressing my way through life in an awfully clunky way. I definitely am trying too hard. But you know what? Those five perfect pirouettes that you see a dancer pull off on the stage are the result of many trying-too-hard, eight-ten-twelve-pirouette practice sessions in the studio. But you wouldn't know that—they don't blog about it!

Homeschoolers have strong convictions

When you're in school you don't give educational philosophy much thought. But homeschoolers give that a lot
of thought—sometimes too much thought. And when you
give something too much thought you become very attached to your thoughts. I am sure I'm no exception to this.
The fact is homeschoolers do not all think alike.

When we became homeschoolers a simple Google
search pointed me to two groups in our area. (I'll write
about the homeschooling community later.) I immediately
connected with our local groups and they were as kind and
generous as anyone could hope for. We quickly learned
of their regular park days where we were welcomed and
found lots of wonderful people. I of course got on the
email lists of these groups. With one group I had some interesting correspondence that made me aware of the diversity of the homeschooling population.

When I joined the list and introduced myself I said that
I call ourselves "freeschoolers." Here are some conversations that followed with some "unschoolers" in our group.
Unschoolers are followers of John Holt who believe children should be allowed to follow their own inclinations and
learn what and how they choose. These are some of the
group emails we exchanged.

Patricia:
Hi Clara. How would you describe "freeschooling"
and how would it be different from "unschooling"?

Clara:
Hi Patricia. I'm just sort of playing around with
ideas... My idea of "freeschooling" is teaching kids
like college students, minus the term papers and
grades. I just pick a topic—literature, history, philosophy, the arts—pick some good books (or works or

performances) and study different aspects of them. I don't think kids need "textbooks" in the sense of things written for them. I think they can learn from real books/works, primary sources, as in college. I also don't believe that they need to "prove" that they have learned something, so no need for tests or term papers. My kid is 10 so I think later we might do projects or papers on various topics, but not now. Now, I want him to just enjoy good books and learn what he can from them.

Right now we're reading Jules Verne's *Around the World in 80 Days* and studying geography and history through it. And math. We just started homeschooling so I haven't found the right math book yet but I'm looking for a good beginning algebra book. I think math will be the only subject my son will have "homework" on. Any ideas on a good beginning algebra book anybody?

So I'd say freeschooling is unschooling philosophy plus good books in different fields. That might be a little of a contradiction but I guess that's what happens when you invent things as you go along!

Thanks for asking! Would be fun to hear different people's educational philosophies.

Patricia:

I agree that the bottom line is what works. I am generally a pretty enthusiastic reader and love to delve into things once they catch my fancy. I have no problem coming up with ideas of things to do. Sometimes and with some of my kids this worked great. We did periods of study just as you are describing. However, at other times this approach didn't work. My interest or enthusiasm didn't catch on or was a deterrent to reading or investigating certain things. In the end it was more reliable for much of the time for the kids to come up with their own ideas or spend time "doing nothing". I don't do a lot of "nothing" and that is not useful (sorry about the double negative). I could use a little practice in just sitting around.

Clara:

You're right. You can never be sure beforehand what's going to work. And I'm enough of an unschooler to be OK with a good amount of doing nothing. I'm also pretty sneaky at having kids do things that feel like doing nothing...!

Patricia:

I wonder about your use of the word "sneaky". That is something that I've thought a lot about. I ended up deciding that the kids' autonomy and an authentic relationship between us precluded sneaky parenting on my part. These values were more important than any particular academic achievement. If I felt nervous about them not knowing spelling I would tell them, "I am feeling nervous about spelling," rather than trying to do something to get it in the back door. On the other hand, if they really needed to or wanted to write something I would encourage correct spelling and tell them why. They were free (at least I hoped they felt free most of the time) to reject my suggestions. "Suggestions" that people aren't free to reject really aren't suggestions. What do you think?

Beth:

Hi Patricia and Clara. I have noticed that being sneaky with kids is a pretty popular American pastime. I received, a few years ago, a cookbook titled Deceptively Delicious, written by Jessica Seinfeld. The gift-giver thought my daughter should be eating more vegetables. Mrs. Seinfeld was then on talk show after talk show promoting her nutritional sneakiness with much applause and approval. No one that I saw even questioned her, just more sly smile and the nudge, nudge, wink, wink kind of attitude. It just felt dishonest and condescending to me. I showed my kids the cookbook and they decided to try one of the recipes. It was brownies with zucchini. We all tried to like them, but they just didn't taste good, so we didn't make any more recipes.

I think it's pretty standard in our culture to think it's fine (and good) to trick our kids into doing things that we deem are good for them, and that we assume they wouldn't choose on their own (not that I'm saying the op was doing that). But it's definitely worth thinking about!

Clara:
I'm much more playful with my words than that. Don't take them so literally!

I felt that I had a particularly discordant note. Luckily a fellow homeschooler came to the rescue of this clueless newcomer.

Martha (to the group):
Welcome :)
I have really used slyness on my kids (don't hate me cause I'm slick) :)
I have taken dangerous objects from my babies and pretended that they disappeared. There is always Santa, the Toothfairy, the Easter Bunny (who lays eggs, filled with chocolate!)... "It's not gonna hurt", "We're almost there", "Dad and I aren't fighting" ;) Aren't all those a form of deception? Here is my best one... ready: "Be just a minute..." insert "I'll," "we'll"...
How's that for sneaky? LOL
I know you'll say that's not the same, what's the

harm... Just trying to keep us all present. Seriously, am
I the only one living in the glass house? :) I try not to
throw stones but I fear there are some cracks...LOL

Guilty of the human condition, Martha

Martha (privately to me):

Just a heads up. There are more than a few Radical
Unschoolers on this list. So any insinuation of pulling
the wool over kids' eyes or, you know, whatever, gets
more serious attention than you may mean it to. Also
you may not find discussions on curricula or teaching
methods here, as unschoolers, radical or otherwise DO
NOT TEACH their children, they facilitate/guide.

With that said, it is a nice group, one of the more
accepting/involved/ community feeling-like groups in
the Bay Area (not including religious groups, I don't
have any experience there). So hope to see you soon.

Patricia in response to Martha's email to the group:

I think that it is an interesting question—whether
and how we try to get kids to do things that they don't
want to do. I don't think that distracting a baby is the
same as telling your 10 year-old that us parents are not
fighting. Some of it has to do with the developmental
stage of the kid and a lot has to do with intention. "I'll
be right there," could be a stalling lie, or it could express the best intention of a busy responsible person. I take it as my challenge to know which it is. "It's
not gonna hurt," is a very interesting one to me. I am a
stoic who tried to encourage that (with some initial success) in my kids, only to have it backfire seriously. One
kid had a medical/injection phobia for years, complete with fainting and concussions. I really wish I had
been completely honest and empathic from the very
start. Not sure if that would have changed the course
of things, but I would have felt a lot better about it all if

I hadn't been trying to get them to do something by a more backhanded route.

I enjoy talking about the theory and intention behind what I'm doing. I never mean to imply that I follow through on all my ideas or ideals. Screwing up is inevitable, interesting and generally not disastrous. No stones are involved (usually).

Clara:

I had an algebra teacher in eighth grade who taught us very advanced concepts as a game. He never said, "Today's lesson is..." He said, "Let me show you something really interesting. .." At the end of the lesson he would announce, "And what you learned today is..." The kids would all look at each other in amazement and glee: "Wow, and we thought that concept was going to be so hard."

I think in the history of humanity—any culture, any place, any time—there have always been people who have delighted in playing games with children. Some of those games are play and some are lessons—and most, mixed. Playful deviousness, in both children and adults, is something that has delighted the hearts of some people, and confused others who then reprimand and scorn it. Perhaps the twain shall never meet in spirit, though they can certainly be civil to each other and wish each other the best.

Obviously I belong to the category that delights in sense of humor, playfulness, and the twists and turns in human navigations, so I am biased in its favor. But I have also observed that this flexibility makes for less strictness, hence requires more toleration and forgiveness.

I'm with you Martha. We are the guilty and the imperfect. Mea culpa—but then, out of this deviousness of spirit art and science are born.

Are homeschoolers entitled to summer vacation?

This is our first summer as homeschoolers. Jack left school in February and I did some official "teaching" from March through May. Come June, however, Jack started rebelling against our "lessons."

I put "teaching" and "lessons" in quotation marks because what we basically did together was read. And look at maps, discuss topics that came up, look up some of the things we didn't know, etc. It wasn't that different from reading together when he was in school. We are a reading family. But the fact that Jack was now officially a homeschooler made him look at reading together differently. He saw reading time as teaching time now.

Being in transition and often overwhelmed by all the changes that quitting school had brought on, I can't say we even read that much together. We finished *Great Expectations* that we had started while Jack was in school and read *Around the World in 80 Days*, his first official homeschooling book. We were halfway through Steinbeck's *Travels with Charley* when Jack demanded a summer vacation. The book was a little slow going which made summer break that much more appealing.

I really don't like to leave projects unfinished. I am so conditioned by my own schooling that I think not finishing your work by the end of the school year means you have flunked the grade. It feels like getting an "Incomplete" in a college course. How do you leave John Steinbeck stranded in the middle of nowhere in some Midwestern back roads and ask him to wait for you to come back in three months?

I had also set the goal—very modest, I thought—that Jack should complete a record of the important books he has read over the years. I designated a notebook, a Book Log, for him to record the following information about every major book he has read so far:

Title of book
Author
Original language of book
Year of publication
Three other titles by the same author
Date the book was read
A short paragraph of comments about the book
Age group Jack recommends the book for (just for fun)

These are the books of substance that Jack has read, or has had read to him, since second grade and he is to enter into his Book Log:

Little House on the Prairie (second grade)
Harry Potter series (third grade)
Tom Sawyer (fourth grade)
Huckleberry Finn (fourth grade)
Percy Jackson series (fifth grade)
Great Expectations (fifth grade)
Around the World in 80 Days (fifth grade)
Travels with Charley (fifth grade)

Nice assignment, isn't it? And it really is not much. You can do all this on way less than two hours of reading and writing every day.

But did we do it? No!

The old college professor in me freaked out at the idea of abandoning a book in the middle and not completing the final report. But alas, I did not have the grading weapon to wield against my kid. He let out one loud "It's not fair" and I officially declared summer break.

The question is, do you deserve a summer vacation if you have only worked less than two hours a day during the school year? And if I am doing away with all the traditional trappings of schooling—grades and tests and homework and mandatory attendance and whatnot—should I also be doing away with the traditional breakup of time into "school" and "vacation"? Shouldn't I be "teaching" my son that when learning is fun it is not necessary to take a "vacation" from it?

Obviously these questions arise out of my own years of conditioning. We adults are so shaped by our own school and work experience that we end up sticking to our own unconsciously held (mis)conceptions even when we are trying to do things differently. But what I noticed was that Jack was also driven by his misconceptions. Here's an example.

The books that we had read with Jack in second through fifth grade up until he left school, were evening family-time reading. They were "fun" not "work." But the minute he was out of school, reading together became "homeschooling." And of course any kid worth his salt has to resist homework, right? Wouldn't it be totally "uncool" to just read a challenging book without putting up a fight?

The moral of the story is this: If you don't have cause for rebellion, you invent it.

I figure I'll spare Jack becoming a rebel without a cause. We'll pick up where we left off as soon as possible in the new school year. Meanwhile Mr. Steinbeck will have to sit in Rocinante, sip his bourbon-laced coffee and wait for us. And once he has safely returned home and put away his gear I will promptly demand my book log entries.

I think I will provide a cause so Jack does not feel deprived of his rebellion.

The Homeschoolers' Conference

One of the first pieces of advice I received from fellow homeschoolers was: *Don't miss the conference!* One far-sighted mom made me make my reservation right on the spot, sitting at the kitchen table of another homeschooling mom, on my iPhone. I'm sure glad I did.

The conference is an annual event organized by the

Homeschool Association of California, held in Northern California. I dutifully registered for the conference and booked our rooms way in advance. I am now sitting in our motel room, reporting.

It is a blast! I had not seen such an eclectic group of free-spirited people for a long time. Kids run around in various groups or singly all day. Curfew is 1:00 a.m. The swimming pool teems with splashing kids and is circled by adults lying on their towels like beached whales. On the grass naked toddlers somersault and the esplanade is traversed—back and forth, back and forth, all day—by mohawked teenagers and skipping little girls, arms linked.

The hotel where the conference is held is big and sprawling, with lots of outdoor space: courtyards, pools, outdoor stage, many gathering areas, a pond... It is large enough that you can actually take little walks. Excellent choice. The kids can roam independently and yet be contained. The staff is super friendly and doesn't mind kids' antics.

And then there are the events. From chess and Yu Gi Oh tournaments to all-day Math and Brain Games Salon. There is a Construction Zone, Bead, Fiber, and Paper Art Salon, and an Alchemy Alcove. There is a Recycled Resource Room (books, toys, crafts kits) and the Swap-O-Rama-Rama where you can alter, decorate, and swap clothes and accessories. Every night homeschooler bands perform on the stage and kids dance with their parents or with their "first dates." The San Francisco unschoolers hosted a party in one of the courtyards last night and a nice big group of people sat together under the stars, drank mojitos, and talked about everything and nothing in particular.

All day long, of course, there are also sessions. I won't list the obvious ones: lots and lots of art, science, writing, and resource and self-help workshops for parents. Martial Arts and dance. Yoga. Story-telling... But let me list some of the more unusual ones.

For little kids: Battle of the Ninjas vs. the Pirates; Make Your Own Fairy Wings; Doll and Stuffed Toy Hospital; Tea Party; Make Clothes for Your Toys.

For adults: Homeschooling the Gifted/Sensitive/Special Needs Child; Benefits of TV and Videogames; Teaching Quantum Physics to Young Adults; Internet Resources; Conquering Homeschooling and Parenting Anxiety; Families-on-the-Road: Lifestyles, Philosophies, and Budgets ("spending less than living in a traditional stick house"); In Defense of College.

For teens: Music Industry; Sex Ed; Transitioning In or Out of School; Youth Activism; Indescribable Sexiness ("people with totally average looks"); How to Help a Friend in Trouble ("you may never use drugs, but it is highly likely that you will know someone who does get into trouble"); Wilderness Survival; Web Design.

For everybody: Bird Walk; Civil War Confederate Artillery Demonstration; Light, Illusion, and Fire; Owl Vomit ("why owls make pellets, where to find them, and dissecting them"); Noise and Explosions; The Discovery of Electromagnetism; Atomic Spectra; Duct Tape Creations; Storytelling: Real Life Heroes.

Before we came we printed out the schedule and highlighted the sessions we wanted to check out. But did we? No! The first evening and the next day all my son did was run around with old and new friends. Room to room. Area to area. Talk, talk, talk. Swim, run, eat. Crash at midnight. And I spent most of my time in the motel room catching up with work and just plain resting. I've had a hard few weeks. My mother broke her leg and I've been in and out of hospital and rehab, and on the freeway driving back and forth between San Francisco and Santa Cruz. So the first couple of days I did nothing.

Today is Saturday, the peak day of the conference. Nearly one thousand people have already arrived. One thousand! This is the biggest turnout in the twenty years of this annual conference. You keep hearing that more and more people are leaving schools and that homeschooling is turning into a movement. There's certainly evidence for that here. It is fascinating to observe.

And today I finally feel rested. No more sitting in the motel room behind the computer. I will now close down shop and go join the fun. Wish you were here!

"Amazing Opposites"

Jack gave the title to this blog.

I have gotten some interesting feedback on my recent blogs about my experiences with schools and homeschooling. A very good friend of mine, Sadie, wrote this in an email:

> I loved going to school... and I went to school when I had high fevers from nasty flus, in spite of my mother's objections... and once I think I even fainted in the classroom from the fever!... For me school was an opportunity to get to know what was outside of home... and since my parents were not educated people, school maybe was the only opportunity to get to know the outside world, and it turned out to be a golden opportunity for me, given the friends that I made in school... Years ago a roommate of mine mentioned that her music teacher and his wife had decided to homeschool their kids. I became so agitated that I called it a criminal act!!!... adding that I knew that the origin of schooling came from religious doctrine but nevertheless no parent should be allowed to keep their kids from going to school!!!... Is knowing the outside world about knowing a 'better' world or is it about knowing a 'different' world?

A reader, Rebecca from Canada, wrote comments from

a very different view point in response to this blog. She did not think much of my attempt to get Jack to read books that I consider the basis of a good education.

> I'd much rather my kid read the books he enjoys and wants to read than to "make" him read books I think are "good for him". See, if he loves reading, he'll likely find his way to those books on his own time. If you push him toward those books, making them 'compulsory', then chances are you will have a kid who continues to resist reading (and you). I don't think he's finding something to rebel against because he doesn't have school anymore. I think he's tasted freedom and he likes it and wants more of it.
>
> I do realize what you were saying about what was fun is now work... but I don't buy it. I've been involved in alternate ed and home education for, oh my gosh, 17 years now. I've seen kid after kid "deschool"... and seriously, if your kid had ever really enjoyed those books the way you think he did, I'm not sure he'd be so resistant to them now. A kid just doesn't switch off something he "loves", if you know what I mean. And I also think the books are irrelevant, really. He's likely still deschooling and needs time to make any activity he's previously associated with school or learning to lose that association so he can make it his own. So, yeah. Take a loooong vacation so that he can come to that point on his own, authentically.

I was going to write a blog contrasting these two different views: one in favor of schools (and formal education) and one very much against it. I was going to write that I really do see the valid points of both sides. In fact I empathize with both of them. I was also going to write that it is very difficult to find your own way when you see the sense in views that are opposite. Taking charge of my son's education is giving me an ongoing opportunity for self reflection. When you think about what your child should learn or what you should teach your child, you inevitably ask yourself some very intimate, and philosophical, questions: Who am I? What do I value? What should I want for my child? Etc.

As I was sitting behind the computer trying to articulate some of these thoughts, my son came over and started reading over my shoulder. He read the quotes above. He became very interested. He asked to go back to the blog where Rebecca had left her comments and wrote an answer to her. I then asked him what he thought about the contrasting views of Sadie and Rebecca. I asked him to give the blog a title. He came up with "Amazing Opposites" and ended up finishing this blog for me. Here are his comments:

> I think it's crazy that two people can have two thoughts that are completely opposite. One being that kids should have complete freedom and the other that they should be strictly in school. But they both sound so friendly and so much the same. The way they write it just seems like they're twins. Because they sound like each other even though the meanings are the exact opposite, like a two-piece table: there's one end and there's the other end, but right in the center is the split. And where that split is is where the two opposites meet and sound alike. Have you ever seen where two major rivers merge to form the Amazon? One of the rivers is completely clean and the other river is filled with mud, so muddy that it looks like tea with half-and-half in it. And they stay apart and split for at least a mile, or five or six miles, and then finally they merge. And during that merging they work together and form a color that works perfectly with nature. And that's exactly what happens between these two people's comments. They work perfectly with each other to form one thing.

And that thing is not easy to describe and it would take pages and pages to describe and so I'll say the simplest answer possible. That answer is a match of pairs.

A little muddy maybe, but excellent commentary—isn't it?! I won't give you my interpretation of what Jack is trying to say. In fact, I don't think I could say it any better. Somehow we both felt the validity of two opposing currents and the mysterious way in which they connect to form something "that works perfectly with nature."

The many rivers of thought that merge into one magnificent river—the Amazon of the intellect—is education.

Time for some major changes

Change Number 1: No Screens

One day I had a meltdown. I woke up sobbing. I just couldn't take it anymore. What I couldn't take above all was all the time Jack was spending in front of the computer screen every day: no reading, no music playing, no building or making something, no drawing or painting, absolutely nothing but the computer.

That day my husband stayed home from work to take Jack out so I could have a couple of hours of breathing space. By the time they returned from their outing I had packed away the VCR, DVD player, Xbox, and Jack's computer. No more screen time. Cold turkey in cold blood! Having seen me sob uncontrollably that morning Jack looked around with wide eyes but said nothing.

You see, I hate doing law enforcement work. I dislike and am very bad at patrolling my son's every move, timing his activities, issuing citations, and carrying out "justice." And children—especially boys—being consummate negotiators, I just did not want to endlessly fight off his attempts to push limits. You know how it goes: Any allotted

screen time will definitely run over if you do not materialize immediately to enforce the rule. If the allotted time gets
interrupted there is going to be the future negotiation, and
disagreement, over exactly how much time is left. Does
screen time accumulate if one day is missed? How does it
apply to times when friends come over or friends are visited? And on and on.

Right now I am too overwhelmed with demands on my
time and energy to take on any arrangement that requires
ongoing negotiation. So I unilaterally decided against all
screens: Off with its head!

And you know what? Jack accepted it with practically
no resistance. I really didn't expect this. I was prepared for
battle but none ensued. It is now over two months of no
screen time. I have modified the rule so that when friends
come over the Xbox may come out of storage, half an hour
per child. Also, Jack is allowed to watch TV when we visit
my mother, but only in the mornings before everybody
wakes up. I have to admit, I came pretty close to allowing him to watch TV a couple of times in the evening at my
mother's but managed to muster up my resistance and,
boy, was I much happier for it.

Result? Jack now reads a lot more, listens to and plays
more music, and generally finds something to do. In the
car, not being allowed to play on the iPod he chats and
looks out the window. Whew... what a relief. And it wasn't
as hard as what I had braced myself for!

Change Number 2: Less Work

The second change I made was that I cut back and
changed my work hours. There was just no way I could
spend even four consecutive hours a day working. Expecting a ten-year old boy to entertain himself for hours and
hours in an apartment is just not realistic. I now work for
a couple of hours in the morning and a couple of hours

at night, either after dinner or after my husband and son go to bed. It's a lucky thing that I am somewhat of a night person. Still, though I do my best to work as efficiently as possible, I am far from able to be as productive as when I had all day to myself. The bottom line is that my work has suffered. But there's nothing that I can do about that right now.

Change Number 3: The Move

The biggest change we decided to make, however, is to move out of San Francisco. My husband and I are both city people and as for me, San Francisco is the smallest of the cities I have lived in. I used to live in New York City and I still dream of living there again. But... I cannot bear to see my ten-year old cooped up in a city apartment all day. It was a whole different story when he was in school. In fact, one reason I preferred public to private schools is that publics generally have much bigger space for kids. My son's former public school had a big yard complete with a good play structure, garden, and space and equipment for all the usual ball games.

It was a no brainer. My husband and son quickly agreed with me that we should move out of the city. The bad economy came to our rescue. We could now even look for a house to buy in Marin County, which is a beautiful area north of San Francisco where kids have a lot more roaming space. It is a perfect location for its proximity to San Francisco (we can maintain our friendships and continue many activities) and to Sonoma County where there are a lot of farms. I have always wished for Jack to learn about growing things and taking care of animals, so this is a great opportunity. And there are many homeschoolers in both Marin and Sonoma counties.

My job as a writer, editor, and publisher can be done from anywhere. But moving out of the city is not going to be easy for my husband who will now have to commute close to an hour to and from work. Luckily he is an early morning person so he can hit the road at 6:30 a.m. and avoid the worst traffic.

So, you see, yanking your kid out of school is not as easy as all that. We have had to make some major adjustments—dare I say sacrifices? I am not going to pretend that I am over being angry at my son's school and all related parties for having pushed us into homeschooling. But then again, perhaps we needed a push. I am totally convinced that all's well that ends well.

I am also totally aware that we are lucky to be able to do what it takes to "end well." Who would have thought that being able to make sacrifices for your kid is actually a privilege?

The dusting of books

Well, the move out of San Francisco is upon us. We're packing, loading, cleaning, painting, etc., hence my laxness in writing blogs.

Packing books is an interesting activity for a homeschooling mother who is a bookworm. Every book I picked up and dusted I evaluated from the point of view of using as a teaching tool. I say "tool" because I don't expect to be "teaching" every book or having my son read all the books his father and I own. But I do think about using books to demonstrate points. For example, if Jack's fascination with Greek mythology continues I will at some point casually walk him past our Plato/ Aristotle/ Homer/ Herodotus/ tragedies shelf and let him see that there were also historical characters in ancient Greece. It wasn't all mythology. If he shows interest I'll take it from there.

And some books I just want him to be around even if he doesn't read them. Let him pick up from the corner of his eyes those volumes of Chekhov, Tolstoy and

Dostoyevsky. Let him see all of Shakespeare and Jane Austen in one place, or the many accounts of the French Revolution. Or let him see those rows of Trollope—and if he ever asks I will tell him how Trollope wrote on horseback on his business trips for the post office and that the idea of mailboxes on the corners of streets is his brainchild. Again, a place to start.

(I know I lose a lot of readers by writing about the classics. I apologize, but I'm going to write more.)

A couple of days ago I leafed through the two fat volumes of *Don Quixote* and *Divine Comedy*. I know very well that Dante and Cervantes are not the kind of authors you can force anybody to read. Frankly, I never finished *Don Quixote* when I was younger—it was too long and too infuriating. And *The Divine Comedy* is certainly rather esoteric. I packed the volumes with an inner sigh. "Will Jack ever read these—or Manzoni or Gogol?" I lamented.

(I apologize again. I really love this stuff and I want to share them with my kid.)

So last night a very good friend of mine, Indu, invited us to dinner. We met when our kids were in preschool and of all my newer friends she is the closest one to me in my intellectual interests. I described our new house to her and all the coincidences that led us to it. "You never find a house. The house finds you," she said. I agreed. But it turned out that something else was also about to find us.

In the corner of her dining room there was a stack of books. "You must have these," she said. Her son Arun is a splendid boy who is happily engaged with his school and increasingly enamored of tennis. She was a little disappointed that he wasn't interested in those books but we all know that her kid is as excellent as they come. Nevertheless I made a bet with her that someday Arun will come back to these books. I will hold them for him until that day.

The books...? A series under the title of *My Book House*, edited by Olive Beaupré Miller, first copyright 1921, thirty-fifth printing 1953. There are about a dozen volumes for elementary through high school "boys and girls." The two volumes I have before me give you an idea. One is called "From the Tower Window" introducing children to epic literature from different cultures—Greek, Persian, Indian, Biblical, Nordic, Germanic, etc.—and legendary historical figures like Charlemagne and Joan of Arc. The other, "Halls of Fame," introduces children to famous writers: Dante, Cervantes, Chaucer, Shakespeare, Goethe, Tolstoy, etc. The books are beautifully illustrated and just looking at the pictures and reading the captions is an engaging pleasure. I gratefully borrowed the books to explore with Jack while holding them in safekeeping for Indu's son Arun.

Now, these books are not very fun to read. The prose is pseudo-archaic and the "retold" stories are wordy and so densely told that they are sometimes hard to follow. But no matter. These books are amazing teaching tools. I will assign chapters for Jack to read on his own and study others together, augmented by the actual texts from which stories are "retold." But great teaching tools are many. What struck me about this particular series is that I was reminded of two things. First, the cultural and intellectual content of children's *education* was much richer in the past. And second, the cultural and intellectual content of children's *entertainment* was much richer in the past. In other words, kids used to be brought up with excellent materials used for true Aristotelian purpose: to instruct and to amuse.

(Again, I apologize. I know I am often seen as old-world and "elitist." People on the political right eye me with suspicion as ultra liberal, and people on the left dismiss me as reactionary and old-fashioned.)

While I was dusting and packing my books I mused over why I feel so strongly that my kid should be surrounded by Shakespeare and Dante and Dostoyevsky. I am certainly not going to force him to read anything he doesn't want to. I *am* going to do my best to make great literature interesting to him but I know very well that real interest can never be forced on anyone. But what I am certainly shooting for is to get this message across to him: Art, culture, and intellectual pursuit EXIST.

I feel that the greater part of the culture in which our children are growing up now denies—and denigrates—the greatest accomplishments of human beings throughout the world and throughout the ages. The books that found me at my friend's house reminded me that this denial and denigration is a relatively recent phenomenon.

But then, maybe Disney and Pixar will not succeed in muting Homer and deleting Joan of Arc. Perhaps a restoration, even a renaissance, is in order. Perhaps we should start with kids.

The school calls me about an anti-bullying program

Early in what would have been Jack's sixth grade I received a call from a new PTA member from his former school. She invited me to a meeting they were having about what to do with the bullying that was continuing to go on. I agreed to attend and did a little research so I would have something constructive to contribute.

As I comb the media for news about children for my website I notice that school bullying is often in the news: more savagery in schools, more suicides, more hand-wringing on what to do... In the most recent newsletter from Edutopia there was a segment titled "Creative Solutions to Prevent Bullying: Boosting Emotional Intelligence to Battle Bullying—A Brooklyn program gives kids an emotional tool kit."

The "emotional toolkit" was more mumbo jumbo about "I-Messages" ("I feel...," "What you're doing hurts me," "I hear you say...") to let the bullies know how they are hurting the bullied one. I watched the video demonstrating this approach with Jack to get his reaction to it. He right away recognized the same-old-same-old and smirked. I jotted down his comments verbatim:

> They tell you how to react when someone hurts you but you don't want them to hurt you in the first place. If you react like this lady says that's good, but normally you get hurt and then you lose yourself. Kids don't control themselves that well unless they're the daughter of a king or someone like that. Kids can't stop and think about how to react, they just react. It's really stupid that you think a kid would stop and think.
>
> They should teach kids not to hurt anyone in the first place. We're young but when you teach us things like this lady says you treat us like babies. You've got to be strict about this. It won't work to just go blah blah blah... You should be a little harder on us. I'm not saying you should punish us for every word we say off topic but you have to take bullying seriously. You don't take bullying seriously. This video talks about how some bullying turns into drug and gang fights. Many people can get caught between that. It is a big thing. Now unfortunately some bullies in high school have killed people. You can't take this lightly. Duh...
>
> You have to start when kids are really young and try to teach as hard as you can—but don't go hard on kids in first grade. Get harder on them through the years. Get serious. In elementary they don't teach you enough to prevent bullying. Teach kids before they become bullies. If you are strict with the leaders they would never lead other kids into bullying.

What I understood from Jack was that he thought this "I-Message" approach is too soft and babyish. He speaks from experience. This was the method that was tried in his school and it didn't stop anyone from bullying him. According to his experience this is what happens with I-Messages:

Bullied kid: "I feel hurt because..."
Bully and friends: "Aw, shut up..."

After this video I showed him the work of Michael Pritchart who is a local comedian and anti-bullying advocate. He is one of a number of inspiring people I have "met" through my website. His approach is to call a schoolwide meeting and let the bullied children talk. After that he lets the community at large make comments. This approach completely absorbed Jack:

> This is a way better approach. It's so cool, so awesome that I don't know what to say. It's the best method ever. All teachers should do this: be funny and let the kids talk. One day I walked into the teachers' lounge at my old school and I heard one of the teachers—unfortunately I think she quit—say, "The kids don't like me, they hate me. I try my best to be one of them but I can't." That's the best thing I heard a teacher say. But if she tried this method she might have gotten lucky with the kids.
>
> This guy sounds like an awesome dude, I want to meet him. I wonder how he came up with such a great method. He was not telling the kids not to be bullies but really showing them and explaining to them how it felt to be bullied. But he was not telling the kids to explain it in the moment of feeling bad... His way works much better. Normally if you're able to control yourself and say all the things that they tell you to say the kids don't believe you. They think it's completely fake. They tell you to shut up.
>
> This method is just more real. If you're a bully and you feel affected by what the bullied guy or girl is saying, then if you have bullied someone you might come up and apologize. That might bring some pressure off of you.

In the beginning one of the girls said she was trying to understand how the bully was feeling and realized that that they were hurting too. The bully hurts himself and just can't keep it inside. He needs to release it and takes it out on another kid. But that's not a good way to release the negative energy. What I've learned from a teacher is to take it out on a ball or a brick—but I recommend you don't do the brick because I hurt my toe doing that.

Michael Pritchard's comment about grief turning into anger especially hit home with Jack:

When I get bullied I get mad and I want to hurt the person who hurt me. I used to hate my life, how it hurt me—that was the grief part. Then it turned into hatred. I just hated the people who were doing it. Finally it turned into rage. Now if anyone bullies me even a little touch I want to hurt the dude. That's when I take it out on a ball or a wall or a brick. Eventually the hatred turned against the teachers: rage was against the bullies and hatred was against the teachers. All their planned stuff like I-Messages and stuff just didn't work.

I summarized Jack's reactions in a note to take with me to the PTA meeting along with links to the two videos:

• A nice lady holding up a heart-shaped piece of pink paper containing an I-Message does not give the impression that she's taking bullying as seriously as it ought to be taken.
• A big guy with a double edge of humor and toughness is more effective in getting the message across that he means business when he talks about bullying.
• I-Messages and the like are seen by kids—younger as well as older—as fake and babyish. A kid doing an

I-Message is often setting him or herself up for being made fun of.

- Real self-expression is *free* expression. In Michael Pritchett's video the kids expressed themselves in their own words, not according to some phony formula. This is what made their words effective.
- Kids do not like to be talked down to no matter how young they are. And if anybody would listen they would talk—and listen to each other.

Here are some of my own observations:

Trying to teach kids to react in a calm and proper manner in the moment of being bullied is wishful thinking. Yes, we should all be superhumans and able to "manage" our anger at a moment's notice but we have to be honest. How many people, no matter what the age, are able to do that? It is certainly extremely useful to learn some basic techniques for surviving awful situations right in the moment: observing our breathing, averting our gaze, removing ourselves... But to concentrate solely on these techniques is actually laying the burden of exertion on the bullied person. What about the bully? Kids don't see this as fair and square.

Bullying must be addressed in a community. Bullying is not something between two people that can be settled with a little dispute resolution. The entire community must face the problem and address it openly. And of course the kids themselves are the most relevant part of this community. They must be given the chance to speak their own minds in their own words. That's the first step, and one through which a lot gets resolved without need for further intervention. But it is a step that needs support and some simple nudging from adults who are perceived as both very serious and very compassionate.

Nothing fake works.

I had done my homework to offer experience and suggestions at the anti-bullying meeting at Jack's old school. I rose my hand a number of times to make comments but I was passed over. After two hours, when I finally realized I was not going to be called upon to talk, I left. My presence was not going to be acknowledged. Not even the new PTA member who had invited me to the meeting introduced herself to me. I never learned who she was.

Bad blogs and negative resistance

This is definitely not an invitation for abuse but I do like it when readers challenge my thoughts or downright say they don't think much of something I write. It gives me a little jolt and makes me look at myself.

In response to my most recent blogs someone (didn't leave a name!) said that it wasn't a very good blog. He/she is totally right. Before I posted the blog I realized that I hadn't made my points clearly enough, which basically means I hadn't thought them through. But I decided to post it anyway as a way of recording the various aspects of homeschooling. One of those "aspects" is me—and my limits. I simply have very little time to do anything right nowadays. And this is what I want to write about here.

You see, being a mother is already a full-time job, even if you have the easiest-tempered child in the world. Add to that other work inside and outside the house. And other family obligations and care-taking. And keeping up some semblance of social life so you don't feel isolated from the world. This is already a heavy load—and then place one huge load on top of it: homeschooling. It would break any camel's back.

But the fact is that human beings are not camels. We can carry much heavier loads, because we have to. I know I'm not going to break under my load because I see that my friend who has an autistic daughter has not broken. Another friend taking care of a twelve-year old daughter, a mother in early stages of Alzheimer's, and a sister recovering from a severe stroke, has not broken. We come up with whatever strength is required of us, *because we have to.* It's as simple as that.

So I know I'm not going to break. But there is no question that the quality of my work suffers. (I won't even talk about the quality of my life!) So, yes, some of my blogs are going to be sloppy, reflecting my fuzzy-headedness. But I'm very curious to see how things pan out in the long run. I picture my blogs as a series of snapshots—snapshots at various times of various aspects of raising a kid. These include snapshots of the nuts and bolts of raising and educating a kid, as well as snapshots of my own emotional and even intellectual states.

I always feel I should apologize when I interject myself into the picture when I talk about raising or educating my son. The pressure is so strong—and so internalized—to airbrush the mother out of the child-rearing picture. Or rather, we are allowed to be in the picture as "mother" but not as someone in our own right. I, as a person, should basically just vanish!

But another fact is that human beings don't really vanish. I make a point of writing about myself in these blogs, purposefully resisting that awful voice that keeps telling me "it's about your child, it's not about you; if you can't go away then at least airbrush yourself." I do put up that resistance. And resistance takes many forms. Let's call purposefully writing about yourself positive resistance. There is also negative resistance.

Negative resistance shows itself in omissions. Either you are omitted from the picture or some quality of yourself is. In a fuzzy-headed blog, for instance, what is omitted is the clear-thinking part of yourself. And when there is enough indication that you are not just fuzzy-brained then what is missing is the time to hone your work to reflect your ability to think clearly. TIME is what is seriously omitted from my life right now. And that omission is going to show itself in various ways in what I do. The absence of something can very much have a presence.

In effect I am very much present in my shortcomings. My bad writing, fuzzy thinking, short temper, even unhappiness and frustration, all do reflect the absence of my other, opposite, sides. So I feel that my good sides are present in their absence. My better and more competent side puts up negative resistance by making itself absent from what I do.

So... bad blogs? Yup, that's me. Bad mother? Yup. Bad teacher? Ditto. Just bad bad bad...

And this gets me thinking about "bad boys." Negative resistance. That's probably what they're up to too!

Time, time, time—or quantitative un-easing

I'm not finished with my negative/positive resistance topic—and I am going to interject myself into the child raising/educating picture some more.

I think having time is the biggest factor in feeling that you exist. When you have very little time to yourself, your "self" doesn't exist anymore. Or rather, it *feels* that it doesn't exist anymore. But the self fights back. As I wrote in the previous blog, you start to exist by negative resistance to non-existence: *I make myself absent, therefore I exist.*

But I'm not going to talk about existential matters. That sort of thing is endless. What I want to do is to free associate about time.

I think one reason that we suffer from "not having time" is that we quantify time. We are so conditioned to do that. And I'm not going to say a whole lot of clichéd nonsense about how bad "conditioning" is. There are good reasons and legitimate purposes for a lot of the conditioning that we receive. The problem, and the suffering, arises when we lose our autonomy and sense of control to conditioning.

There are all kinds of good reasons to quantify time. We need hours and minutes and days and years—a lot of the time, but not all the time. Sometimes we need NOT to quantify time by breaking it up into measurable quantities. Sometimes, I think, not measuring time gives you more time.

Take my teaching for example. I started out our home-schooling journey setting time frames for things: this many hours of screen time and that many hours of reading time; this long for "academic" lessons and that long for music; this much for being outside in fresh air and that much for "socializing." I'm not knocking myself or others who set out this way. It's not a bad place to start—but it's a place you put behind you very fast! (Experienced homeschoolers smile knowingly as they read this!)

For starters, if you want to stick to schedules you have to turn yourself into an alarm clock. Perhaps there are kids out there who can self regulate by the clock: at the strike of 9:30 turn off the video game and open the book; at 1 dab their lips with the napkin at the lunch table and move behind their desk for math homework; at the stroke of 5:00 stop their game of tag and buckle themselves up in the car so mom can get home in time to cook. I'm sure there are kids like this somewhere, but I sure don't know any.

As for my kid, even turning myself into an alarm clock won't do the trick. To dislodge him from doing what he wants to be doing requires a pair of pliers. I won't go into the unpleasant scenes we can get into as a result of this. I don't know about him but I lose a lot of self-respect over this issue. For one thing, no one acts pretty when they have to monitor and police another human being. For another thing, when I can't enforce my own rules and time-tables I feel like a nagging or screaming fool. I don't imagine my son gains any respect for me either when I can't enforce my own rules, and that makes me doubly frustrated. So this kind of measuring and allocating time doesn't work. This is one side of the coin.

The other side of the coin, however, is that you—or at least, I—can't completely leave a kid to his own devices. I just can't live with a kid who spends endless hours in front of various screens, which is what my son would do if I don't turn myself into a pair of pliers and yank him away from it. I am not kidding. This is the reality of children his genera-tion. Even their socializing, their friendships, are conducted behind a screen: texting, playing games, on Skype, Face-book, you name it. I know a lot of homeschoolers and un-schoolers who think this is OK. I don't. I'm not going to get into an ideological battle about it. I just can't live like that. Period.

So, how can you have some regulation in life without quantification of time? This is not just an intellectual exer-cise; it's an existential challenge! But it's also a very prac-tical and everyday problem that I have to find a solution to. How do I accomplish the teaching/learning goals I very much insist on without assigning timetables to them? I feel that I have to do some experimentation now.

What I'm going to experiment with is to become more subjective in my approach—which goes against all advice in child rearing.

You are always told to make sure the child knows what is expected of him. OK, this sounds fair enough. But per-haps the problem is that we *quantify* what we expect of our children: spend this much time, read this many books, complete so many assignments, exercise for so long. What if we make clear what we want the kid to do without as-signing a time or other quantification to it? What if we just regulate his activities with "enough" or "not enough"? This sounds awfully subjective, doesn't it? I mean, aren't we conditioned to think that the clock is objective while mom's judgment of "enough" or "not enough" is subjective?

But to hell with the "objectivity" of the clock. I'm going to try subjectivity of judgment now. I know that "subjectivity" sounds arbitrary and authoritarian but maybe it's actually less arbitrary and authoritarian than setting time schedules. Isn't turning yourself into an alarm clock or time police just as authoritarian?

The fact is that we are in the position of authority with our kids, so why pretend? Why relegate this authority to our conditioning to quantify?

When would you like to eat?

My mother is eighty-three years old and has always been very active, creative, and deeply connected to many people in her life. She is a celebrated educator, author, artist and any number of other things. But old age catches up with everyone eventually and she has had to slow down. She lives with my brother most of the time but stays with us a week or ten days out of the month. In fact, one reason we moved out of the city was to have a bigger house so she can live with us more comfortably.

What my brother and I try to do is make sure her active and social life does not suffer the effects of age too much. We try to support her in her activities and habits as much as we can. But for someone as full of energy and imagination as my mother you could always be doing more. New projects are constantly bubbling out of her and the phone rings off the hook. She likes to write, teach, do art, cook, etc., while keeping in touch with her wide circle of family and friends—and she needs a little help with each little task. Her life runs into all hours of the day. She likes to eat late.

My husband keeps very early hours. He wakes up between five and six in the morning and is on the road as early as possible to avoid rush hour commute. By the time he gets home around six o'clock he is tired and hungry.

My son is eleven and spends most of his day at home. The afternoons are the only time he can do things outside the house, spending time with other kids or skateboarding at the park. I of course want him to do this as much as possible—what is more necessary for a kid than doing good, healthy things with other kids? So I try to make sure he spends his afternoons exercising and enjoying being with friends. He too is usually awfully hungry by six o'clock.

Getting home in time for cooking, serving, cleaning is all done in a mad rush. From the car to the kitchen I only have time to set down what I'm carrying. The last thing I want to do while still out of breath with the preparations is to sit down and eat myself.

My mother likes to eat after going for early-evening outings. I myself like this schedule better, but not when I've already gone through one cooking shift. I cater to people of strong and uncompromising preferences.

So how do you spend all your afternoon outdoors but also get home in time to cook (presuming that you have done all the shopping and preparations in advance)? You get home, plunk down whatever you're carrying (bag, jacket, etc.) and get going on dinner. "What's for dinner?" someone asks. "When's dinner?" says another. "I'm not hungry," says yet another. You continue with what you're making, having thought in advance about what to make so it can be warmed and served later with minimal extra labor—so you can wash the pots and pans after the first group eats and all that would be left to do later is to warm up the food using minimal crockery. Think about it—it's an awful lot of juggling. Day in and day out.

I only feed my husband once a day at dinner time. But for my son and my mother I have to think about meals two or three times a day. (I won't mention snacks and the little evening drink and munchies for my mom.) Just keeping up with the food needs of our household (planning, cooking, serving, cleaning) is more than enough work for me—forget about keeping up with my own working life, homeschooling, and all the other unnameable parts of being a decent mother, wife, daughter, etc... Let's just stick with food. And the fact that nobody compromises. Breathing down my neck is not noticed. If I bring it up it creates bad feeling.

I was thinking today that I am often asking someone, When would you like to eat? There is coordination to be done so I need to know. Then I realized no one ever asks me that question! I have never heard anyone say, When would *you* like to eat? So I thought, why don't I ask myself that question? Suppose I take my own preferences into consideration? Suppose I decide when I would like to eat instead of fitting my own eating into others' schedules?

And you know what? The very thought of taking yet someone else's wants and preferences into consideration exhausts me—even when that someone else is me. I realized by thinking about pleasing myself I would be turning myself into yet another person to cater to and please—and who needs that! I'd rather just eat whatever and whenever than add another person to the people I have to take care of.

Eating is not that important to me. To be quite honest, I'd rather eat very simple foods that requires minimal labor. I cook because I feel it's my duty to feed my family well, especially my kid. So whatever I eat of what I basically make for the family is quite good enough for me. And the time I eat doesn't matter much either. I generally eat at the time when it is most expedient in terms of reducing cleanup time and other labor.

What I can't live without is exercising. In fact, that's the one and only way I keep sane. If I don't go to my dance classes or work out I know I will take a deep emotional plunge. I can't afford that. I compromise with eating time but not with exercising.

So when would I like to eat?
I don't know.
Do I have a choice?
I suppose.
Do I even care?
About what?

Still struggling with screen time

Last spring, following a melt-down I had, I banished all electronic screens from my son's life. We don't have TV reception so the ban meant no computers, no Xbox, no iPhone, etc.

There is no question that I was much happier without a screen always glowing in my son's face. He didn't do too badly either. But... even when in total desperation I put away all screens, I knew that it would not be forever. I have a strong suspicion that banishing all electronic screens may be winning a battle but losing the war. I think the best way to foster obsession with something is to banish it. So at some point in the summer screens started making a come-back one at a time—slowly, slowly...

One of the things I keep writing in my blogs is how much I hate playing screen police, or any kind of police or patrol. I'm really really bad at it. And Jack knows it. He keeps pushing and sneaking and generally being very un-pleasant to get his way because I just can't stand having to enforce rules and regulations. He knows how much I hate being a disciplinarian and he has learned from experience that a lot of times I give in to his unpleasantness just to get away from it. I wish I were better able to stand up to him but I just am not. My bad.

So where does this leave us...? Back to lots and lots of screen time. Again, unless I materialize on the hour and end up in some kind of unpleasantness (push and whine and bargain on his side, exasperation and yelling and

screaming on mine) the damned screen never goes off.
Games, YouTube, Facebook, and hours of mindless Skyp-
ing take over the air and sound space of our house, not to
mention Jack's semi-conscious consciousness. It just hurts
to be part of this.

One of the accusations that I throw at him in my moments of frustration is that he has become addicted to the
screen. I tell him that to keep doing something that you
know is bad is called addiction. I yell that he has no control
over himself and he shouts back that if I let him do it his
way he will prove to me that he has self-control. He spent
his Christmas money on some kind of device that allows
him to play Xbox games with others online. "Playing with
others will be more fun and satisfying," he said, "so I won't
spend as much time behind the screen."

"Whatever," I thought to myself. I didn't really believe
it.

But I do have to report one improvement. Jack is starting to feel that he needs to prove to me that he can have
self-control. I think calling him a screen addict did not sit
very well with him! He does make some effort to prove me
wrong. Hey... I take whatever I can get!

Nevertheless, there is still too much screen presence,
more that I can take. I previously wrote about my "subjective" and less quantitative approach to limiting the time.
But here's a more detailed version of how that is translat-
ing into our everyday routine.

I take away the computer at night before going to bed.
When Jack wakes up in the morning (which is usually earlier than me) he has to read and do math homework. When
I wake up and need my couple of hours to do some work
I let him get on the computer. Then we do our lessons or
reading together and have lunch. After lunch it's outing
time. Most days he likes to go to the skate park and meet
up with his friends. Other days there are other activities:
park day with homeschoolers, roller skating, or occasional

classes. In the evening again he can have the computer for a couple of hours. Ten o'clock is electronic device curfew, which means that the cell phone and texting activities have to cease as well.

I think this is a reasonable schedule. It is still way more screen time than "experts" recommend but let's get real. On the homepage of this site a little while ago I posted a survey by the parenting website Netmums that showed that many mothers lie about all kinds of things, from how much TV their children watch to what they cook them for dinner. So let's be real indeed. My son still has too much screen time, and certainly way too much for me. But that's where we are... Let's see how successful we'll be with this new regimen!

Homeschooling, a year later

Exactly one year ago on this day I pulled my kid out of school.

It's been quite a year. Our lives changed in a lot of ways. The most visible change has been that we moved out of San Francisco. We exchanged the gritty charm of the city for the beauty and ease of life in a small town. As for Jack, it is much easier for him to go free range here than in the city. It's much safer here and much more user friendly for the average kid. The skateboard park, the local youth center, the friendly board-game shop—this sort of thing makes for a much more pleasant life than the restricted and guarded life a kid lives in a city. And the fact is that my son quitting school was what made me realize we actually were free to make other changes in our lives. Funny. I would never have thought my son's lousy school was what was keeping us in the city.

But as I think about how things have turned out for Jack the word "change" doesn't seem quite right. When someone becomes more oneself it's hard to call it "change." Jack is more himself now. He is not so reactive. He makes his own choices more regularly and is consequently more relaxed. It just seems like he breathes with more ease now. (Has *he* changed or have the circumstances?)

My friend Flavia claims that Jack is more affectionate since he quit school. She says he is more polite and engaging. I'll be happy to take her word for it but what I can say for my part is that he certainly has not become any worse of a kid! He has also made new friends with whom he is happy, unlike most of the kids he knew at school. We don't have to deal with any real conflicts now, with kids or teachers.

I would also say that he has learned a lot more since he left school. Even though we don't spend an awful lot of time in official "lessons" together we have covered a lot of material. Interesting stuff. Good writing. History. Intro to social sciences. He has also had time to play and learn a lot more music. He has learned recording software and is now learning Photoshop. He even embarked on writing a novel less than a month after he left school. (It was abandoned about ten pages later, but still!) I have to admit that we haven't kept up with math as much as I would like and Jack himself feels bad about math not being his best subject any more. We will have to remedy this soon.

Our routines have changed. We don't get up in the morning and rush out the door. (He still is an early riser but I stay up late and sleep in—those late night/early morning hours are the only time I have to myself.) But we do an awful lot of driving. The first question most people ask homeschoolers is what we call the "S" question: "But do the kids socialize enough?" Yes, the kids socialize plenty—and guess who gets them from here to there and there to thither to do the socializing. We're on the road an awful lot.

There's also the driving from interesting class here to enriching activity there. And as the kid indulges in interest and enrichment yours truly kills an awful lot of time waiting in the car, chit chatting on pavement, or sipping tea at kitchen tables. Killing time is no fun. I hear the clock ticking awfully loud in my ears. Maybe it's because I'm getting old that I really don't like killing time. I don't think I have that much of it left anymore.

Altogether, there is no question that Jack's life and education have improved since leaving school. He is happier with himself and with others and is learning more. My life has also improved in that that I don't have to suffer from witnessing my child's unhappiness and I don't have to struggle so hard trying to improve things—and failing at it. But my life has not improved as far as doing things for myself is concerned. I can barely manage to keep up with my greatly diminished work let alone anything else I might wish to enjoy.

So one should do one's best and sacrifice what one can to homeschool one's child. Right?

I am not sure. Even if a parent's overriding passion in life is to raise and educate her children I am not so sure being so very much at the center of your children's lives is such a great thing. I make no qualms about my own frustration at perpetually putting my own life and work on the back burner on account of having had a child. I don't pretend to be such a selfless mother and I frequently write about it here. But it's not just for my own sake that I am not entirely happy with being my kid's ever-present companion. A kid needs many people in his life on a regular basis. He needs a wider horizon to take off toward every day. Just as it is sweet to come back to home and family in the evening, it is fresh and exciting to run out the door first thing in the morning. School can be that great "outdoors," full of activity and pleasure of new and challenging things. Alas, this was my own school experience...

In the past year I have met many people who are homeschoolers at heart. Many of them are really great: open-minded, bold, sharp and accepting at the same time, and truly fulfilled—both kids and adults. Truth be told, I don't feel I am one of them. And I think it will be some time before my son can really assess how fulfilling homeschooling has been for him.

So the verdict at my first anniversary of being a homeschooling mother? This: Homeschooling is infinitely better than a bad school but not as good as a good school.

Sometimes I get intimations of a terrific school I can now design. I think that my homeschooling experience is giving me some very solid ideas for creating such a school, complete with teaching methodology. (Here my third-generation educator side shows itself.) I thought I left teaching when I quit my job in academia but I guess my situation has turned into one of those "you can take the —— out of the —— but you can't take the, etc. etc."

And I have to record that on exactly the first anniversary of taking my son out of school I spent the day helping the mother of his old school friend Anoah complete their homeschooling paperwork. Their new school, Hazelwood Olympus School, was established exactly a year after Jack quit school. You should have seen the smile on Anoah's face!

So how fun is it?

Homeschooling has forced me to abandon a lot of expectations and non-expectations, so I don't waste time trying to sort out what should have been how and why. But the question that always runs in the back of my mind is, how fun has it been?

Now that we've been homeschooling for a year I think I am ready to give my assessment. Homeschooling is one-third miserable, one-third hard but rewarding work, and one-third just great.

So the first third, the awful times... Here is a list of things that make for bad times.

Fighting: Jack and I end up fighting way too much. These are the times when he won't cooperate, or puts up unfair resistance, or just can't help himself pushing limits and my buttons (he's always been good at this, hence this website). These are also the times when I am exhausted, or pushed by others, or just plain upset and I somehow take it out on him. We are both guilty of sometimes picking a fight with the other.

Getting on each other's nerves: I really do not think parents and children should be together 24/7—or let's say not all people are wired in a way that they can take to being in company of anybody 24/7. You inevitably get on each other's nerves. This is not fun.

Boredom and tediousness: There are definitely lots of times when Jack is bored—alone, uninspired, understimulated, etc.—and a lot of times that I have to do things that I find tedious—too much driving, too much waiting around, finding too many things uninteresting.

Wasting time: Jack spends a lot of time on things that I consider a waste of time and they usually involve a screen. Watching him spend way too much time in front of a screen—playing games, "socializing" on Facebook, following link after link on YouTube, that sort of thing—is really painful for me. In fact this sort of thing is exactly the kind that sends me over the edge and leads to arguments and fights.

The second third of the time is spent doing things that are difficult to do or not necessarily fun but rewarding. A lot of our "studying" falls in this category. The reading we do together or the "lessons" that we have are challenging. Jack doesn't particularly like the intellectual stimulation. He'd almost always rather be doing something else. His assignments or our discussions are certainly not uninteresting to him but he does not jump for joy to be doing any of it. Nor do I jump for joy to remind him to do his assignment or call him to sit down to work. I also most often would rather be doing other things. BUT… once we do settle into our readings, discussions, or explorations, we can get totally absorbed and carried away. And I certainly see the fruit of my labors. Jack is developing a very impressive capacity to think. I take pride and great joy in that, even if it is certainly a hard-earned joy.

The third third of the time is fun, pure and easy fun. We drive by so many schools that resemble prisons, children behind bars, weighed down with books that I do not care to open myself or have my son burdened by, interactions between children and/or adults that make my hair stand on end… We cruise right by these places and gloat in being free from them. We meet up with other homeschoolers in parks, in company of other children and families who are comfortable with who they are and with each other, nobody competing with anybody, nobody giving in to pressures that distort their being and make them unhappy, kids running free, late for nothing, afraid of no disapproval or judgment… We check out places—museums, cultural centers, libraries, play parks, whatever strikes our fancy—and do as we please. We don't have deadlines. Jack doesn't have to prove to me that he has "mastered" anything and I don't have to prove to anybody that I am indeed "teaching" him.

Pi Day

Today is March 14, or 3.14—or shall we say π?

I had never heard of Pi Day. Apparently math enthusiasts—or geeks, as Megan put it—celebrate Pi Day all over United States.

Megan is not exactly a "geek" herself. She's a writer, radio producer, dancer, singer, and any number of other hot stuff—including a closet student of math and physics. She is also my niece who is living with us right now, a splendid young woman and a real delight to have around.

Megan woke up this morning and announced that she was going to bake a pie in honor of Pi Day. Naturally, of course, we all heard "Pie Day." Nobody's going to argue with someone (a good cook, I might add) volunteering to bake a pie, but what is pie day, we wanted to know. So she set us straight and walked down to the grocery store to buy different kinds of apples for a little pie tasting. We just got up from the table eating terrific fresh pies and having a little π appreciation.

I won't bore you with listing some "educational" points here (even though we did use the opportunity for a little "homeschooling" at the table). Here's a chance for you to have a little π appreciation of your own at the official website of Pi Day: www.piday.org.

As it turns out March 14 is also Albert Einstein's birthday. And Megan pointed out that a particularly interesting Pi Day is coming up in 2015 when the date will be 3.14.15.

So here's to π, Einstein, and Megan—and here is the beauty itself in partial, 1,120 decimal-digit, splendor:

3.1415926535 8979323846 2643383279 5028841971
6939937510 5820974944 5923078164 0628620899
8628034825 3421170679 8214808651 3282306647
0938446095 5058223172 5359408128 4811174502
8410270193 8521105559 6446229489 5493038196
4428810975 6659334461 2847564823 3786783165
2712019091 4564856692 3460348610 4543266482
1339360726 0249141273 7245870066 0631558817
4881520920 9628292540 9171536436 7892590360
0113305305 4882046652 1384146951 9415116094
3305727036 5759591953 0921861173 8193261179
3105118548 0744623799 6274956735 1885752724
8912279381 8301194912 9833673362 4406566430
8602139494 6395224737 1907021798 6094370277
0539217176 2931767523 8467481846 7669405132
0005681271 4526356082 7785771342 7577896091

7363717872 1468440901 2249534301 4654958537
1050792279 6892589235 4201995611 2129021960
8640344181 5981362977 4771309960 5187072113
4999999837 2978049951 0597317328 1609631859
5024459455 3469083026 4252230825 3344685035
2619311881 7101000313 7838752886 5875332083
8142061717 7669147303 5982534904 2875546873
1159562863 8823537875 9375195778 1857780532
1712268066 1300192787 6611195909 2164201989
3809525720 1065485863 2788659361 5338182796
8230301952 0353018529 6899577362 2599413891
2497217752 8347913151 5574857242 4541506

"Smart Shock"

I recently came across a note I had taken a few years ago of a conversation with Jack. He must have been seven or eight.

"Mom, have you ever gotten a smart shock?"

"What's a smart shock?"

"It's when you know what a word means when you've never heard it before. You probably heard it before but you don't know what it means. I had a smart shock when I was five. I suddenly knew what the word 'independent' meant. I suddenly knew it meant working solo, single, solitaire, all of that."

This is the same kid who thinks he is cheating when he gets perfect score in spelling: "But I don't know how to spell, I just have photographic memory."

I think this is a good example of how fast the brain works. Kids learn without knowing how they're doing it. Sometimes *what* they know surprises them and they feel confused when they can't figure out *how* they've learned it. The moment you become aware that you know something but you don't know how you learned it is a bit jolting. I think "smart shock" is a great description!

Jack and "The Good Citizen at School"

As I've mentioned before I like serendipity. I love exploring elements introduced by chance into everyday life. As a book-oriented person a lot of those elements are books and publications that I come across by chance.

One of my recent chance encounters was with a little book I picked up in a used bookstore, *The Good Citizen's Handbook: A Guide to Proper Behavior.* This is a collection and reproduction of materials from the 1920s to the 1960s on how to be a good citizen. On the front cover is a drawing of a handsome young boy in overalls with his hand on his heart. The back cover describes some of the ways in which readers can perform their "duty." It mentions topics like these:

Penmanship
Proper respect for authority
Cleanliness
The dangers of delinquency
The importance of a meat dish
The benefits of cheerfulness
Why it's never right to poison the neighbor's dog

The book's decidedly quaint and old-fashioned—and more than slightly ridiculous—aspects notwithstanding, it's full of a lot of common sense and good advice. Look at these definitions for example:

Sin An act contrary to a person's conscience.
Vice An act harmful to a person or a person's morals.
Crime An act that breaks the law.

I like this advice:

Remember that the best way to reduce crime is to

prevent it by proper methods of training at home and at school; and that the best way to deal with criminals is to make good citizens of them.

Good common sense, and fair enough.

I decided to read some of the book with Jack and get his reaction. The "good behavior" in the subtitle and the pictures of extremely clean-cut, white, suburban people of course brings out a sneer in any "cool" kid nowadays. But I persisted. Here are some the conversations and revelations that ensued.

"I know all this stuff," Jack said when I introduced the book as a subject of our lesson of the day. "Be a good boy blah blah blah..."

Upon my insistence that we look at some of the advice in the book Jack said: "Look, one of the reasons I was bullied in school was because everyone saw me as a goody goody. I was on time, I didn't miss class, I didn't make fun of weird teachers. I was only popular when I came up with awesome excuses for not doing my homework. Everyone came to me for excuses."

This was news to me! As far as I knew Jack did do his homework. And he must have turned them in because in his report cards teachers always commented that his homework was done. So could it be that he was embarrassed about being "goody goody" in doing homework and lied to his fellow students that he didn't do his homework? I also wondered whether he was perceived as "goody goody" because of my being active in the school, the PTA, etc. But I'll probably never know. Children are constantly reinventing their past.

The *Good Citizen* book is organized into seven sections:

In the Family
At School and Work
In the Neighborhood

In the Community
Starts with You
In Your Country
In the World

To go over some specific instructions we read from "The Good Citizen at School." The first advice was: "Obey School Rules." Jack had trouble with this at the first word! He sneered:

> Obey school rules... Kids know the rules. If they break them it's because they want to have fun. Like the stupid rule 'Don't run on the black mat' [the mat under and around the play structure]. Running is one of the things of fun. Every game I know involves running: hide and go seek, tag, cops and robbers, zombie... It's no fun if you walk on the play structure. And if you run into someone, well, they should look out for themselves.

Common sense from the children's side, isn't it? To make a rule that kids should not run in the playground is ridiculous. So naturally, kids won't "obey" it and will not think much of rules either.

What Jack did agree with were "The Laws of Clean Play." "In playing you should follow every rule," he said. We went over these "laws" one by one. I've put Jack's comments in quotation marks:

1. Don't cheat. "Or admit it if you're cheating."
2. Treat your opponent with respect. "Unless you're playing football."
3. Play for the success of the team and fun of the game. "Yes yes yes..."
4. Be a good loser or a generous winner. "You'll never have friends otherwise. You'll be a jerk in everyone's eyes."

It was interesting to me that when it came to games rules were OK in Jack's eyes. He did not sneer. There's surely a lesson in that for adults setting rules for children.

By the way, I have to add an interesting thing parenthetically here. This book has very few pictures of anybody with dark skin. But in the picture accompanying the section on the "laws of clean play" there is an illustration of some kids playing basketball, and sure enough there is the black boy shooting hoops!

It was not easy or pleasant going over "rules" or any discussion of "good behavior" with Jack. But it did lead to these revelations from him:

> The kids who do not do the right things at school get a lot of attention. The reason I was such a bad boy is because I got a lot of attention. I would even do stuff like steal an extra spork just to get attention from my friends. I had fun with grownups getting mad. When everyone picked on me I let all the bad behavior out. I didn't keep anything in. What pleased me about getting into trouble was that teachers were afraid of being fired for being bad teachers. When we got into trouble the principal thought they were bad teachers.

Lots to think about, but I won't go into it...

It never fails to amaze me that if you give kids a chance they will tell you what they think. And what they think is definitely what we need to know if we want to get anywhere with them.

The Question of Discipline

A great deal can be and is said about discipline. I am not going to engage in ideological battles about it. One reason that I don't like engaging in those battles is that most of the time people who passionately debate each other are not clear about what they mean by discipline.

What I mean by discipline is this: a regular schedule that works for all involved, and the stamina to stay with a project. Perhaps there are people with temperaments and lifestyles that can do without regularity but I'm not one. There are certainly people who swear by accomplishing great things by fits and starts, but I'm not one of those either. The way I am may be unfair to my son but kids are inevitably caught up in the way their parents are, so there's no point in pretending otherwise or even desperately trying to *be* otherwise.

So... I need regularity and I believe in developing staying power and commitment. How do I set a schedule and goals for my kid who is bent on fighting me all the way?

One of the things that I absolutely abhor is telling people what to do. I am not a good task master at all and even worse at policing. I used to be a great boss at work because at the slightest resistance from my staff I would just do the work myself. I have yet to learn how to "supervise" others—except my highly motivated college students. Alas, my own kid does not behave in a "highly motivated" fashion with me and tends to take advantage of me the way my staff used to. One major problem of teaching your own kid!

Perhaps I should look at the power/authority dynamic that I am faced with in teaching Jack as a sort of existential challenge, having to do what I really don't like to do. The challenge is this: staying true to who I am (disciplined and committed) without falling into power dynamics that I hate and that my son, in his perpetual quest to push limits, is constantly driving me toward.

I also have the character defect of having a bad temper. I get worked up and I do blow up. This certainly doesn't help matters, and while I am constantly trying to improve my temper I can't say I expect that I will ever be a model of "equanimity and poise" (hah!).

The reason I say these things is to put my attempts at

"discipline" in context. I have written about being deeply troubled by Jack's never-ending hunger for more and more screen time. It really is a constant battle that I keep failing at.

I have tried setting time limits: this much time for screen activity, this much time for reading, this much time for this and that. When you are dealing with a kid who never "remembers" boundaries he has agreed to, loses track of time, and is endlessly bargaining and resisting, it is not easy to enforce time limits. If you set an alarm clock for him you have to set one for yourself too, which means that you have to interrupt what you are doing (which is often work that needs concentration) to go and engage in an unpleasant and disrupting (to your own work) encounter with an eleven year-old.

So last year I gave up on setting concrete time limits. The best I could do was to come up with a "schedule" that I posted up in Jack's room. "Every day Jack has to do three things: Studying, Free Reading, Outing." The rest of the time he was free to do what he wanted, including screen time. It roughly worked out like this: in the mornings Jack had free screen time and did some reading (both assigned by me as part of "study" time, and books of his choice as part of "free reading" time). In the afternoons we had lessons together and then he went on an outing (park with other kids, skateboarding, the afterschool program he has joined, etc.).

This was roughly the schedule. I say "roughly" partly because I had a lot of distractions myself (family and work responsibilities) that interfered with me holding my end of the "regularity" bargain. And once I had a difficult time sticking to my own rules, how could I blame Jack for pushing and trying to extend his limits?

Still, I think this idea is the most workable: setting down general guidelines for what you expect to get done every day and not quibble over exact hours and minutes assigned to each one.

In recognition of summer vacation I took down the sign in Jack's room reminding him of the three things he must do every day. Right now, it being summer, I don't care if he "reads" every day and certainly don't expect him to "study." But... that has only made the beast of screen time raise its ugly head with a vengeance. With days a little too hot for skateboarding and friends either out of town or with too much time on their hands, sitting in front of screens and playing or surfing the net has become all-consuming.

Back to arguments and fights... and my own meltdown. This time around my husband had to get involved in setting and enforcing limits. Two hours of screen time every day. That's it. Dad says so. No use trying to bully mom.

Whew... nothing like a little male authority!

More on discipline

While we're on the topic of discipline I will interrupt *Clara's Clearing* to interject a couple of blogs by one of the contributors to the Mothers of Bad Boys website. These blogs appeared in the site's "Manners and Morals" series and are of particular relevance to the topic.

Culture and Discipline   by Pendar

I have not seen any comparative studies of how children learn discipline in different cultures. Here are some of my own observations.

I was born and raised in Iran. We had many American friends and I was always amazed by how disciplined the American kids were compared to Iranian kids. They went to bed at certain (early) hours. They kept to the designated children's areas when the grownups had parties. They did not play on the streets or with neighbors. And they really listened to their mothers.

I remember one episode that for some reason really left an impression on me. We were sitting in the living room with the American mother of some friends and one of the American kids said that he was going to get something from the fridge. The mother said No. The boy kept walking to the kitchen, ignoring her. I expected the mother to follow the kid and stop him or turn him back. But she just sat there. The kid cried from the kitchen: "I'm opening the fridge." The mother again just said No—and to my child's ears her voice was loud and resonating without being a yell. And there came no sound of the door of the refrigerator opening or closing and her wayward son came back smiling a little sheepishly. Young as I was I thought to myself, wow, what authority!

In our household in a similar situation my mother would have had to scream at us, or at my brother really. (I was a good girl.) She would have had to walk over to the kitchen and have a shouting match with my brother. All manner of unpleasantness would have followed. Tsk tsk... very uncivilized. My mother did not have the same authority as the American mother. Or, actually, I should say, she did not have the same *kind* of authority. Her authority was demonstrated under different circumstances. I'll come back to this.

In comparison to American kids our lives were quite free. We did not have very strict bedtime rules so we often fell asleep on the living room floor or in the car coming back from somewhere. In fact, one reason we often fell asleep away from our beds was because we participated in our parents' lives. If there was a party, the kids were there too. If our parents went to the movies they took us too. Our lives were totally mixed together. We felt sorry for the American kids who lived under such strict curfews.

But in the end we did learn discipline. Our schools were a lot stricter and more formal than American schools. Everybody knew that the academic demands on us were much more rigorous and we had no choice but to meet those demands. We sat down and did our homework when we had to—and often not in our own separate rooms but at the kitchen table while grandma cooked dinner and mom and dad argued. Perhaps we learned to manage distractions this way.

But what I think really taught us impulse control and discipline was the formality that was required of us. If we went to a party at someone other than our closest friends and relatives, we sat very politely and quietly. In presence of older people, our grandparents' generation for instance, we particularly held our tongues and made no more than eye contact with our cousins who were equally antsy to get away underneath their calm and polite exterior. And no matter what manner of goodies were spread on the table in front of us we did not touch—or look, for that matter. And that's when the authority of Mom showed itself in full splendor. Just one look and we were on such exemplary behavior that nobody would have the faintest idea that outside that stiff and formal living room we would all be running wild, with our mothers on our tail screaming at the top of their lungs.

Another example of unshakable Mom authority was when we had guests ourselves. God forbid if some younger spoiled brat took a liking to our favorite possession. One look from Mom and we offered up our best toy like a sacrificial maiden. In observance of extreme politeness there was no room for argument. Early on we learned that not only was it extremely bad form not to immediately heed the dictates of Mom but it was thoroughly useless to try. Good form über alles.

What's interesting is that thinking back, I don't ever remember any kid being punished for impolite behavior or bad manners. Not even my brother, for instance, who was as unruly as any boy I've ever seen, was ever guilty of bad manners. There was no need for punishment because bad form was simply not an option.

In fact, one of things that struck us about American kids is that they were subjected to all kinds of exotic punishments. No dessert. (What dessert?! For us food was food, not compartmentalized in different orders: what's good for you, what you must eat, what you like to eat, etc.). Go to your room. (What room?! We had our bedrooms too but space was not compartmentalized either: good space, bad space.) Confiscated allowance. (What allowance?! Even if we had official allowances it was useless to threaten to take it away when grandma or an uncle or older cousin were always there to spoil us in case we were suffering too much.)

Don't get me wrong. I'm not trying to say our parents were always nicey-nice. Slapped hands, faces, and fannies were not at all uncommon. And they were certainly done in the heat of the moment: "QUIET!" Mom would yell—and then, Slap... There were threats galore: "One more time and I'll slap you till you can't breathe..." Or the worst threat of all: "I'll tell Dad when he comes home." Tsk tsk again... very uncivilized. Hysterical. Bad bad bad.

It looked like we Iranian kids grew up under a kind of arbitrary chaos while the American kids grew up under rules and order. The upbringing seemed so different, even contradictory. But you know what? The end result wasn't that different. We all ended up getting similar education, having similar work, and living similar lives. I think we just ultimately learned the same things: impulse control and discipline. Only the pedagogy was different.

Discipline, Power and Democracy   by Pendar

"As the husband lost his power over his wife, both

parents lost their power over their children." So writes Rudolf Dreikurs, whose 1964 book *Children: The Challenge* is still one of the most practical and decidedly untrendy books on raising children.

I imagine a lot of us strong women cringing while reading that line. We like to talk about freedom, equality, and all kinds of lofty ideals but get a little queasy looking the question of power in the eye. But Dreikurs is right. The question of power is at the heart of all social relationships and it plays a very important part in both the upbringing and the development of children.

What Dreikurs repeatedly points out is that it is good that the old power structures have crumbled. He welcomes equal rights not just for women but for children as well. He recognizes that there is no going back to "obsolete traditions" and that is certainly cause for celebration. "Children are particularly sensitive to a social climate," he writes. "They have been quick to catch on to the idea that they share in the equal rights of everyone." Children no longer tolerate "an autocratic dominant-submissive relationship."

This is certainly well and good except that it has a negative side. "Our children have reached the point where they defy restrictions because they assume their right to do as they please," Dreikurs writes. "If each member of the family insists on doing as he pleases, we have a houseful of tyrants."

And this is where discipline comes in. We need to learn to curb our "do as we please" impulses to be able to live peaceably with others and to grant others the same freedom we want for ourselves. Dreikurs begins his work with the observation that while parents recognize that the old-fashioned and autocratic ways of beating discipline into children are neither desirable nor effective any more, new methods have not quite replaced the old.

How do we replace top-down, heavy-handed discipline with "new methods based on democratic principles"?

Dreikurs' work and the work of Jane Nelsen (both based on Alfred Adler's theoretical framework) provide some very useful tools on how to create democratic environments in which children participate in decision making. Dreikurs' "Family Councils" and Nelsen's "Family/Classroom Meetings" are very practical and effective tools in avoiding "autocratic" power dynamics. I really recommend their books. I've tried their methods and gotten good results.

The "discipline" I'm interested in, however, is not just the one required for social harmony and respectful behavior. I'm wondering how the democratic principles that Dreikurs talks about can be applied to teaching the kind of discipline that is required for a child to concentrate on a project, stick with it, and bring it to completion. I'm interested in the discipline that a child needs to make something of him/herself.

"Democracy is not just a political ideal, but a way of life," writes Dreikurs. I wonder how this "way of life" can create motivated children and accomplished young adults. I realize I am not posing an easy question. How do you modify "democratic principles" to apply to children's emotional and intellectual development?

One place to look for an answer is in what Dreikurs calls "The Fallacy of Punishment and Reward." "Punishment and reward belong properly in the autocratic social system," he writes. "Here, the authority, enjoying a dominant position, had the privilege of meting out rewards or punishment according to merits." It is easy to see how the reward and punishment method is widely used in our school system: good vs. bad grades, "gifted" vs. "special needs," "well-adjusted" vs. "at risk," etc. Evaluation of children, whether it's academic or psychological, is very much based on this reward and punishment, good kid/bad kid, model. "Dominance, force, and power must be replaced with egalitarian techniques of influence," Dreikurs writes.

I think the lack of motivation that we see in a lot of kids

is very much related to their perception of the "dominance, force, and power" that Dreikurs talks about. We know how sensitive boys are about questions of dominance and power. How can we fail to see that pulling power rank over boys can kill their motivation to exert themselves?

And where there is no motivation, there is no learning, no hard work, no success—what appears to outside observers as no discipline. The inner discipline that we would like to see in our kids is very much connected to how they perceive authority. If kids see the adults in their lives—parents, teachers, etc.—as engaging in this reward and punishment method of imposing their power, it is no wonder that they rebel against it. And unfortunately, by rebelling against that illegitimate authority they also misguidedly rebel against their own best interest. They miss out on tapping into their own motivation to exert themselves and developing the discipline that will translate into the pleasure of getting good at things.

Again, I think Dreikurs offers a useful idea. He says dominance must be replaced with "egalitarian techniques of influence."

But what exactly is "egalitarian" influence? I can imagine a lot of people objecting that it is a contraction: influence by definition involves imposing a will. But does it necessarily? Can we imagine a situation in which a child, or an adult for that matter, is influenced without somebody imposing their will on them? Isn't it in fact quite common to be influenced by people who in no way engage in power struggles with us? Don't artists, thinkers, loving mothers, favorite uncles, best friends, etc., influence us without exerting force?

So I wonder: Could it be that lack of discipline in children is a direct reflection of the undemocratic environments in which they live? Could it be that a little more democracy—and real freedom—can create more motivated and disciplined children?

Back to *Clara's Clearing*

What exactly does it mean to have no life?

What people usually mean by "having no life" is having no time to do what they want. That's one thing.

Another thing is actually losing a sense of yourself. I'm somebody who feels things best physically. To me a big part of having a sense of myself is the ability to feel my movements freely.

One of the things I was very aware of when my son was a toddler was how my every movement was interrupted. The natural cycle of movements got broken repeatedly. Say, when you get up from your seat to go to the kitchen: You get up with a certain momentum, build up a certain speed, cover a particular distance, and finish the cycle of your movement at, say, the refrigerator. Not so when you have a little kid. When your attention is on the unpredictable movements of a toddler you may be interrupted at any point of the cycle of your movement. Or you may have to slow down or speed up. The natural rhythm of your movement is disrupted, often repeatedly.

Or, remember what it was like to walk down the street with a small child? First of all, you can't even stand up straight. You are constantly hunched over protectively. You don't swing your arms like your normally do when you walk. You hold them steady and immovable, usually ahead of you. Then there are all the stops-and-go. Taking two steps might take three minutes while the next moment you might have to sprint full speed to catch the kid before he does something dangerous. The unnaturally slow pace and the stop-and-go is really nerve wracking. Ever been stuck in a really bad stop-and-go traffic jam? That's what it feels like, except on foot.

I might be particularly sensitive to this disruption of the natural rhythm of movement but I bet everybody feels

the effects of it even if they can't articulate it. To somebody like me this break in natural motion feels like losing a
sense of myself. It feels like my whole lifecycle is constantly
intercepted.

Of course the older the kid gets the more your sense
of natural movement is restored to you. And when they're
away, at school or something, you go back to your own
life and life-motion rhythm. This is one of the reasons that
women get accused of being hysterical. It's not just PMS.
It's the craziness of not being able to make it to the bath-
room at the pace you are used to, or need to.

And this is just physical activity. What about mental activity? How many times can you go back to what you were
thinking, or trying to figure out, after being interrupted?

Really, ever thought about it? Interruption is a form of
torture.

Jack London Park: What it means to close it

Last June Lilly, one of the homeschooling mothers,
came across an article in the New York Times about the
permanent closure of Jack London State Historic Park. She
brought it to our attention and immediately started organizing a trip to the park and, equally importantly, a campaign to add our voice to those opposing the closure.

It only makes sense that we speak up against the closure of Jack London Park. We live in California, not too far
from the park in Sonoma County. A lot us live in the San
Francisco Bay Area where Jack London was born and lived
most of his life. We are also homeschooling our children,
which means that we are quite involved in our children's
education—and Jack London has certainly been part of
a good education for generations of children around the
world.

Our group decided to read *The Call of the Wild* prior to
the trip and one of the mothers volunteered to prepare a

presentation on Jack London's life. After much organizing effort on Lilly's part August 21 was picked as the date when most people could make it. On a beautiful and thank goodness not too hot Sunday morning the group met at the entrance to Jack London's living compound.

What a splendid place!

London's "Beauty Ranch," as he called it, is located in the beautifully named Valley of the Moon in Sonoma County. It is where Jack London and his wife, Charmian, lived happily and worked quite creatively—on writing, farming, wine-making, raising animals, and building. The ranch consists, among other things, of the cottage in which Jack London lived and died, the remains of the magnificent Wolf House that was built by London but destroyed by fire before he had a chance to live in it, and the "House of Happy Walls" that was built by his widow in his memory and has been turned into a museum.

If the park closes, all of this—London's personal effects, typewriter, collection of books, furniture, and everything thoughtfully collected by Charmian and others in the museum—is to be packed and stored in an undisclosed location. The houses will be dismantled and the objects boxed up and scattered. Perhaps many will disappear into private collections. What belongs to the history and people of United States may very well end up in private hands, out of context and inaccessible.

What greatly struck me was how lovingly the building and the grounds have been maintained over the years. The frayed authenticity of the place speaks volumes of the care and appreciation that have gone into its preservation. Everybody—from the tour guides to the park rangers and the volunteers of all ages—exuded love for the London legacy and pride in taking part in preserving it. I wondered if there was a chance that the park would be auctioned off by the State of California to developers and turned into some commercial abomination—as happened to John Steinbeck's house in Monterey County. But the staff said that as far as they knew it was to be shut down and the contents boxed up and stored in Sacramento.

The depth and extent of the love that Jack London inspires was most tellingly on display at his grave site. London's grave is a simple boulder placed upon the spot where his cremated remains (and later those of his wife) were buried. Inside the small fenced-in area of the site we saw piles of ashes. These were the remains of recently deceased folks who had asked that their ashes be scattered at Jack's grave. I wondered how many people had had their ashes scattered there over the years, to be washed away with each year's rains. This is love. This is what will be eradicated when the park is closed to people who take strength from Jack London—the strength to live with courage and compassion and to earn success unaided by anything other than raw talent and hard work.

We were so glad we went. When we read *The Call of the Wild* Jack was painfully shocked by the brutality it depicted. People who have close contact with children know how terribly pained children become to witness cruelty to animals. Jack London does not spare his readers the shock and devastation of brutality, whether it is to animals or to poor and working people. His deep compassion—and his unbounded courage—is born of this understanding of raw cruelty, both in nature and in civilization.

Perhaps the message of *The Call of the Wild* is that the only force as powerful as the call of the wild is love. I thought visiting Jack London's various houses of "happy walls" in the wilderness of Sonoma County was a good point of departure for contemplating these forces. Certainly Jack London is one of the very few writers in whom the call of the wild and the call of love intersected so clearly.

Did the kids get any of this? I don't know. But we started them on it.

Sadly—very sadly—only four families of the 11 or 12

who had given their word actually came with us to the park. We picked up a fifth family along the way. After visiting the Jack London Museum there were only three middle-school boys left who sat and listened to the little presentations that we gave. My contribution was very brief. I pointed out to the boys the collection of Jack London translations in dozens of languages on the second floor of the museum: "All around the world kids grow up reading Jack London and marveling at the man and his life. Isn't it a tragedy to wipe out his legacy in the country where he lived and produced his great works?"

Lilly's contribution was perhaps more in the spirit of Jack London himself. She gave a presentation on how to "fight back"—in the form of a lesson in civics! The kids wrote letters to various state representatives to be delivered in person in Sacramento. That trip will be planned soon. Meanwhile we will try to join efforts with other groups fighting to keep the park from closing—though it appears that the closure is a done deal and not merely a "scare tactic," as the New York Times article pointed out.

But as I watched three unruly middle school boys perched on logs by the stone building of the Jack London museum attempting to compose letters to state representatives, I did not just see kids learning about the democratic process. I saw kids embodying the call of the wild and learning to channel that force.

As for me, I'm too old for the call of the wild. I just love Jack London.

CHAPTER 4

The Teaching Part

In Jack's sixth grade I started a new blog, *Educating My Boy*, to chronicle the "academic" part of what I was doing with him. Educating my boy turned out to be a grueling but rewarding experience. I took the teaching part very seriously—maybe too seriously—with the consequence that I burned myself out by seventh grade!

This chapter describes the teaching materials and some of the "lessons" I incorporated in Jack's education. It includes teaching methods I experimented with, good and bad ideas I tried out, ambitious projects I abandoned, and some insights I hit upon.

Let me confess that as I reread these blogs I see how hard-nosed and almost coldly intellectual I was at times with Jack. I'm embarrassed about it. But it's also true that that is only half the story. I have not recorded all the slack I cut him behind the scenes! At any rate, the blogs are sketches of our actual teaching sessions, just to give the reader an idea. They contain a lot of plans that were not followed through and ideas that could have been expanded ad infinitum. But everyday life has its way of putting the brakes on all flights of fancy, including the pedagogic ones. If I were to dedicate my life to educating children perhaps I could do some fleshing out of the skeleton laid bare here.

I also want to say a word in defense of intellectual training for children. One of my favorite psychologists and researchers on how children learn, Peter Gray, recently published a wonderful book, *Free to Learn*, named after his blog on Psychology Today. This is an insightful and learned study of the role of play in children's learning and its gradual elimination over the years. (It also contains a concise history of the notion and purpose of schools as well as an instructive comparison with the Sudbury Valley school which can serve as a great model for "democratic" schools where children are "free to learn.") My one gripe with that book, and a great deal of "alternative" educational theories, is that they rarely include intellectual activity, and indeed intellectual training, as a form of play. In the blogs that follow I have recorded the lessons through which I tried to get Jack to engage in intellectual play—i.e. the play of ideas.

Like all play, intellectual play is not fun unless there is some friction involved. Ideas have to be posed, pushed to limits, refuted, experimented with, reshaped, etc. It is actually a kind of wrestling. Wrestling is no fun if no one ever pins their opponent's shoulder down and yells "I win!"

Sixth Grade: Educating My Boy

So what *do* we teach?

Obviously one of the first questions you ask yourself when you decide to homeschool your kid is, What do I teach?

I won't go into all the different approaches and philosophies people adopt when they ask themselves this question. Among homeschoolers the two extremes are the "Classics" people who have a strict curriculum complete with Greek and Latin, and the "unschoolers" who allow the kids to completely follow their own interests. Most homeschoolers fall somewhere in between these two approaches.

I have always believed that most kids are capable of the same kind of intellectual rigor that is (hopefully!) expected of college students. I'm not talking about expecting kids to do college-level research and write term papers. I'm talking about the capacity of children to think. I'm also talking about exposing them to original sources, i.e. important books themselves and not baby versions of them or secondary writing about them. As I have written before, my approach to education is: good books plus math. My approach to homework is: reading assignments plus math practice. In short, I will go by what I remember learning from as a kid. I will not try to include "curriculum" that I found tedious as a kid and a waste of time as an adult.

I will blog about the day to day "lesson plans" I have come up with and the ups and downs of the teaching and learning process. But before I embarked on my present approach I did some soul-searching, as it were, on what I *can* teach. And my answer to that is this: I can only teach what I love.

What do I love?

There is a quote from Oscar Wilde that has lodged itself in my consciousness since I read it when I was quite young: "We are all in the gutter, but some of us are looking at the stars."

What we love are the stars we lock our gaze on through thick and thin. I want to teach my son to look up at those stars: to see them, and also to get into the habit of returning his gaze to them after being distracted. It is perhaps a kind of meditation I want to teach him, like acknowledging distractions and unpleasant sensations and then returning to the breath. It is a skill to learn. And like all skills the more you practice the better you get at it.

Sometimes I have to grab hold of my son's face and almost forcefully tilt his head to look up. You know the urgency of the feeling. The gutter runs over with nasty distractions. Children are bombarded with advertising—for products as well for attitudes and "values." The temptation to conform and consume blindly is great. "Peer" pressure can crush. Wonderful children can in a few very short years turn into unwell and unhappy adults. I think looking up at the stars is a matter of surviving the gutter.

Beauty, knowledge, freedom, compassion. These are the "stars" I want my son to see. I want him to get practice in returning his gaze toward them after each distraction. The way I can teach him to always find those stars is through what I love: great books and great art. Luckily, in the history of humanity a good deal of these have been produced. I have loved them and learned from them and I will try to pass on the gift—and the secret about surviving the gutter—to my kid.

So a great deal of my homeschooling effort will consist of splashing around in the gutter with my son, groping to find his chin, and forcing him to look up. This, I think, is going to be the gist of his middle school education.

The Role of Chance

At the official beginning of sixth grade I want to start by sharing some of the "lessons"[1] that I prepare for Jack. But before I embark on the planned part of our curriculum I want to pay homage to the role chance plays in what Jack studies. In fact the very "curriculum" that I'm going to blog about came to us by chance.

I wrote a previous blog about how a friend of my mine unexpectedly gave me a series of books that she had read as a child. The series is called *My Book House* (first copyright 1921, thirty-fifth printing 1953) and has twelve books for "boys and girls" from elementary through high school. As I looked through the volumes I decided to use the series as a guideline for organizing some lessons for my son's sixth grade education.

As I wrote before, however, I don't at all think that all the volumes are well written. There are excerpts from famous writers in English, but also lots of retelling of stories and translations that are not very well done. One of the challenges that I have set for myself as a teacher is to give Jack an idea of what good and not-so-good writing are about.

I am also going to try to turn my son's education into an intellectual challenge for myself. Some of the material that we will cover is going to be an education for me too (reading and/or looking up things I have put off) but mostly I am going to set some problems for myself to solve. The first "problem" is how to transform random material into teaching tools.

The *My Book House* series is going to be my first teaching tool. We are missing volumes 5, 6, and 8 of the series but to stay on the "chance" course of events I am not going to try to find the missing books. There is no index telling

---

1   These "lessons" are not necessarily one-day sessions. Most of them are a condensation of a few lessons spread out over days.

me what the missing volumes cover, but so what... We'll just read what we have.

Something that has always bothered me is that kids are given a lot of books that they never read. Practically every kid I know has bookshelves covered with books that he or she has received as presents or inherited from older siblings. My son has rows and rows of books that he has not even opened. Good books. Books selected for him carefully. Volumes of stories, science, art, etc. Books sit on shelves and everybody is too embarrassed to admit that they never get looked at, let alone read. This has always bothered me.

Interestingly enough, a lot of the books sitting on my son's bookshelves—from nursery rhymes and fairly tales to the classics—can be incorporated into the *My Book House* lessons. It's not a surprise of course. There is continuity in the education that children are given in any culture. I think this continuity should be encouraged and in fact pointed out to kids. It forms the basis of the culture into which they are born.

As for me, the first lesson that I have learned is that pretty much any random choice of educational material will reflect this cultural continuity. I will use the "curriculum" I have chanced upon to explore the cultural threads that run through a series of books copyrighted in 1921 and the bookshelf of an average kid born in 1999.

It's fascinating to discover a systematic transmission of culture and education at the heart of "chance"!

First things first: Aristotle in the nursery

Volume One of my "teaching tool," "In the Nursery" from *My Book House,* is all nursery rhymes. The editor, Olive Beaupré Miller, has done a fine job of collecting nursery rhymes from all over the world: Europe, Asia, Americas (including Latin American, Native and African American), and Africa. (Not bad for 1920s, eh?!) There are also short poems in English from famous poets: Shakespeare, Shelley, Lord Byron, Wordsworth, Christina Rossetti, Robert Burns, Keats, Langston Hughes, etc.

So how do you put an 11-year old boy to work on nursery rhymes?

I started with a famous quote from Aristotle: "The purpose of poetry is to amuse and instruct."

Here are some points I made while reading some of the nursery rhymes with Jack. (I am not going to belabor these points because any adult can catch the drift.)

1.   Poetry and art have been used to amuse and instruct children from a very young age in all cultures and throughout history.

2.   Many different art forms are used in nursery rhymes: Poetry (rhyming of words and rhythm of language); music (singing and playing of songs); and visual arts (especially after the invention of the printing press).

3.   Before books were widely available nursery rhymes were only "oral" literature. They were memorized by adults and passed on in oral form to children.

4.   Rhymes and music make memorizing easier.

5.   Poetry, music, and pretty pictures give entertainment and pleasure.

We then talked about what children learn through nursery rhymes, what they are "instructed" in. Here are some the things children are taught:

a.   Language
b.   Poetry, music, art
c.   Right and wrong
d.   Fun and games

We also looked at Jack's own collection of children's

books (which included contemporary children's literature) and concluded that Aristotle's purpose is still being served! We analyzed Dr. Seuss books for how they "amuse and instruct." Kids love to elaborate on whether they "learn" from Dr. Seuss or is it just fun. Really, try it with a kid. They will come up with things that are wilder and crazier than Dr. Seuss himself.

While our lesson was going on, Jack was sprawled on the living room floor, fetching and chewing gum, and occasionally bursting into some physical exertion.

After we read some rhymes from Shakespeare, he was reminded of a mock Shakespeare line he had composed a while ago. He recited with exaggerated diction: "Let us grabbeth hold of reality and taketh it for a ride, shall we?"

When clowning became too intense class was dismissed.

What's the purpose of stories?

"Story Time," Volume Two of *My Book House,* is a collection of fairy tales, folk tales, animal fables, stories from the Bible, and a few anecdotes about actual people (Chopin and George Sand, for instance). Again, the editor, Olive Beaupré Miller, has done a fine job of drawing on sources from all over the world: Aesop's Fables (Greek), Panchatantra (Indian), Jatakas (Buddhist), Kalileh-va-Demne (Persian/Arabic/Indian), as well as Native American and African stories.

I had assigned a number of stories from this collection for Jack to read before having our lesson. On the day of the lesson I was curious what he remembered from the first lesson.

"What did Aristotle say was the purpose of poetry?" I asked.

"To entertain and to educate," he replied.

Good. He remembered!

We then discussed the stories he had been assigned to read. He brought up an excellent point about how what stories "instruct."

"The morals of stories make a bigger impact when they are told in stories," were his exact words. "If they just tell you 'do this' and 'do that' it is not education. Stories show you what to do and why to do it and what happens if you don't."

From our discussion of individual stories I could see that Jack had no trouble identifying the "morals" of the stories, i.e. what "lessons" the stories were trying to teach. Then I took the discussion a step further. I brought up the question of how these stories "entertain"—i.e. amuse and give pleasure. (Doing this is not always as easy as with Dr. Seuss!) We both thought it was much harder to pinpoint how stories, or poetry or art or music, give pleasure.

It was much harder to find answers to "why do you enjoy stories" than it was to find out what instruction they were giving. We acknowledged the difficulty and left it as that.

During the lesson, Jack was again sprawled on the floor, engaging in all kinds of unrelated activities. At one point he crumpled a piece of paper so thoroughly that the sheet became quite limp and, when he spread it out, much smaller compared to a non-crumpled sheet. He asked me why that was. I said that surely there are scientific explanations for it but I have no clue. We left that at that too!

Introduction to the art of writing

Volume Three of *My Book House*, "Up One Pair of Stairs," is also a collection of folk and other stories and poems but there are more original texts (as opposed to retellings) than in the previous volumes. Children are introduced to the unadulterated language of literature. I assigned Jack poems by Robert Louis Stevenson, Emily Dickinson, and

Wordsworth, and stories from the Grimm brothers, the Old Testament, and retellings of a couple of stories from Chaucer.

Now, please don't imagine that I expect a whole lot from my son. Alas, the average middle schooler of today can only handle very simple language; my son is no exception. I have no idea what age group Olive Beaupré Miller, the editor of these books, had in mind for each volume but I would bet anything school children in the 1920s were much more sophisticated readers than kids are now. I only mention this so my readers don't think that I am overly ambitious with my son or that he is any kind of prodigy. I read everything with him and make sure he understands it.

The poems I assigned were short and simple. Here is Emily's Dickinson's "The Sea" as an example:

> An everywhere of silver
> With ropes of sand
> To keep it from effacing
> The track called land.

During this lesson I went back to where we left off in the previous lesson, which was how it is more difficult to say why and how you enjoy a piece of writing than point out what you "learn" from it. So I asked Jack which poems he enjoyed more and why.

He said that the Robert Louis Stevenson poem was not "realistic" so he did not like it. Wordsworth was more "realistic" so it was better. His favorite was the Emily Dickinson poem which he found most realistic even though she used "metaphors" and "similes." I asked what metaphors and similes were and he said metaphor "is what something looks like, like the sea is silver" and simile is "something that is similar to something else." Good enough. (To give credit where it's due, he must have learned this at school.) I left his ideas as they were. I neither asked why he thought one poem was more realistic than another, nor why he preferred realistic poems, nor asked him to find metaphors and similes for me. He had heard those words; that was good enough for me.

We moved on to the stories I had assigned him to read and the discussion of things one learns from stories. This time, however, I made a distinction between learning the "moral" of a story and the other things one learns from reading the same story. I introduced some ideas.

Discussing the Grimm fairytale I brought up the topic that some people think some fairytales are too gory and violent and children should only read the cleaned-up versions of them. Jack said: "Kids should know what's real, including violence. But it also depends on the kid. Kids will eventually be exposed to gore." It got him to think about other things kids might be learning by reading fairytales. I thought it was clever to use his interest in blood and gore to stimulate his imagination. Imagine what a great topic of conversation this would make with a group of kids!

Other pieces I had assigned were the stories set to music by Edward MacDowell and Charles Gounod. I made the point that you can tell stories in words, but also with music. I meant us to listen to those pieces and hear the story in them, but we didn't get around to it. (Fact of life!) I reminded Jack of Prokofiev's "Peter and the Wolf" which he had liked as a young kid. We got inspired to listen to that again, but haven't gotten around to doing it yet either!

Then we went over a couple of stories by Chaucer. These were retellings in modern English with a few lines in the original language here and there, just to give the reader a taste of the language of Chaucer and his time. And we ended our lesson with the story of Moses. We had a brief conversation about the three Abrahamic religions—Judaism, Christianity and Islam—and even touched a little on modern Middle East politics.

My purpose in glossing over so many topics? To fire up his imagination, point out some things, throw out ideas, and get Jack thinking. I believe that kids learn by picking things up, absorbing them into what they already know, and change and grow in response. Jean Piaget called this process assimilation and accommodation. Kids don't need to be beaten over the head to learn, or prove what they have learned by some kind of demonstration (as in taking a test). I like to leave things as they are.

After our lesson an interesting thing happened. Jack said that he noticed a pattern in the order of my assigned readings. He saw a progression in there. These are his exact words describing this progression:

1. Beginning of life/creation (Robert Louis Stevenson's "The Swing")
2. Growing up (the Grimms' "The Little Girl and the Hare")
3. Life coming to an end (Wordsworth's "Kitten and Fallen Leaves")
4. Old age and a final experience (MacDowell's "Tailor and the Bear")
5. Your death (Gounod's "Funeral March of a Marionette")
6. Ages of life (Dickinson's "The Sea")
7. First ever colony and creation of man (the story of Moses)
8. Next age of man/Knights of the Round Table (Chaucer's "Chanticleer")
9. Former-day man who believes in this (Chaucer's "St. Valentine's Day")

Well...! First of all, the selection of the pieces was completely random as far as I had anything to do with it. I had just picked some pieces and Jack read them in the order that they appeared in the book. And as for the particular pattern and wisdom he saw in the pieces, I'm not quite clear. Nor is he probably. But so what! The kid is reading and thinking—generating some ideas. That's what I want.

Getting technical: genre, interpretation, editing, annotation

Usually, at the beginning of a lesson I revisit points that we have brought up, or "covered," before. The reason that I put "covered" in quotation marks is because I don't think of learning as a linear progression where you cover or learn a "fact" and you move on to the next one. In my blog "Uncertainty, Improvisation, Approximation" I wrote that I think it is much more accurate to think of learning as achieving approximations, through multiple revisits.

Much of this revisiting is a kind of review that happens automatically at each lesson. Reminding Jack of some of the things that we had talked about before is a kind of intellectual warm-up and a good way to start a new lesson.

One topic I revisited with this lesson (Volume Four, "Through the Gate") was the difference between prose and poetry. (I made a mental note to read Molière's *The Bourgeois Gentleman* with Jack at some point: "That which is prose is not verse and that which is verse is not prose"—I think kids would get a kick out of that!) We quickly touched on some points and observations we had made before. One was that both prose and poetry can be used to tell stories. Jack thought poetry was better at describing things while in prose it was easier and more straightforward to tell a story. I introduced the words "descriptive" and "narrative" to help him articulate his thoughts better.

Jack offered his own definition of poetry: "Poetry is a little segment of musical writing." A very nice little definition! His definition of prose was not quite as—shall we say—poetic? "Prose is like a book—hard to say what book, could be any book. It's up to you to choose which book is prose." Good enough for now. We moved on.

I then reminded Jack about the difference between oral and written tradition in literature and how in the oral tradition rhyme and rhythm, hence poetry, were used to

help listeners memorize a piece and to pass it on to others. I also pointed out that in oral tradition there are many
retellings of a story because no particular narrative is fixed
in writing. Different retellings often give different interpretations and different interpretations "amuse and instruct"
differently. To demonstrate these points we looked at two
different Cinderella stories that I had assigned him to read.

First we looked at the retelling of Cinderella from one
of the books that had been sitting on Jack's bookshelf for
years, *Classic Fairy Tales*. This book, a colorful and cheaply
produced book (printed in China) with washed-out medio-
cre illustrations, cited no editor. The title of each story is
followed by "retold by" and the name of some obscure author. I pointed out to Jack that when a collection of stories
does not have an "editor" we don't know who chose these
particular retellings and why.

I contrasted this to the Cinderella story in Volume Four
of *My Book House* series. This series does have an editor,
Olive Beaupré Miller, a noted author of children's stories
herself, who in her introduction to each volume explains
many of her editorial choices. Most importantly, I pointed
out to Jack, she cites the source of her particular stories in
her footnotes. In this case her source was the French *Tales
of My Mother Goose* by Charles Perrault in 1699, translated
into English in 1729. The footnote also explained, "These
stories, centuries old, were told Perrault by an old nurse"—
a good reminder of how oral tradition works.

As we looked at the citation and comments in the footnote I explained what footnotes are for and how a good
editor uses them to cite her/his sources and make comments, clarifications, references, etc.

My husband and I are in the publishing business. So
far Jack's understanding of editing had been limited to
"correcting" writing: copy-editing, fact-checking, proof-
reading, that sort of thing. I used this opportunity to teach
him about other aspects of editing. I pointed out that any

collection of writing is "edited" by someone. I showed him how in the fairy tale collections he had in front of him someone had made the choices of the individual stories and particular retellings of them. A good editor has good reasons for making these choices, explains those to her readers, cites her sources, and may choose to make other relevant comments.

We compared the particular retellings of the Cinderella stories and the ways in which each interpreted the story differently, or emphasized different aspects of the story. In the *Classic Fairy Tales* collection Cinderella ended up forgiving her ugly stepsisters, sharing her glamorous new life with them. Jack didn't think much of this "moral lesson" and thought it ruined the story. (Children like bad people to get punished!)

Jack wrapped up the lesson with this comment about the crystal slipper: "Nowadays they would do a DNA sample to identify the right girl."

During this lesson he was playing with Bakugan toys, decorating his bed frame with them (they are magnetic), and frequently interrupting me with: "I just want to show you..."

Useful metaphors, aesthetics, "social studies"

For this lesson I had assigned a number of stories for different reasons.

I wanted Jack to read the two stories, "Stone Soup" and "The Emperor's New Clothes," for their metaphorical value. I asked him what he learned from "Stone Soup" and he said that the lesson of the story was that it was better for people to pool their resources together and create things together. We noted that the twist in this particular "lesson" was that sometimes you almost have to trick people into doing that.

"The Emperor's New Clothes," he said, showed how a

trickster can fool a stupid and vain person and how others will go along with the lie for different and opportunistic reasons. Jack enjoyed the part of the story that it took a child to call the bluff. Mainly, however, my point in assigning these stories was to introduce "stone soup" and "emperor's new clothes" as metaphors that can describe situations that one observes in everyday life.

The second set of assigned stories was two retellings of the fairy tale "The Selfish Giant." I had Jack read an anonymous retelling from that flimsy collection, *Classic Fairy Tales,* and compare it to a retelling by Oscar Wilde. I wanted to know which one was more "enjoyable" to read (back to the "amuse and instruct" theme). Jack said the Oscar Wilde one was better: "It was funner to read"—and something to the effect that it flowed better. I asked whether he was saying that to please me, since he knows that I like serious writers. He denied vehemently!

Our most interesting conversation, however, followed an old Greek story that I had had him read. "The Battle of the Frogs and the Mice" is a parody of Homer's *Iliad*, composed about a century later. It is about a war that breaks out between frogs and mice because of an incident that occurs between the prince of mice and some frog. The mouse prince, running away from a cat, asks the frog to carry him across a pond. The frog agrees but while the mouse is on his back he runs into a snake and ducks underwater. The prince of mice is inadvertently drowned and a bloody war breaks out between frogs and mice, avenging the killing of the mouse prince. The story is a parody of the interminable fight between the Greeks and Trojans in the *Iliad* and pokes fun at the absurdity of war.

Obviously I had an ulterior motive in choosing this story! I wanted to point out the idiocy of one group of people turning against another, and how once this sort of thing starts it perpetuates itself and is very difficult to stop. I reminded Jack of the family feuds between the Capulets and

Montagues in *Romeo and Juliet* (we had seen the Zefirelli's film in third grade) and the feud between the Grangefords and Shepherdsons in *Huckleberry Finn* (we had read it in fourth grade).

So far so good. Jack did not object. Then I took the discussion one step further. I said that since one group of people can turn against another group over very stupid things (and once they do this it is very hard to get them to stop and think) some leaders create wars by deliberately turning one group against another.

Jack grumbled at this. He knew where it was going. But I didn't back off. "Whenever you have a war," I said, "you must always ask the question, What do leaders gain by making wars between people? Who benefits from a war?"

"I don't want to think about this," Jack blurted out angrily. "Because my body wants to do something about it but I can't. I don't want to know. It ruins my life."

The comment about his "body" was very interesting to me and I made a mental note of it. But I insisted some more. "I'm teaching you social studies through literature," I said. But he was very upset: "I don't want to know. I don't want to learn this until I'm 18. I can't even vote now."

I was surprised at how upset Jack got. I know that children are very sensitive about the brutalities they notice in life. It makes them feel helpless and angry—and surely quite scared. But I also learned a lesson from Jack's outburst. Some social and political realities are just too harsh for children. They "ruin" their lives in that they not only make them feel helpless in improving things but also guilty in enjoying the security and good things they enjoy in their own lives.

I dropped the lesson and the topic. But it got me thinking about how to teach "social studies." Actually, I've always disliked the title "social studies"—it sounds babyish and condescending. I reminded myself to keep to my approach of teaching Jack like a college student. When it's time to do "social studies" I'll introduce *social science* and its various branches. In fact, this ties in very well with teaching science in general (observing, experimenting, hypothesizing, inductive and deductive reasoning, verification, etc.) and the introduction to Aristotle as a natural scientist. I'll be working on this!

Fiction, folklore, and "fakelore"

We are still on Volume Four of the *My Book House* series. For this lesson I assigned stories about three American folk "heroes": Pecos Bill, Paul Bunyan, and Johnny Appleseed.

The main difference between Pecos Bill/Paul Bunyan and Johnny Appleseed is that the first two are total fiction—"tall tales"—while Johnny Appleseed is a historical figure. Pecos Bill and Paul Bunyan were literally larger than life (very big dudes), capable of acts of stupendous strength.

Pecos Bill was a "straight-shooting, hard-riding cowboy," who played with knives as a baby and was raised by coyotes. The story begins with his mother saving him from vicious Indians who wanted to abduct him and goes on to tell of his superhuman battles with bulls and bad guys.

Paul Bunyan also had superhuman powers and led his company of loggers "over Maine and Michigan, Wisconsin, Minnesota, Illinois, the Dakotas, Kansas, Iowa, Utah, and wherever there were trees." He chopped down an awful lot of trees and established logger colonies.

Johnny Appleseed planted apple trees. He is generally depicted as a kindly, generous man (clothed in nothing but a burlap coffee sack) who collected apple seeds from cider mills back east, scattering them randomly all over the Midwest and the West. He was such a gentle creature that not even the Indians ever bothered him. He walked the land free and in peace. (Here I pointed to the contrast between this and the way Indians are usually portrayed in American folk tales: Could it be that Indians did not always attack well-meaning and harmless people? Hmmm...)

I really don't like to encourage Jack to use Wikipedia for research but it sure was convenient for learning some more about these American heroes. We found a few interesting historical details about Johnny Appleseed and noted how historical people can be fictionalized. For example, Johnny Appleseed did not randomly scatter seeds; he planted orchards. He subsequently sold those orchards and made good money. By selling his trees he brought business to the cider mills who gave him free seeds. He really was a generous and altruistic man but the saintly semi-clothed old man babbling and strewing seeds is fiction.

(Writing this line reminded me of Edna St. Vincent Millay's "April comes like an idiot, babbling and strewing flowers..."—great poem! Contrast with T. S. Eliot's "April is the cruelest month, breeding lilacs out of the dead land..."—Sorry, off topic!)

We came across an interesting concept on Wikipedia: *Fakelore.* Fakelore is folklore that is deliberately invented instead of mysteriously springing up and taking root on its own. In America fakelore is often connected to advertising. Paul Bunyan was adopted as a sort of mascot by the logging industry and used to put a folksy face to logging companies massacring the environment. There are huge statutes of Paul Bunyan in many logging towns.

I plan to come back to heroes and legends: epics from many parts of the world and legends based on historical characters, like Charlemagne and Joan of Arc. In this lesson I just wanted to make a distinction between total fiction and fictionalized actual people. But the little research on Wikipedia took us on a tangent. I asked Jack what he thought of folktales versus faketales.

"Not much difference between them," he said. "They're all stories."

"What makes some fake, then?" I asked.

He thought for a minute. "I guess what makes them fake is that they start out as fake. It's like once you're a liar or a thief you're always a liar or a thief. Once you're a fake you're always a fake." Then he added: "But I like the stories anyway, even if they're fake."

Analyzing stories: "plot, character, details"

An ancient Egyptian tale, "Rhodopis and Her Gilded Sandals," is the oldest version of the Cinderella story. Jack's assignment was to read the Egyptian version in Volume Seven of *My Book House* and to compare it to other tellings of the story.

In the Egyptian story, Rhodopis (Greek for "rosy cheeked") is a beautiful young woman bathing in a river. One of her dainty slippers is picked up by a "royal eagle" and dropped in the lonely king's lap. The king has all the maidens of the realm try on the slipper, to no avail. Then a grateful subject, a man whom the king has set free from the burden of unjust taxes, leads the king to the river where Rhodopis bathes. Her little foot fits the slipper, she produces the other one, and then she and the king get married and live happily ever after.

Jack mentioned some of the differences in the Rhodopis and Cinderella stories: there was no fairy godmother, no ugly sisters, and "Cinderella" herself was not a servant. There was no ball or pumpkin carriage either. Jack also mentioned that in the Egyptian version the moral was not to forgive bad sisters. The moral in Rhodopis was that the king reaped the rewards of being a good and just king.

The next assignment was the Greek myth, "Phaeton." Here an interesting thing happened. On his own, Jack offered a nicely systematic analysis. I asked for a "synopsis" of the story, a brief description of the plot. I asked him if he knew what "plot" meant. "It means what's happening in the story," he said. Then he added: "The plot is the spinal chord of the story. The characters are the add-ons, like arms and legs." Good start!

The main character in this story is Phaeton, the "non-listening kid" (according to Jack) who boasts to his teasing school fellows that he is the son of Apollo. The other kids don't believe him and to prove it he decides to ask his father to allow him to drive his chariot of the sun. His mother, Clymene, warns him not to do it and Apollo says that is not a safe thing to do for a youth. But Phaeton persists and Apollo yields. In the end Zeus has to come to the rescue when Phaeton, unable to control the powerful and unruly horses drawing the chariot, nearly destroys the whole earth with the fires of the sun. Zeus zaps Phaeton to death and saves the world.

Jack described Clymene as the "kind mother" character and Apollo as "the kind father who can't stop his kid." Then he took his analysis a step further: "The characters are the arms and legs of the story, and other details, like the horses in this story, are like the muscles that keep the body together." Very nice, I thought.

The next story he was assigned to read was a Welsh folk tale, "The Youth Who Wanted Some Fun." I asked what this story was about and Jack said that he did not quite understand this story, neither plot, nor characters, nor details. "I only remember one of the pictures but not sure what that showed either." I had a strong suspicion that he had not read the story. But since there had been too much time between the time I assigned the story and when we had this lesson, and also since he did such a good job analyzing the other stories, I let him get away with it!

I introduced the concept of "analytical tools" and said that the three aspects of the story that he had called "plot, character and details—spinal cord, arms/legs and muscles" were like "tools" that could be used to analyze any story or movie. To demonstrate how these tools can be applied to any story I suggested we look at the book we are reading together, Mark Twain's *The Prince and the Pauper.*

I asked Jack to give me a synopsis of the book. "I'd like to finish the book before telling you that." I realized that I had said that a synopsis is a brief description of the plot. We hadn't finished the book so technically he couldn't give me the plot—Okay, fair! So I asked him to tell me what the story is about. He said he didn't understand me. I asked him to tell me what Halo Reach was about (the computer game he is very interested in playing right now). He gave me a quick summary of what the "characters" are in Halo Reach and what they're trying to do, but would not do the same thing for *The Prince and the Pauper.*

After I gave him an example of what I mean as a synopsis of the novel—a beggar boy and the crown prince exchanging places and the adventures they run into—he said, yeah, yeah, yeah, gave me a similar synopsis, and walked away.

This lesson was an interesting example to me of how intelligence and boredom work together. Jack is obviously reading and absorbing stories in a very intelligent way. But then he gets bored with too much of what he thinks is the same thing. Perhaps the Welsh story was one too many folk tales for his taste at this point (we've been reading many of those). And he definitely doesn't like to demonstrate something that is too obvious to him, a synopsis being one. Stating the obvious, in an oversimplified manner, does indeed seem boring!

King Midas brings homeschooling crashing down

One of the stories I had Jack read was the story of King Midas. Midas was the king who so coveted gold that he dreamed of having the ability to turn everything he touched to gold. When his wish was granted and he turned his most beloved daughter (and every plant and flower, as well as his food) to gold he realized his mistake.

I had Jack research the origin of the story (Greek or Roman?) and read Nathaniel Hawthorne's telling of the story as a little shot of good writing. While mentioning the moral of the story, my main idea was to discuss how we come to "value" thing: is gold more "valuable" than bread when you're hungry? That sort of thing... but we didn't get to that!

I asked Jack what the moral of the story of King Midas was. "Not to be greedy," he said. "Money isn't happiness."

"What is happiness?" I couldn't resist asking.

"Happiness is a good home, good parents, couple of pets—a second class economy." (By "second class economy" I think he meant a middle-class life! I really don't know where he picked that up.) Then he went on: "Try not to be famous till later in life. If you're a kid and you have famous parents you're not going to be happy because your parents don't spend time with you. Like in *The Prince and the Pauper*—having a king for a dad doesn't necessarily make you happy."

"What makes you happy?" I asked.

"It's different for every person," he said—and then for some reason he got mad: "I don't know what makes me happy..."

As we were talking I was taking notes, as I always do during our lessons hence these blogs. But suddenly Jack was angry at me for taking notes.

"You care too much about what I say, if it's interesting or not... Can't you not care?"

I told him that I can't "not care." I can't help it if I find what he thinks interesting. I also said that I take notes of our lessons and conversations for the blogs I'm writing and that I hope to make into a book.

"I feel like a guinea pig. I don't like it," he said.

He was right of course. In fact I had already given some thought to how to defend myself if Jack charged me with treating him like a guinea pig. My plan was to show him my favorite Piaget book, *The Origin of Intelligence in Children*, and how Piaget observed his babies the way Aristotle observed the natural world. I wanted to show him that while Piaget closely observed his children, the kids were not exactly "guinea pigs" to his experiments. I was going to read some of Piaget's observations with Jack to let him see for himself that "studying" something or someone is not necessarily an obtrusive or disrespectful activity. I also wanted to make the point that while Piaget was interested in *how* children learn to think, I'm also interested in *what* they think. (Maybe introduce the idea of philosophy?)

But... I realized I was thinking about an ideal teacherly world. Sometimes you just have to quit your teacher role. This particular conversation came on the heels of an especially challenging "lesson" when Jack was extra fidgety and not at all cooperative. I could see that the lesson was not turning out fun for him, but neither was it for me. So I figured the best way to deal with the situation was to be really honest.

I told Jack that homeschooling is not easy for me. Some parents who homeschool learn along with their kids. I certainly do learn some things as I teach Jack but mostly I teach him what I have already learned. What makes homeschooling interesting for me is to "study" him, as it were. What I learn is from watching him learn. As a writer, and a student of how and what kids learn, I can't help wanting to take notes and share my observations in the form of writing. I told Jack that in all honesty if I can't have my own version of "fun" while homeschooling I really don't want to do it, and the fun of it for me is studying how and what young people learn.

I also said that I thought he had been very resistant to any work lately and that maybe we should think over the whole homeschooling idea. "I don't want to have to force you to learn," I said. "But if you're studying with me you have to want to learn from me and also to let me do what is interesting to me."

I shut the book and said we should take some time thinking about whether we want to continue homeschooling. We needed to come to an agreement about it.

The next day after our Midas meltdown Jack said that he thought about it and he does want to continue to be homeschooled. He said that he agrees to my condition of making homeschooling interesting to me as well as to him.

I was very glad to hear it but I certainly do see that in a way I didn't really give him a choice. The option I gave him was a bit of a "my way or the highway" kind of choice. That's one way of looking at it. Another way of looking at it is that ultimately kids don't really have a choice but to put their trust in their parents. So Jack's decision to continue homeschooling was his way of putting his trust in me over a school. He trusted that I do not disrespect him and have only honorable intentions.

I do value this trust—all the gold of King Midas be damned!

Poetry

"Reading is more important than writing"—Roberto Bolaño

One of my pet peeves is the way children are introduced to poetry these days. It's similar to a lot of music education going on. Children are asked to write poetry and make music as their first introduction to poetry and music. This is totally absurd. Children should first *hear* poetry and music, they should become sensitized to it. Making poetry and music is impossible if you don't hear them first.

Through our year, Jack's sixth grade, I read out loud to him the poems from Book Seven of *My Book House* that I have assigned. Every single time he says that he hates poetry. The only comment he ever makes about poetry is that a particular poem is or is not "realistic"—not that he can tell me what he means by realistic, but I never push him to give me a definition either.

I had marked three poems to read to Jack from Volume Seven: "The Cloud" by Shelley, "The Bells" by Poe, and "The Peddler's Song" from Shakespeare's *A Winter's Tale*.

First Shelley:

> I bring fresh showers for the thirsting flowers.
> From the seas and the streams;
> I bear light shade for the leaves when laid
> In their noonday dreams...

I pointed out the visual part of the poem, the images that are evoked and the "realistic" scene that is painted in words. "Very realistic," said Jack, "but I don't like poetry."

Then, Poe:

> Hear the sledges with the bells—
> Silver bells!
> What a world of merriment their melody foretells!
> How they tinkle, tinkle, tinkle,
> In the icy air of night!
> While the stars, that over sprinkle
> All the heavens, seem to twinkle
> With a crystalline delight...

Here I pointed out the "realistic" sounds evoked by the poem. Tinkle, sprinkle, twinkle—all imitate the sounds that bells make. The repetition of words—"tinkle, tinkle, tinkle," and later in the poem "time, time, time"—also imitate the repetitious sounds of different kinds of bells. I pointed out the pitch differences between words, from higher pitched "tinkle" to the progressively lower pitches of "time" and "bell"—all resembling the difference in pitch between smaller and larger bells.

Then we moved on to Shakespeare. In "The Peddler's Song" the travelling peddler is advertising his wares:

> Will you buy any tape,
>   Or lace for your cape,
> My dainty duck, my dear-O?
>   Any silk, any thread,
>   Any toys for your head
> Of the newest and finest, finest wear-O?
> Lawn as white as driven snow,
>   Crepe as black as e'er was crow.
> Gloves as sweet as damask roses
>   Masks for faces and for noses.
> Bugle bracelet, necklace amber
>   Perfume for a lady's chamber,
> Golden quoifs and stomachers,
>   For my lads to give their dears,
> Pins and poking sticks of steel
>   What maids lack from head to heel,
> Come buy of me! Come! Come buy! Come buy!
>   Buy, lads, or else your lasses cry!
>   Come buy!

Jack picked up the advertising going on here and smiled. I recalled for him some songs and chants from my own memories of hearing peddlers in the streets when I was a child, but also of not so long ago on subways in New York City. I asked Jack to condense this poem into a short advertising jingle (media time is expensive, I explained!). This is what he came up with:

> Will you buy any tape
> My dainty duck, my dear-O?
> Any thread of the newest
> And finest, finest wear-O?
> Come buy, come buy, come buy,
> Or else laddies your lassies will cry

As serendipity would have it my husband had marked a very nice poem for me to read in the *Times Literary Supplement*. I had read Kate Bingham's "By the River Lau" the night before and decided to read Jack a few lines from it to see how he would react. The poem is a long one; here are the first three stanzas:

In Mino by the River Lau
there lived the artisan
who pressed and dried the pulp that made
an origami man.

Like onion silk her washi paper
crackled in the air
long-fibred fine as a sheet of light
a single shining square

that held between her fingertips
she folded in her mind
until she had by heart a map
of intersecting lines...

I had planned to only read a few stanzas to Jack. But as I started reading he stopped his fidgeting and listened attentively, so I didn't stop. I read the poem in its entirety and he listened with rapt attention. My niece who was working on her computer nearby also stopped and listened. She noticed Jack's rapt attention as well. (Who would have thought!) So I asked him what he thought. "Dumb and boring," he said.

A few week later, I don't know what inspired Jack to write a poem. There is a very cute poetry-writing formula in one of my most favorite books, *The Boys' Book: How to Be the Best at Everything*. Jack had written a few poems before, following the formula. He came up with this new one (punctuation and lack thereof included):

   "Water"
Blue and calm.
Swooshes, falls, and runs.
Is it gods love?
The first creation

This concluded our sixth grade poetry class.

The Prince and the Pauper

The "lessons" that I have been blogging about have been on readings from *My Book House.* But we've done other readings and other "lessons" as well. I will blog later about the reading list I've been going through with Jack.

On the reading list for this year was Mark Twain's *The Prince and the Pauper.* Alas, I read this book on my own in second grade but had to read it to my sixth-grade son. But no matter. He has to get certain books in his consciousness, by hook or by crook! One of the reasons for reading *The Prince and the Pauper* was to lay a foundation for introducing him to sociology, which is on my agenda to take up as part of our social science curriculum next year.

My opinion of the book as a second-grader was that it was boring and not very good (compared to a short novel I had read by Pushkin that I had found very good!). Reading the book again after decades I still found myself of the opinion that it was boring and not very good! Now I can certainly articulate better what is wrong with the book: the writing is belabored, there is too much false archaism, the plot is crammed with many abandoned threads and too much implausibility, etc. I had to plod though it back in second grade; I had to plod through it now, dragging my kicking and screaming boy behind. Once a plodder, always a plodder. Important message to my kid: you finish what you start. But back to the book...

As we read *The Prince and the Pauper* we talked about

many things, mostly history. The "prince" in the book is supposedly Edward VI, the son of Henry VIII. The history of Henry VIII and his many wives makes of course a good story. I pointed out some connections that Jack already had to this particular history. One connection is in the nursery rhyme *I Had a Little Nut Tree* where "the king of Spain's daughter" refers to Catherine of Aragon, the spurned first wife of Henry VIII and mother of Mary I, known as "Bloody Mary" (an anecdotal connection Jack enjoyed!).

The beheadings and other executions ordered by Henry VIII and his daughter Mary were very disconcerting to Jack, as were the bloody intrigues and backstabbing going on at court. And since in the novel appears a hermit whose excommunication from church and parish has turned him homicidal, I had to explain something about the bloody wars between Catholics and Protestants in England at the time. Jack really hated all this. The executions in the Tower of London and the witch-hunting executions of a couple of women in the book were very difficult for him to hear. The oppression of poor people that Mark Twain depicts in the book is also not pleasant. The stories that the band of pauper/criminals tell around a campfire of how they ended up doing what they do is Mark Twain at his most observant.

History was certainly not intended as entertainment for children—so what do we do? "Protect" children from history by keeping them ignorant of it? A sort of Siddhartha experiment where the prince's father tries to keep the future Buddha from becoming aware that disease, old age, and death exist? I don't know. I just plod.

At any rate, as we read the book (which took an ungodly long time—we had to renew the library loan three times) we did talk about a lot of realities and ideas that the novel presents. As I do with most novels I read with Jack I often stop to explain what's going on—I can't stand leaving comprehension to chance. We had had a number of conversations while reading the book but for this "lesson" I wanted to have a more formal discussion. There were areas I particularly wanted to explore, which also touched on Aristotle's "to amuse and to instruct."

I wanted Jack to pay attention to what we learn from this particular novel about three things. One, how being born to a social class, a totally random chance occurrence, can determine your life. A prince and a pauper can be virtually identical except that one, well, is born a prince and the other a pauper. Two, education is often the first step for bridging the gap between social classes. After all, the reason the pauper in the book could even be remotely taken as a prince was because of the little education that he had received at the hands of a kindly priest.

These first two points Jack could quickly grasp as soon I pointed them out. But the third point—that language itself is a key element both demonstrating one's education and bridging social gaps (which still is true of England and the English language) was a little trickier and I tied it in to the topic below.

I drew Jack's attention to the question of plausibility in fiction and what is called verisimilitude. I introduced the word: "veri" as in verity ("realness") and "similitude" as in "similar and simile," words that Jack knew. How close to "reality" was *The Prince and the Pauper*? "The plot was semi realistic," said Jack, unable to elaborate a whole lot on what he meant. I had anticipated this, so before this discussion/lesson I had had us watch the movie *My Fair Lady*, with Henry Higgins changing Eliza Doolittle's cockney into King's English.

"So how likely do you think it would have been for the little pauper Tom Canty, who most likely spoke some version of cockney, to pass off for a prince who would have spoken high English, regardless of the Latin that the priest had taught Tom?" I asked Jack.

He acknowledged that it was not likely. I pointed out that the book then failed on account of lack of verisimilitude. I pointed out that then perhaps the book was more successful in "instructing" us than its deficiencies allowed it to "amuse" us as a great book.

This was a pretty advanced lesson. I told Jack that this could very easily be a session I would conduct in a college literature class. I also told him that if this were a class for a higher grade than sixth I would give two topics for students to write on:

1.   What do we learn from *The Prince and the Pauper* about social class, education, and the English language in the England of a few centuries ago?
2.   What does and what does not make *The Prince and the Pauper* "realistic"? Explain the concept of "verisimilitude."

Now, if Jack was the overachieving type (or if I was a card-carrying Tiger Mom) I would probably give him this option to write on: Analyze the novel with the "analytical tools" that you came up with a couple of lessons ago: "plot, character, and details."

Jack was flattered to be reminded of his "analytical tools" and he said, yeah, plot is the backbone and spine of the story. And he elaborated: the characters expand the story, like arms and legs make a body bigger, and details are what make the story interesting. "A story without details is boring," he said.

To conclude the lesson I said that if he was not the type of kid to give me so much trouble I would give him a writing assignment. "If you were a good boy I would give you a big homework right now," I said. He gave me a funny look.

Speaking of giving me trouble, through this discussion Jack was busily doing things with his hands, folding paper, popping ollies with his little finger skateboard, etc. Once he lifted his foot to his nose and sniffed it. When I said that was gross he said he was just trying to touch his heel to his nose as a stretch. (Yeah, right!)

Also, as is usual during our lessons, he seldom looked at me. "Your eyes don't have to be on the person to hear," he said. "The stupid teachers always said 'give me your eyes.' That's so unreasonable. People don't hear with their eyes."

Too complicated?

I'd like to add a note for readers who might think that this lesson was too complicated for an eleven-year old. I would say that the points that we covered in this lesson may be too difficult for a kid to *remember* but they are not too difficult for him to *comprehend*. These blogs are brief and condensed versions of long conversations between Jack and me. I don't gloss over any point I am trying to get across to a student, be it a college student or a middle schooler. I make sure they comprehend at the moment but I don't worry about remembering at a later time. I introduce certain ideas and ways of looking at things and leave the remembering to future encounters with those ideas and angles, during the revisits.

The fact is, we all do read fiction for the plot. Children like their fiction action-packed (as in Harry Potter) and more sophisticated readers like intricacies of plot, character, prose, etc. The "whodunnit" or "what happens in the end" questions keep the reader going. The Sanskrit *ketam hatat* (corrupted by my distant memory!) is the epitome of the question that opens any story: *And how does it [the story] go...?* This is the frame-tale enquiry that unfolds the stories in the old Indian *Panchatantra,* and its subsequent reincarnations in different languages. Setting ultra literary connoisseurs aside, this curiosity is what propels the telling or reading of stories. So I always make sure my students know exactly how the story goes.

Back when I taught Shakespeare to undergraduates the first thing I made sure of was that they understood every nuance of the plot of the play we were reading. To make *Hamlet* more accessible, for instance, I showed a film first. (I chose Mel Gibson's version and not Laurence Olivier's to make it less intimidating!) Once we were done with discussing the plot we revisited characters, motivations, philosophical questions, even the beauty of the language. One class time in particular stands in my memory as one of the sweetest in my life. We had returned to the scene where Ophelia, instructed by her father and against her own wish, is returning Hamlet's tokens of affection. It is a conversation between two heart-broken lovers, one weeping and the other raging. My students—inner city, street savvy, minority and immigrant young men and women from the Bronx—sat in total silence as I read to them. At one moment I looked up from my book and took in one of the loveliest scenes I have ever beheld in my life: a bunch of bright young people, heads bent over their books, brows knitted, too spellbound to say a word or make a move! But I digress...

It is quite unfortunate that children now don't read the kind of literature that challenges and develops their reading comprehension, hence their own use of language. I see it in my own kid and there's not really anything I can do about it. (Even if Jack were the kind of kid that you could force into doing things I still wouldn't want to resort to force.) I saw the future of kids like him in my college students. But... once you get around the comprehension block (hold students' hands through it if you have to) they certainly can grasp and appreciate the depths of good literature. Perhaps once their eyes have been opened to this depth they might become inspired to plod through comprehension barriers on their own and someday actually read real literature for pleasure.

I don't know what else might work!

Teaching what I don't know: Physics

Most of what I worked on with Jack this year was what I knew. I studied social science (developmental psychology as an undergraduate) and the humanities (literature in graduate school), and I have taught literature and writing in college. I can certainly do a passable job teaching literature, history, philosophy, the arts, intro to social sciences, and even some scientific methodology. But what about fields I know very little about...?

I used to be a math major in college (before switching first to music, then to psychology, and finally to comparative literature) and while I remember hardly anything from all the math I did in college I do remember the pleasure of studying mathematics. I also studied a good amount of physics and chemistry but I am sad to say I found no pleasure in that. Weird to say, I was not interested in the practical applications of math. I have always loved abstraction. Maybe weird but true.

I know a lot of homeschooling parents whose approach to teaching their kids is to study things with them. This is a fantastic approach and I've seen families who have achieved great results doing this. What tends to happen is that the kids at some point get better than their parents and take off on their own, which is wonderful to see. But I have felt very insecure taking on subjects I don't know anything about—this is the flip side of having experience teaching subjects I am familiar with! I feel a lot less adventurous than a lot of homeschooling parents I admire. Also I just don't feel old dogs should force themselves to learn new tricks.

Still, I had no choice but to challenge myself a bit. How do I teach physics, I asked myself?

Years ago I had seen a book that I had been meaning to look into some day: *The Physics of Dance* by Kenneth Laws. I have been a student of dance, particularly ballet, for many years. I have had some truly awesome teachers who influenced me more deeply and lastingly than my Ivy League professors.

So, not knowing how to approach something I don't know I went back to dance. (Whenever in doubt I turn to ballet.) I looked up *The Physics of Dance*. Thanks to the gods of electronic communication I not only ordered my copy but came across a string of books on the physics of all kinds of sports, including—most relevant for me—the physics of skateboarding. My very un-team minded son only does solo sports, namely skateboarding and snowboarding (and a little skiing and ice skating). I immediately ordered *Skateboarding: How It Works* by Emily Sohn.

This is a small illustrated book covering some basic concepts in physics: Newton's three laws of motion and other important and useful concepts such as centripetal and centrifugal forces, torque, kinetic and potential energy, momentum, gravity, friction, etc. The skateboarding context for teaching physics really worked for Jack. He was able to grasp the concepts quickly and actually feel them in his body. I, meanwhile, applied what I was studying with Jack to my own experience with movement, namely in ballet. So the two of us went back and forth between skateboarding and ballet, comparing and contrasting concepts in actual different movements, turning for instance. Lo and behold, for the first time in my own life I actually enjoyed physics! It's wonderful how you can take a few basic concepts in science and keep exploring them in different contexts. Now I feel I have the vocabulary to do this with Jack.

Our experience with learning physics gave me some more ideas. I went back to my days of studying kinesiology many years ago and another area I had stored in the back of mind to someday explore more: the planes of movement. As I looked up that old interest I realized you can learn three subjects through studying movement: anatomy, three-dimensional geometry and physics. You learn about all three when you study how the skeletomuscular structure is capable of moving in 3-D space and what forces and laws of physics propel or hinder the body moving in space. Maybe I'll make it a sort of class for a couple of home-schooling mom/kid teams.

Okay, so far so good for physics. But don't ask me to teach chemistry. I really have no idea about that and no passion for it. I don't know how to link it to dance either—maybe nutrition...? But no matter. I'm resigned to not "teaching" some subjects. Either someone else has to step in and cover for me later, or the kid will be left to his own devices somewhere down the road.

Failing math

I'd say this year was not a successful one for math. Robert was in charge of teaching math and since because of our move and his long commute we knew he would not have a lot of time our goal was a modest one. The plan was to use sixth grade to get Jack to become sure-footed and fast in using the multiplication table and to continue with basic arithmetic.

Well, it didn't work out. I realized half way through the year that Robert was simply not going to have enough time, or energy, to take on teaching math to Jack. (And I know from experience how much energy is required to teach an uncooperative fidgety kid.) I myself felt pretty overwhelmed by all that I had to do too so I looked into getting some outside help in teaching math.

When Jack was in school math was his favorite subject and he was in the GATE (gifted and talented education) program mostly on account of his math scores. In fourth grade in a letter to President Obama in class he wrote: "Dear President Obama, I get advance on my math test. Can we be friends?" He took pride and pleasure in his math abilities and I wanted him to continue enjoying that.

For outside help I first looked at Kumon. I like their approach to teaching math, which involves a lot of repetition until kids are fast, confident, and ready to move on. Concepts and operations are introduced in a way that kids pick up quickly and get more challenging slowly and gradually. I have to say I prefer the Asian school of teaching math as opposed to the American way, which involves too much verbalization for my taste and patience. I can't quite explain what I mean (I am not at all up on math pedagogy!) but I think using too many words to describe or explain math is a waste of time and confusing for the student. It's much easier to "show" math to kids than to explain it in words. I think words slow down the math brain. I think the idea of "math facts" is ridiculous; as if we need some word to give math legitimacy!

Kumon requires that kids do 20 minutes of math every day, which is fine. The problem for me was that they require that kids do that every day of the week, no breaks. Now, I think working on anything seven days a week is excessive and I know that my kid would rebel against that. I remember loving doing math; it kind of felt like it scratched an itch in some part of my brain. I would love my son to experience that pleasure. I knew that forcing him seven days a week to work on anything will not sit well with him and will turn him against it. "Nobody works seven days a week," I told the Kumon lady. But she was very strict about it so I gave up on Kumon. I didn't want to pay $120 a month, get into tugs of war with Jack, and end up killing his love of math once and for all.

Next I checked into what another homeschooling mother uses for her daughter. EPGY—Education Program for Gifted Youth—is run through Stanford University and has an online interactive curriculum that students complete at their own pace. It has review courses which would have been particularly good for us. The price tag? About $600. The price and the emphasis on the "gifted and talented" put me off. I find that using that label tends to go along with a competitive approach that is the opposite of what I want to accomplish for Jack: the pleasure of learning.

Doing a little online research I realized there are a great many online courses for teaching math. In our homeschooling email lists I have seen lots of advice and resources on finding good math curricula. Before forking out $600 for EPGY I decided to do some more homework and consult our various homeschooling communities. I wrote off sixth grade as an "F" in math (for myself as a teacher!) and Jack will have to catch up next year.

The plan for next year is to involve Robert (who is now working three days a week, which means he has more time and we have less money—so definitely forget about costly courses in any subject) in finding a good math curriculum for Jack and for him to be in charge of "teaching" it. I simply can't keep up with everything.

One of the lessons one learns in homeschooling a kid is one's own limits. Obviously we all have limits in what we know but we're also limited in what we can take on, period. Especially as kids grow up one needs help in doing a good job teaching. I am hoping my husband will come through in math. But even if he can't meet all the demands on his time (the days that he doesn't "work" he works in publishing) I hope we can somehow keep the pleasure of math alive in Jack so that someday he will immerse himself in it and catch up.

I believe that in one summer one can *voluntarily* learn something that has been forced on one for years in school. With math I will have to put my trust in this belief.

Other curricular and extracurricular activities

Here are some of the things we have done with Jack in addition to the official "lessons" I have been blogging about. Many of these activities we would have done even if he were in school but certainly not all.

Song writing and recording

Last summer Jack took a song writing and recording summer camp with the San Francisco Rock School, which has been created by Mona Lisa, a fellow homeschooling mom. It was such a success that the summer camp developed into a three-month long weekly workshop. Mona Lisa hosted the workshop at her house (all day on Tuesdays) which was a blessing to the rest of us moms! Jack got a Mac computer for his birthday so he would be able to work with the popular recording software used nowadays. That was in the Fall.

Pamela Parker, a gifted San Francisco musician and teacher, taught this class, gave private lessons in guitar and singing to Jack, and led the kids in a rock band that performed at Golden Gate Park. She continues to be an inspiration to Jack and his friends.

Drama class

In the Spring some of Jack's friends enrolled in an improvisation drama class which he was inspired to join. The class for homeschoolers was given by New Conservatory Theater Center in San Francisco, taught by very cool actors and drama teachers.

Galileo and Iliad

A friend of ours, Valentina, stepmother of one of Jack's school friends, is a talented actress and part of a theater ensemble, Inferno Theater. She invited us to two of her plays which were of particularly educational value. One was a dramatization of the letters of Galileo to his daughters and the other a contemporary dramatization of *The Iliad*. The latter fit in nicely with the parody we had read of *The Iliad* and the former was a good introduction to Galileo, his life and times as well as his science.

The Smith Rafael Film Center

One of our luckiest finds is the California Film Institute at the Smith Rafael Film Center in San Rafael, where we now live. I discovered the cinema fairly late in the year and only saw a couple of movies there during Jack's "sixth grade." The most valuable film from an educational standpoint for Jack was *The First Grader* which was based on the true story of a man in Kenya who decided to go to school for the first time at age eighty. Wonderful film and a good introduction to the history of Kenya (and many other developing countries).

Books

We read four classics this year: Steinbeck's *Travels with Charlie,* Dickens's *A Christmas Carol,* Mark Twain's *The Prince and the Pauper,* and Jack London's *Call of the Wild*.

The Exploratorium

While we no longer live in San Francisco we are still lucky enough to be able to make fairly regular trips to the Exploratorium. This is an excellent interactive science museum and interesting for kids of all ages, as well as grown-ups. Jack and his dad made quite a few trips to the Exploratorium this year. I'm sure Jack learned some science there, though that's definitely not my department!

Middle school interactive course

An old friend of mine, Jaleh, gave Jack as a present an interactive series of courses which I have to admit I never had a chance to really check out. Robert would occasionally assign some "lessons" from it and Jack spent some time fiddling around with it and discovering things on his own.

Marin Youth Center

Last but not least, Jack and I quite by accident discovered Marin Youth Center in San Rafael. This was an afterschool program for middle schoolers and high schoolers, run by a group of wonderful young people. Really, the center was almost too good to be true, complete with recording studio, metal working and other art studios, pool tables, an organic café run by high schoolers, etc. The courses offered were fantastic, from state-of-the-art software to organic cooking. And there were field trips: skiing, kayaking, mini-golf, etc. The center was open every day in the afternoons and for $45 a month the kids could drop in any time and stay as long as they wanted.

Terribly sadly, MYC lost its funding and will not be around after the summer. It was such a godsend for us. Jack got to be around kids (all public school kids) and a very nice young staff, learn a few things and get exposed to other things, and I could count on a few hours of free time when I needed it. All the kids were very disappointed at the news of the shutting down of the MYC. Jack started a letter writing campaign and collected signatures to show community support for the center, but unfortunately it was of no use.

I record all these activities and resources just to give an idea of what a rich world we live in. Of course my family lives in a particularly resourceful part of the country but I am constantly reminded that any community can offer a

great deal of educational opportunities for kids. Take colleges for instance, both community and four-year colleges.
The average drama or music or dance department has performances that they would love to have an audience for. If
there are no movie theaters showing films other than commercial ones there is Netflix. One can visit websites of good
theaters anywhere in the country, learn about interesting
films, and then order them through Netflix.

I won't mention libraries and electronic resources because that's just too obvious. One quick trip to the public
library will open up more opportunities than I need to even
give examples of: reading and interactive materials as well
as activities. Really, we live in the age of links: all you need
is to start somewhere, anywhere, and then get linked to
infinity.

Speaking of links, the California Homeschool Association website is a starting point in the infinite chain of links
for homeschoolers. As far as I'm concerned a lot of homeschooling resources are just as valuable for school kids. I
think the boundaries between school and homeschool are
blurring.

It is all a question of time.

Wrapping it up: overview and self-evaluation

To wrap up sixth grade I did two things. First I reviewed
what we had covered during the year. I went over the notes
I had taken for and during our lessons. Jack certainly didn't
"remember" everything. I had to put things that he didn't
remember in context and then it would ring a bell—or not!

But as I put it before, I'm not very concerned over kids
remembering everything they are taught. "Remembering"
is often a form of demonstrating that you have "learned"
something. Learning is more invisible than that; it takes
place on a much deeper level. Kids can't help learning. So
I was happy to just go over what we had read or talked
about (revisit them), whether Jack "remembered" or not.

He just listened and made an occasional comment. That was good enough for me.

The second thing that I did was that I asked Jack to write a self-evaluation for sixth grade. I got the idea from the children's program of a ballet school. (I'm always learning things from teachers of dance!) I thought it was a great idea to get kids to think about how they did during the year. I think that's a much better indication of progress than how *we* think they did.

Here's Jack letter of self-evaluation to me, exactly as he wrote it:

Dear mom-teacher,

This year I think that I did well, but to you I probably didn't reach your expectations. It was fun at times and it is fun homeschooling though I do have a feeling that I will go back to high school to experience real school and to get a high school degree. Yes I do understand that I can get one through homeschool but still I am straying away from the subject, this year was interesting, strange, but fun. It could get annoying at times, but it was enough to understand that it wasn't just torture—like in school –, it was also learning so that is sort of why I think homeschooling is for me. Most of all this was a hard year, but I LEARNED and that was the whole point! If I was to say that I learned as much as I could have, I would be lying. There was much we could have done, but just as everything, there is a reason! That reason is that we were new, so we had to get used to it and lots of things happened such as the move! I also appreciate the effort you put into it! Next year I hope it will be better—no, you know what? I will make it change!! I will work harder, I will do my own research, and best of all, I will go out more!! ☺
    Love,
    Jack

Contrary to what he says Jack did indeed reach my expectations in all things "academic." My only complaint, as always, was too much screen time which took him away from going out and doing more physical things. So now all my readers are witness that he promised to do more going out—and playing—next year! (Is that too much to expect?)

Reviewing my notes I came across this comment of Jack's that I had not incorporated into any of my blogs. It is actually a relevant one for this "wrapping up" blog:

> Our lessons together are more boring than school—in a sense. In the sense that in a classroom there are other kids and that makes things more fun.

Sadly, I can never match school in providing other kids. Jack definitely misses being with other kids (does he "remember" how miserable he was when he was with other kids?) and I think that is the main reason behind his contradictory feelings about being homeschooled. In his self-evaluation he says that he wants to someday be in a "real school" while in the next sentence he says "homeschooling is for me."

One question that a lot of non-homeschoolers have is why we teaching parents don't create classes for kids. This is a long story. Let me just say that organizing classes is much more complicated that it appears. Homeschooling families tend to be very individualistic and have strong ideas that are sometimes hard to reconcile with others. But even with like-minded homeschoolers, because life tends to become pretty scattered in the absence of routine, it is difficult to organize things. The only successful one was Mona Lisa, who organized San Francisco Rock School—but she's a supermom who cannot easily be emulated.

I think once we have worked out the misery and the conflicted feelings of Jack's elementary school years we will all be much happier—whether or not Jack decides to return to school. (And I have to admit I hope he does.)

Seventh Grade

The Crash: Jill comes tumbling down

By the time "seventh grade" rolled around I was thoroughly spent. What had exhausted me was not "teaching"—in fact I quite got into that. It was the daily struggle to get Jack to sit his bum down and pay attention to me. Or to go outside and do physical things. Or to keep his word after making an agreement to *anything*—any schedule, any activity, any plan... What I had on my hands was a highly uncooperative twelve year old whose only "fun" was computer games and sneaking candy. His idea of friendship was to do these same things with friends.

Jack is not a rude or aggressive kid but his capacity for resistance and his gift for finding just the right buttons to push cannot be overstated. That, and kids' need to take out their frustrations, anger, power-plays, etc., on those closest to them, usually the moms, is really hard to take with no school or other adults to give you a break. So in seventh grade I decided to withdraw and not "teach." I knew that the fights and bad feelings that would ensue every time I tried to make Jack do anything were simply not worth it. Before I describe more of what happened that year, a word about the wars children wage.

The strategy Jack excels at is the battle of attrition. With this strategy if you engage him you lose fast, and unless you strategically retreat you lose slowly by being worn out. Kids have only the parents to take on whereas parents are juggling an assortment of responsibilities and urgent matters. Our multi-tasking and fear of doing the wrong thing is no match for kids' single-minded, no sense of consequence, all-out unleashing of their full force. Parenting books instruct you to approach retreat and engagement as "strategies." Therapists enquire about and advise you on "strategy"—as if this is 1812 and we're talking about Napoleon and the Russian general Kutuzof. In reality the average parent is not contemplating military strategy, just trying to do what they think is the best thing given who he/she is and who the kid is. The strategies "how to" books advocate tell you how to engage, when to retreat, and when to go for the kill (enforce "consequences", i.e. punish). Maybe this is one way of looking at things but I, for one, had a serious case of battle fatigue. But then, after all, it was old man Kutuzof's battle fatigue that lost him some battles (by not engaging with the Czar) but won him the war (by retreating from Napoleon).

In seventh grade I backed off and trusted Jack in the hands of others. Before I describe that I will share the last two blogs I wrote on my website. I had no more energy to run the website either so that went dormant too. I told myself it remains to be seen whether Jack and Jill will in the end fetch their pale of water, or that their fate is closer to that of Sisyphus, rolling the boulder up the hill to repeatedly tumble down every time they reach the top. But then again, I thought, the fate of Sisyphus is definitely preferable to pushing buttons in front of a glowing device. At least Sisyphus got some exercise.

The last blogs on *Mothers of Bad Boys*

I'm on sabbatical already (and why)

I've only homeschooled Jack for a grade and a half and I'm already in desperate need of a sabbatical.

Technically, our "school year" has started. Since Jack really fell behind in math in the last couple of years I feel justified to have him work mostly on math this year. My husband who is in charge of math is working three days a week now so he has more time and energy to teach math. In addition, we have signed Jack up at an interesting math program offered by Dominican University in San Rafael, CA.

The program is called Math Circle and meets one evening a week with different lecturers on various math topics.

On Mondays Jack goes to an outdoor program called Dirt Time which I think is a godsend for kids (I'll write about this more later). All day long a bunch of homeschooled kids roam in the wilderness and explore nature, directed by a young and very knowledgeable group of naturalists. The kids learn all kinds of things about our local flora and fauna, as well as skills like animal tracking, fire making, whittling, etc. At the end of the program the older kids become knife certified, which I think is an absolute necessity for boys especially. I really can't think of any better or more necessary program for children.

My ideas for the "curriculum" this year were basically to introduce Jack to scientific methodology, both in natural and social sciences. Dirt Time is a very good beginning point for learning to study science. After all, scientific methodology begins with observation. It's wonderful for kids to learn to observe closely. I couldn't be more grateful for Dirt Time.

I was also going to do a few more lessons in fiction, what we started last year. Specifically, I wanted to explore epic and historical legend.

But… all this has to wait until next year. I can't teach right now. I am burnt out.

There are two kinds of homeschoolers out there. When one explores homeschooling options one invariably comes across those homeschooling families who are mostly having a ball doing it. These are the folks who homeschool by choice and conviction. They devote their lives to homeschooling and are generally quite gung-ho about it. I am very grateful to these folks because without them there would be no homeschooling option, no advocacy, no support, no community. As far as I'm concerned these guys deserve serious accolade.

I, alas, belong to the second group of homeschoolers. Let's call them the reluctant homeschoolers. This is a group who has dropped out of school for different reasons. Some kids have dropped out on account of bullies, some on account of learning issues, or bad teachers, etc. For the most part, those of us in this group had not planned on homeschooling. Sadly, dropping out of school has caused major disruption in our lives.

In one of my previous blogs I got a comment that I sound like I don't enjoy having a kid. I often think that I complain too much too. As I write these blogs I am constantly hearing a little voice telling me that raising and educating a kid is not about me, that I should concentrate on Jack and get out of the picture. But I never manage to do that. I'm always interposing myself. I even told Jack last year that the only way I will continue homeschooling him is if I make it interesting to myself. That little accusatory voice does torment me but it doesn't quite succeed in wiping me out of the picture. I really don't see why I should let it do that to me. Having a kid should not be a death sentence for the mother's life and identity, should it?

Which brings me back to being a reluctant homeschooler. I had planned that as my son got older and more engaged with school and friends I would be able to return to my own work and interests. I sure did not think much of the education he was receiving in school but I always assumed a kid mostly learns from his family and by himself. School was to be a community: friends, adults other than parents, and challenges both good and bad to learn from. And while the kid is learning to navigate through this community, the parents have time to do what they need to be doing.

In the back of my mind then, I am still wishing we didn't have to homeschool. I have tried to make the best of it—and again, I really do have enjoyed the challenge and the freedom of educating Jack the way I think is best. But that little seed of reluctance has been firmly planted in me. It doesn't go away and it has a way of exhausting me.

Doing anything reluctantly is draining. That's why I need a sabbatical.

From the Editor

Farewell to *Mothers of Bad Boys*

It is exactly two years since I launched this site and I am saying farewell for now. I've really enjoyed running this site, "met" some terrific individuals from whom I have learned a great deal. I met Peter Gray whose *Free to Learn* blog on Psychology Today was a great source of inspiration, affirmation, and information. His book, also titled *Free to Learn*, is must-read for parents and a liberating force for children.

I also met Cevin Soling whose documentary *The War on Kids* is a chilling and eye-opening account of the assaults on children by various institutions, from educational to psycho-pharmacological. The parallels he draws between schools and prisons cannot be denied. His book, *The Student Resistance Handbook*, is refreshingly irreverent and a valuable contribution to tell-it-like-it-is literature on schools.

I briefly met Michael Pritchett whose anti-bullying work is the only one I found that was worth talking about. It's the only one that looks at things from the perspective of those on the giving and receiving side of bullying: the children. This work bears the stamp of approval of my son— and he should know!

But I just don't have the time to do it any longer.

My circumstances have vastly changed since I started this site. As I explained in my first *From the Editor* blog, my reason for taking up the cause of "bad boys" was to bring attention to how boys were being treated in schools. I also wanted an outlet to help me and other mothers cope with having our kids implicitly labeled as "bad." I can't overstate how much I have learned—and how much a lot of what I felt was wrong with the way boys are treated has been confirmed. But the fact is that my son in no longer in school and we don't have that kind of "bad boy" problem anymore.

As I blogged about it before, the irony was that while I was trying to understand and find solutions to the "bad" behavior of boys (boy behaviors that are not tolerated anymore and are slowly pushed into the direction of being pathologized and/or criminalized) we had to leave school on account of some real bad stuff. Bullying. Gang behavior. Neglect by schools. And I just gave up hope for changing things after years of trying.

We left to homeschool. I blogged about that extensively and started a new blog, *Educating My Boy*, on the academic part of things. Being a teacher at heart I have really enjoyed being in charge of my son's education. I have learned a great deal about how and what to teach middle schoolers. I hope someday I can do something with this knowledge.

There have been a lot of positive things about our homeschooling experience. But there are negatives too. If I were to put it in a nutshell, the problem is that to make sure that a homeschooled child does not miss out on a full life, the parent—most often, the mother—has to completely dedicate her life to the child. Often this is not possible, nor am I convinced that it is necessarily desirable.

Right now, as I wrote in my last blog, I am burnt out. I not only need to take a break from "teaching" my son, I need to take a break from having my life completely taken over by things having to do with being a mother/teacher. I need to get back to other work.

I will certainly not shut down this site. There is a lot of good material here that is useful to people. Lots of stuff from a couple of years ago still regularly get hits. But I won't be updating very frequently—perhaps a blog here and there, any maybe some compelling news items, but nothing regular.

So, for now, farewell. We'll see what happens next.

In Others' Hands

As I've mentioned before we live in an area that is particularly rich in what it has to offer by way of education. With me out of the "education" picture there were plenty of others to take over.

First, Robert started on pre-algebra with Jack, which I'm afraid did not go very far. But they read an illustrated version of Howard's Zinn's *People's History of United States* together which was interesting to Jack.

The math program at Dominican University continued. While the kids were expected to absorb 30 per cent of the material at best, I doubt Jack learned even that much! But, my hope continues to be that he gets exposed to the brilliant and fun world of math.

Dirt Time and Wild Farmers continued to teach the kids about the natural environment we are living in. For Thanksgiving the children presented a feast made with foraged plants and berries: teas, pancakes and other delicacies made with acorns, huckleberries, miner's lettuce and many other things.

In my unending quest to get Jack involved in dance and performing arts my ballet teacher Charles Torres (a motorcycle-riding, tattooed, spiky-haired, very cool dude) agreed to give Jack stage combat lessons. The studio being nearby, Jack would walk down there with his various weapons and take lessons in stage sword fighting and other dramatized combat. Again in my ongoing quest to make dance studios more boy-friendly I suggested to the owner to start an official stage-combat class for boys. I suggested that since the boys at this age are also exploring music they can each bring a favorite song and choreograph a staged combat piece to it.

I still think this is a great idea but the school did not pursue it. I tried to organize it among the homeschoolers but that did not work out either.

I was also happy to see Jack get involved in doing some work on his own. He made friends with a pet-shop owner in a small town near us, Patty from For Paws in Fairfax, and did some volunteer work taking care of and playing with for-adoption kittens and bunnies. I stayed out of the arrangements and he did a good job of calling Patty to set up times himself. One of the homeschooling mothers with two small boys was also interested in a "babysitter" and Jack volunteered for the job. He made a time commitment and was very good at keeping it. He learned to log his hours and at the end of the job he was rewarded with a big fat iTunes card.

We also managed to take (sometimes drag) Jack to some good films. I wanted him to be exposed to different aspects of life in different parts of the world. Our local nonprofit, indie movie theater was a great resource. As a regular, Jack made friends with a couple of other regulars, both local high school teachers, who were impressed that he was being educated through these films. That gave him a little ego boost. But, I must say, I found it a cryin'-out-loud shame that almost every time Jack was the only child in the audience. Heck, most of the audience is usually the local retired folks.

Here is a list of some of the movies we saw at our great local non-profit cinema, the Smith Rafael Film Center, as well as elsewhere:

> *Hedgehog:* An eleven year-old rich Parisian girl discovers the world of books with the concierge in her building.
>
> *Hero's Journey:* Joseph Campbell on the mythology of the hero.
>
> *NEDs:* Gangs in Scotland.
>
> *The Women on the Sixth Floor:* Spanish "guest worker" maids in Paris.
>
> *Cultures of Resistance:* Battles for peace and justice in

Africa, Brazil, and the Middle East.

Happy: The idea and practice of happiness in different cultures in the world.

Le Havre: An African refugee boy being smuggled through France to London to reunite with his family, with help from French townsfolk.

Opening of the new Bolshoi Theater in Moscow.

Farmegeddon: Raw-milk production and distribution and the laws that inhibit it.

Sleep Furiously: Life in rural Wales on the brink of extinction.

Buck: The original "horsewhisperer," teaching people to train horses by understanding the nature of fear.

Consuming Children: Media teaching children to become consumers.

Exit Through the Gift Shop: Modern street art and its relationship to the art industry.

Waterloo: The historic battle where Napoleon was defeated by Wellington.

My Reincarnation: Tibetan Buddhists in the diaspora and its generational legacy.

This is a very random list of what happened to be playing at the cinema and what I can remember. But my point is that education resources are everywhere and chance is a great guide. We were of course lucky to have a cinema nearby that showed these kinds of films but I have found that these and many other films like them can be found either for free on YouTube or on Netflix on its cheapest membership option. Since these are not money-making Hollywood films they are much more easily and cheaply available. I think watching films and having casual conversations about them with kids, with an occasional look in a map or a looking up of some question, is one of the most powerful teaching tools available. No lesson plans and no homework necessary! The film makers have done all the work for you.

But, ah, the unbearable sweetness of homeschooling...

All the gruesome details of homeschooling said and done, you can't beat its sweet moments, even during a bad year. When your child is at home with you serendipity has plenty of chance to reveal itself in full lovely glory.

When you homeschool you have free, unstructured time, so things happen. Jack came shopping for a rose plant with me one afternoon. We looked at the names of different roses and I showed him the different families of roses (hybrid tea, grandiflora, floribunda, etc.). We came across one rose called Rock and Roll. Later in the day I saw him looking up in my rose book to see whether Rock and Roll was a hybrid tea or a grandiflora.

After lunch one day he sat with his dad during an online presentation of building standards on ventilation systems. A few times after that Robert explained aspects of his engineering work to Jack.

One rainy day as I was washing dishes I looked out the kitchen window and saw a colony of quail taking shelter in our backyard. I called to Jack who interrupted his computer game and came over to watch the quirky birds together, listening to the rain fall.

Another day we took a walk around the block and Jack pointed out to me a prickly pear cactus. I started singing the refrain from T. S. Eliot's "The Hollow Men": *Here we go round the prickly pear/Prickly pear prickly pear...* and ending with: *This is the way the world ends... Not with a bang but a whimper.* Then, still walking and striking various things with our sticks, I told him about T. S. Eliot's "The Wasteland" and its opening lines: *April is the cruelest month, breeding/Lilacs out of the dead land, mixing/Memory and desire...* I told him that to pass seventh grade he would have to take a test:

Question: Which is the cruelest month? Answer: April.

Question: How does the world end? Answer: Not with a bang but a whimper.

This became a running joke between us.

On another occasion driving to join a group of home-schoolers at a park in Napa we passed though acres and acres of vineyard under a clear vast sky. Jack did not take a glance out the window, he was so busy with his electronic device. I suddenly got mad, pulled over and yelled at him to put away the iPhone and look at the scenery. Seeing how mad I was he turned the thing off without resistance. The moment we looked up at the sky together we saw flocks of thousands of migrating birds flying in and out of the most amazing formations. They came together, danced their formation, flew away, and new flocks and formations emerged. It was simply astonishing. We were both speechless.

Homeschooling prolongs the magic moments of childhood. Don't we all long for that?

Eighth Grade

By eighth grade I had recovered enough to start teaching again. Earth sciences and math I left to Jack's continuation of the Dirt Time and Math Circle programs and I concentrated on Social Science and Literature. In addition to being introduced to and appreciating these disciplines I wanted him to gain experience in writing papers and taking tests, both essay and multiple choice.

I started the year with the Delphic Oracle. I had Jack do research and explain what that was:

> An oracle is a person or text that passes on wisdom. The Delphic Oracle was a messenger from the god Apollo. "Know thyself" is the most famous of the wise sayings of the oracle. "Know thyself" is the saying that inspired the Greek in philosophy and science.

Know Thyself became the theme of our studies for the year. I think around age 13 is just the right time to make children start to pay attention to the process of knowing themselves and get introduced to the intellectual disciplines that have emerged out of the efforts of humanity to understand itself.

Social Sciences: Psychology, Sociology, Political Science and Economics

This is a lot, I know. But it is actually not hard to give kids at this age a taste of all the different factors, inside and outside themselves, that make human beings who they are and act as they do. Once kids get a chance to apply what they learn to themselves and those around them they actually become very interested in it.

Again, I received a wonderful teaching tool by chance: a sheet of paper handed around by an art teacher!

I was touring San Rafael High School for next year and walked in on an art teacher who was handing out sheets of paper with the outline of a head with eyes, ears, nose and mouth. She instructed her students to draw what is inside the head and what is outside. Brilliant! This simple concept has so many teaching applications. I used it as my introduction to social science.

I drew a head for Jack and asked him to name what's inside and what's outside.

This is his list of some of the things that are inside versus outside:

> Inside: Happiness, curiosity, feelings, ideas, thoughts, personality, memories, excitement, creativity, wishes, talents.
> Outside: Family, friends, school, sports, video games, city, country.

In the context of "inside" and "outside" I introduced psychology and sociology. Following this conversation it was easy to define psychology and sociology. I had him write down the definitions so that he would better remember:

> Psychology is the study of people and their relationships as individuals. Sociology is the study of people and their relationships as members of a group, such as: nation, religion, economic status (class), race, gender.

Using these distinctions we discussed the social forces that make people who they are, the groups they are born into or become part of, and the lives they live. Jack made a chart of different social "groups" he could think of: girls and boys, "gamers," "rednecks," different nationalities. He then listed the "norms" ("how people are supposed to be and act"), economic conditions (their privileges and opportunities or lack thereof), and political positions (their rights, protection by law, access to power as in elections, etc.) of each group.

In the course of the conversations that arose out of this exercise I pointed out that Economics and Political Science are studies of how economic and political factors affect who people are and what they do. I will not elaborate on these discussions even though I took notes on what we talked about because they actually got quite interesting—democracy, dictatorship, distribution of wealth, education and media, and all kinds of other juicy topics came up!

My purpose was just to open Jack's eyes to these factors and lay the foundation for future study, not to have him take tests in these subjects. I left sociology, economics and political science at discussion level and concentrated on psychology. I find that young people are fascinated by psychology.

Psychology

From an early age children are driven to sketch out a "self" for themselves. Their likes and dislikes, friends and foes, and all kinds of this-versus-that ideas are attempts at finding and distinguishing themselves. By late middle school they are quite ready to get some direction on their road to self discovery. As they are developing and constructing a sense of self it is a good time to introduce them to conceptual tools that bring more clarity to that complicated process. I think a general introduction to all aspects of studying an individual (as an individual as well as a member of various social groupings) is a good place to start, but the individual is what is most relevant to kids at this age. In fact, perhaps psychology is the easiest discipline to get children interested in at this stage of their lives.

I also believe that the insights of some of the best thinkers in psychology are accessible to young people long before college. I started with my own favorites.

Piaget

I have a long-standing interest in how and what children think and I studied Piaget extensively when I was an undergraduate. As a scientist Piaget was very clear about the kind of thinking that he was studying in children: the logico-mathematical process. This form of cognitive operation is, of course, only one aspect of development. Piaget's own studies started at the very beginning, with infants, long before children start "thinking." My favorite book of Piaget is *Origins of Intelligence in Children* which records the observations of his sharp, natural-scientist eyes, as he studied his own three children. (When my son was born I compared what I saw with Piaget's keen observations and realized that I was no natural scientist! Over the years I also realized my interest is not so much in *how* children learn to think, but *what* they think: how they see, understand, and make sense of the world.) At any rate, there are some concepts in Piaget that I think are very graspable and relevant to children. I wanted to teach those to my son.

Here is the "essay" exam Jack took on Piaget:

Explain some important concepts in Piaget's theory and give examples.

The "Sensory Motor Stage" is the stage in a baby's growth where it explores the world through his or her senses and movements.

"Assimilation" is when a person takes in information about things and their mind grows.

"Accommodation" is the way your mind grows after taking in information.

"Object Permanence" is what makes peek-a-boo so fun for babies! They think your face is gone the moment you put your hands on your face, but the moment you take them off, your face is back again. Once the babies learn object permanence they know that when you put your hands on your face and they don't see it, it is still there and that is why at a certain age they lose their peek-a-boo drive.

"Object Permanence" makes a kid rethink everything he or she ever knew. The kid realizes that a person's life does not stop when you are not with them, that a thing does not just vanish into thin air when it is hidden from your sight, and that closing your eyes does not make everything go away. He starts to realize that there are many things that exist that he does not know about! As reality starts to creep up on the child more, the child becomes less self-centered. A self-centered person has not realized that there are many other things going on in the world that do not tie down to that person!

I think it is easy to imagine what interesting conversations children can engage in when these concepts are introduced to them. It could help them to see and understand themselves and others in new ways.

Freud

Freud is full of concepts that make a lot of sense to children, perhaps even more than Piaget. Unfortunately it has become fashionable and politically correct to dismiss Freud; people do this without having read a word of his writing. We started with the "pleasure principle"—in Jack's words: "The impulse that makes you do stuff that gives you pleasure." Then we talked about why sometimes you need to control that impulse, as in sharing or waiting or holding back. We even talked about how we can "sublimate" an impulse—in

Jack's words: "Substitute one action/pleasure/need (A.P.N) for another A.P.N."

Talking about the Id, Ego and Superego was the most interesting. After discussing these concepts I had Jack explain them in his own words:

> Id: The impulses that you're born with. E.g.: what gives you instant gratification.
>
> Superego: The things that tell your Id what not to do. E.g.: your intelligence and conscience. [I swear by the gods that I did not put those words in Jack's mouth. He immediately figured out what legitimate superego is all about!]
>
> Ego: The Ego is what determines your personality by listening either to your Id or Superego.

As we were discussing the Id a song by Queen popped into my mind: "I want it all and I want it now." Jack could immediately relate to that! We tried finding songs expressing the three parts of the human psyche and found that expressions of Id certainly abound in Rock and Roll. Looking for a good example of Superego in Rock and Roll we agreed perhaps anti-war and other idealistic songs may qualify. But looking for the Ego appearing in songs was more difficult. In fact, I realized the Ego is the hardest part of the psyche for a child to understand; it is more complicated that the other two (small surprise!).

As the final assignment I had Jack write essays on his thoughts on the Id, Superego, and Ego and how he has experienced them in his own life. I reproduce the essays here for readers who are as fascinated as I am in how children "assimilate" new information into their existing cognitive makeup and how they "accommodate" them by the way they change in how they see themselves and their world. I am not interested in "correct" answers; I'm just interested in seeing through children's eyes, especially after a new idea or view is introduced to them. As a rule, teaching the social sciences to children at this stage amounts to giving them some interesting lenses to look through. I love listening to them describe what they see. In psychology in particular, who knows, this may even bring about some advances in the field!

Define Id, Superego, Ego, and give examples of how you have experienced them in your life.

The Id

According to Freud the Id is the force that makes us do things that give us pleasure. From time to time the Id can be good, but it is rare. Mostly the Id gets you in trouble by making you do things that hurt you and other people, as well it can be helpful.

How it hurts me:
Once, a long time ago, I wanted to touch a stove top and there was no Superego around to tell me no so I touched it, well you can assume what happened. Another time I wanted to jump off the diving board and do a front-flip, that may not sound bad but I didn't know how to do a front-flip and the only reason I had the idea was because I saw another person do one. Well I back-flipped hard!

How it hurts others:
When I was in elementary school I was a kickball team captain and so one day was choosing my players and my choice was (since I lost the coin toss, so to speak—it was ro-sham-bo): David, the school's best kickball player (he had hurt his ankle and had a bit of a limp), Dylan (small kid but very fast), Juan (slow but a good catch), Emma (fast but a real slacker), and Jesus (he was just all out average!). There were two that I did not have room for on my team and so they didn't get to play. Well so we started

out great! I went first and got a home run, then Juan went and kicked it real far but not far enough, so he made it to 2 base. Then Jesus made it to 1 base, Emma got to 2 base when Juan and Jesus made it to home, but then it went down hill. Dylan got 4 fouls and one out and then David got out instantly! We lost the game 4 to 20. All because I chose Dylan and David when my Id said so and didn't trust my judgment. Man, who knew double Ds could be so bad?

When the Id can help you:
I consider myself a betting man when it comes to playing for fake money, very little money, for an item of little importance, or nothing at all. Well my Id helps with me winning! My mind loves making my decisions for me but when it comes to betting it makes all the wrong moves, but luckily my Id says "Don't listen to him!" and I usually win.

The best song that expresses the Id:
Queen's "I Want It All."

The Superego

The outside and inside forces that cause a person not to give in to the Id. The agents of the Superego are your family, friends, teachers, rules and laws, conscience, and your intelligence.

Bad Superego:
The Superego isn't always right, e.g. laws are not always good. I think that a person no matter what his age should have the right (with proper training) to carry a weapon. Teachers are sometimes bad people.

Good Superego:
I was walking one time and I went inside a store to

get some water then I saw a candy I really like and was tempted to get it, but then my Conscience acted up and said "NO BAD BOY!" so I got my water and walked out without the candy!

Songs of the Superego:
    "American Idiot," "Get Up, Stand Up," and "Give Peace a Chance."

The Ego

The force of which makes your mind either choose or compromise with the Id and the Superego's suggestions. The ego in slang terms is your vanity, but it really means what I explained above. For example: If I were to say that a person had a big ego it would usually mean the person I was talking about would be very full of himself or in other words vain. But if I were to say that person's Ego made the right decision then I would be talking about this concept of the Ego.

When the Ego is at work:
    Once I was hanging out with a friend of mine and a kid I don't really like was there and he was about to do something extremely stupid and my Id was saying "This is gonna be awesome to watch!" but my Superego was screaming "No don't let him!!!!!!" So I compromised and said "That's a stupid idea and you shouldn't do it." But he didn't listen and he regretted it!
    While others may have an image for their Superego and Id such as the Angel and Devil on a person's shoulders, I do not have an image. It is just a force.

English and World Literature

This, of course, is my area of strength and I followed my nose rather than any particular curriculum. As for teaching material I again mostly went with serendipity, using books that somehow came our way. I did, however, incorporate a bit of history of English language and literature into the texts we read.

When we came across excerpts from Beowulf and Canterbury Tales, for example, we did a quick overview of the evolution of the English language. And lo and behold the internet and especially YouTube are full of the most informative, funny, and no-nonsense brief lessons in history of languages. Jack got quite interested in listening to how Anglo-Saxon and Middle English sounded and we even came across rap songs in Old and Middle English. Then we listened to rapped versions of monologues from different Shakespeare plays. It was so much fun. And it was all top notch instruction.

While my first object was to convey my own love of literature to Jack, I also did want him to get exposed to various testing methods. Sometimes you have to "prove" that you know something, so we worked on test-taking and writing various kinds of reports and papers as well.

Taking multiple-choice tests

My friend Jaleh whose daughter had just graduated from high school sent me a big box filled with work books, including Massachusetts Comprehensive Assessment System preparatory tests—whatever! I picked a random tenth-grade MCAS literature book to get Jack acquainted with taking tests in reading and comprehension. The book featured relatively short essays, stories and poems followed by multiple-choice reading comprehension questions.

Jack's homework was to read assigned pieces and answer the multiple choice questions. Together we went through his answers and checked them against the correct ones. In this process we frequently noted that the "correct" answer depended on individual interpretation. He saw for himself that in literature and other fields of humanities taking tests, especially multiple choice ones, do not reflect real knowledge.

Book reports

O ver the years my husband Robert and I have read a number of good books with Jack, even when he was in school. In sixth grade I had him write simple "reports" on the books that we had read. The books ranged from the Harry Potter and Percy Jackson series to Mark Twain, Dickens and Steinbeck. For his report he had to write the title of the book, the author, place and year of publication, and list three other works by the same author. He also had to write down the age group that he would recommend the book for and a sentence or two of comment about his thoughts on the book. Here are a few interesting comments he made:

> Harry Potter series:
>   I would mostly recommend it for ages six and up. I thought it was very thrilling and the plot was well thought out. But a bit hard to read!

> Percy Jackson series:
>   Recommended for all ages young to old. I thought it would be good but it was GREAT! It anyone asked "Should I buy this?" I would say "Heck yah! They're awesome!"

Around the World in 80 Days:
Recommended for ages 10-100. VERY EXHILIRAT-ING! And I enjoyed reading this. It is enough to make someone laugh!

Huckleberry Finn:
16-70 are the ages I recommend it to. Very interesting story line, but a little hard to read. It will get you wanting more! (p.s. Trust me on this one!)

Great Expectations:
Recommended for ages 18-up. Very hard to under-stand if you are under 18.

With the MCAS book I also had Jack look up and jot down some basic information about the author of each piece: name, year of birth and death, country of origin, and three other works. This time I had him write brief definitions or explanations of different topics or works we came across: Tragedy, comedy, origins and development of the English language (Germanic branch of the Indo-European family, Old English/Anglo-Saxon, Middle English, Modern English), Beowulf, Canterbury Tales, the notion of a "frame tale," etc.

Writing papers

The teaching of writing is perhaps one of the most difficult teaching activities. We have all heard about the "writer's block" of even professional writers, and the daunting challenge of a blank piece of paper awaiting what we have to say—or in the case of most students, what they absolutely *don't* have to say. I have experience with teaching the writing process from freshman year to graduate work, even professionals, but teaching children can be the funnest.

The most important thing to keep in mind is that writing, just like talking, is a form of communication. Engaging children in a conversation is the best first step. With Jack I would start by throwing an interesting topic to him and help develop a conversation. Once we had generated enough things that we had to say about the topic I would have him jot down notes on the most interesting or relevant ones. Then I would have him flesh out the ideas in his own words, which would become the first draft of his paper. Coming back to the draft the next day I would help him edit the draft—i.e. cut and paste, add or subtract, clarify, and correct mistakes—to produce the final paper.

World Literature "Term Paper"

The purpose of this assignment was for Jack to learn the format and the rhetorical structure of a term paper. I based the topic on Jack's interest in ancient Greek mythology and expanded it. Now, the fact is that children do not read mythology or epic in original form. The familiarity with Greek mythology usually comes from children's books and popular movies, such as the Percy Jackson series. I think this is a perfectly good place to start. For Indian epic I had Jack read comic books brought from India by friend Indu. Great numbers of Indian kids become familiar with the Mahabharata and Ramayana through their comic book versions. The same thing with the Persian epic, Shahnameh. Jack read the children's versions of these epics. After all, these stories have been transmitted through the oral tradition, such as bedtime stories, for ages. Children have always received these tales in age-appropriate versions!

This is the "term paper" that came out of this assignment.

Compare and Contrast Indian, Greek, and Persian Epics: The Odyssey, Ramayana, and Shahnameh

Summary

This paper will compare and contrast three of the world's oldest epics. It will find the difference and similarities between the different aspects of the epics. These aspects include: The character of heroes, the moral values of heroes, the actions of heroes, moral lessons, and cultural identity.

Definition of Epic

According to Wikipedia: "An epic is a long narrative poem, ordinarily concerning a serious subject containing details of heroic deeds and events significant to a culture or nation." In addition, all epic poetry started as oral tradition and then at some point was written down.

Similarities

Character

Epic heroes are usually bold and strong, mentally as well as physically. They usually have to overcome many obstacles and challenges that usually test their mental capacity as well. But with great power comes great responsibility; what I mean by that is the bigger they are the harder they fall. By harder I mean wider as such: bringing down their family and friends, their country and people, and last but not least, their power. But when they do succeed (which they usually do) this theory is almost reversed!

In the Odyssey, Odysseus is strong, fearless, war hardened, and wise. Telemachus is bold, raging, and kind. Penelope is wise, loyal, and intelligent.

In the Ramayana, Rama is a warrior, demon slayer, wise, brave, strong, obedient, keeps his promises, non-materialistic, wants to do what is right for his people, and powerful. Sita is a loyal and caring wife whose goal is to stay with Rama to show him her affection. Lakshman is a warrior, demon slayer, and a loyal brother who is willing to go through anything for Rama. Bahrata is a loyal brother and he is not greedy or selfish.

In the Shahnameh, Rostam is strong, powerful, and willing to fight. He is as hard as a rock on the outside, but as soft as a mouse's belly on the inside. He appreciates a good fight, but also may be a smart coward when facing an opponent stronger or as strong as himself. Sohrab has almost the same characteristics as Rostam, but much more proud and unwise than Rostam. Sohrab is strong, powerful, and is full of dumb pride, but at least he has good intensions. Tehmineh is a bold and independent woman who does what she wants to do. Gordafarid is a brave and strong warrior who is very wise and tries to protect her home. Kaveh is bold, wise, strong, and a true hero. He is very brave, intelligent, and he wants to do good for everyone. Fereydoun is strong-headed bent on revenge, yet getting wiser by the second. Faranak is a smart and protective mother who wants nothing less than the best education for her son.

Moral Values

In the process of his journey, Odysseus lost many of his men and suffered a lot, so he learned wisdom and humility from the gods.

Rama's moral values were to protect the ones he loved, his people, and to use wisdom instead of violence. He was non-materialistic and spiritual. Sita and Lakshman valued loyalty to Rama. Bharata was loyal and not greedy.

Rostam's moral values were loyalty to his country and his king. Sohrab's moral values were his loyalty to his father and mother and he believed in loyalty to good kings. Kaveh believed in equal rights for people and preventing the death of more innocents. Fereydoun's moral value was punishment of Zahhak the evil king.

Moral Flaws

Odysseus's flaws[1] were that he was vain, self-centered, and he betrayed his wife with other women. Telemachus's flaw was that he wanted to strike out in rage without thinking.

Rama's stepmother's flaws were that she became jealous, greedy, and selfish.

Rostam's moral flaw was that his pride and vanity caused him to kill his own son. Sohrab's was that his pride got in the way of his intelligence. Zahhak faulted by being greedy and listening to the demon Ahriman who told him to kill his father. Ahriman tricked Zahhak by taking advantage of his gluttony. Kavus's moral flaw was that he mistreated Rostam. He was not grateful to Rostam who happened to do everything for him. He was not loyal to Rostam.

Cultural Identity

The epics will all teach you something in one way or another. They will help teach you the best way to act in that culture or at least back then. In each culture children are still named after the heroes in the epics. Even in families that emigrated they still insist that there should be translated versions of the epics for their children so they don't lose their cultural identity.

Differences

Origins

The epics were all composed in different places. For example: The Odyssey was composed in Greece, the Ramayana in India, and the Shahnameh in Iran. But even though the epics were composed in different places they all seem the same to me. Perhaps I feel this way because

---

[1] The seven deadly sins are a lot like the heroes' moral flaws in the epics. Religions are a lot more tough on people by calling people's flaws sins!

they at one point all came from the same people and they were called Indo-Europeans. Now, I have read a little about Chinese and Native American mythology and they seem much different than the Indo-European tradition!

Women

Penelope and Sita in the Odyssey and Ramayana were both strong, brave, and loyal. But in the Shahnameh in addition to being all those things, Tahmineh was bold and independent, Gordarafid was a fearless warrior and Faranak was wise, protective, and wanted her child who would be king to be educated.

Men

In the Ramayana all the heroes had no flaws and were entirely true to others and themselves. They were perfect. But in the Odyssey and Shahnameh the heroes did have flaws and were nowhere near perfect. Rostam and Odysseus had too much pride and vanity. In fact the tragedy between Rostam and Sohrab was because Rostam was so vain![1] Odysseus improved on himself throughout his journey, unlike Rama who started out perfect and ended perfect.

Conclusion

All epics, in one way or another, are similar in that the heroes always want to do what is right for their country and they are brave warriors. They are different in the way that they each have their own unique personality. Rostam is full of pride and strength but has a real soft spot and Odysseus is strong and wise-ish. Rama is a warrior and strong, but at the same time very spiritual. Epics are also similar in the way that they teach the people of each culture moral values and give them a sense of cultural identity.

---

1   In Greek tragedies the tragedy also comes about by the moral flaws of the heroes.

End of homeschooling

By the end of eighth grade Jack was quite sure he wanted to return to school. It was a bittersweet decision for me because I knew there were many things I would miss about homeschooling. But I was also relieved to have time to go back to my own work.

I do have one academic regret. I am sorry that I will not be able to "revisit" a lot of the topics we touched on and elaborate ideas we explored. I am sorry that many of the "seeds" that were sowed will be abandoned. It would have been nice to guide Jack in fertilizing the soil and tending the saplings. But I have to leave that to chance and the elements. But mostly I have to leave all of that to Jack himself—he would not have it any other way.

Now I see that Jack would not have anything any other way than what he wants. Coping with his resistance to how I and others wanted him to be and what we wanted him to do prompted me to start my blogs. So ultimately this book is for the "bad boy" himself. Some day perhaps he will use it to understand himself, me, and the process of his growth and development. I think good teaching is the opposite of controlling someone. It is setting his/her mind free. I hope he'll see that this is what I was trying to do.

As for me, I have had the chance to teach what I love to whom I love. This, ultimately, is great fulfillment for a parent. And the rest of the story is for Jack to tell.

CHAPTER 5

Extreme Mothering

Motherhood is an elusive and unrelenting proposition. There are times when it demands extreme exertion or elicits extreme reactions from women.

Every once in a while mothers hear each other's distress calls. I became especially attuned to these calls when I myself fell apart trying to undo the damage done to my son in school and build a new life for him—working every inch of the way against his anger and resistance. The first time I heard this call was a number of years ago, but suddenly I heard it everywhere.

My friend Kate's daughter was diagnosed with autism at age two. As a tiny toddler Emma had displayed remarkable memory, memorizing poems and maps, so everyone had thought she was a little prodigy. Her mother, though, was becoming suspicious. "She's not learning like other kids," she said. "There is something unusual in the way she's learning." When the diagnosis confirmed Kate's suspicion she said to me, "I feel half dead." It was a good thing she had another baby daughter in her life, otherwise she probably would have felt fully dead. I feel I would have. Just listening to her made my heart sink into my gut. We did not shed tears together but her wail reverberated in my whole being.

I watch a lot of random videos on YouTube. One of my favorite things is to watch the birth of baby animals: dogs, cats, deer, horses, even giraffes and rhinos and elephants. There is one clip, "Baby Elephant Birth Miracle," that is very touching. A mother elephant in a zoo gives birth in the middle of the night as other elephants sleep. The baby has a traumatic birth and does not move after birth. The mother elephant nervously circles the calf, nudging and gently kicking it to get a sign of life. Finally the calf moves and as the mother tries harder to get it to stand up the baby slips under a fence, out of the mother's reach. At this point the mother lets out a wail. Another elephant comes to her help but unable to do anything she lets out more wails. With these last cries all the rest of the elephants and their calves rush to the mother and her friend. There is nothing any of them can do but they keep the mother company until the zoo keepers arrive in the morning and succeed in saving the baby.

We can hear the sound of mothers' distress calls all around us, every day. It can camouflage itself as nonchalant chitchat or betray itself in shrill chatter, forced cheerfulness, or rants of exaggerated convictions. The transcendent form of the distress call is laughter. Kate told me of an evening out with fellow mothers of autistic children. She said that at some point one of the moms pulled up her pant leg and showed her shin that was black and blue from her son's kicks. Her fellow moms, looking the bruised leg up and down, broke into laughter. They then proceeded to discuss how to handle dentist visits and the best "15-step tooth brushing" routine. I may have imagined the whole scene wrongly, but its effect on me was profoundly humbling. I felt humbled by the laughter of those mothers. (And these are the women who not too long ago were called "refrigerator mothers.")

Over the years there have been many stories of mothers of autistic children trying to kill them. Almost always they try to kill themselves along with their kids and sometimes they succeed in one or both. One of the last stories that I followed was Issy Stapleton whose mother Kelli is now in jail for her attempted murder/suicide. Issy had been a very difficult and often aggressive kid who had even sent her mother to the hospital a couple of times. Kelli had blogged about her daily struggles and posted clips on YouTube. The name of her blog is enough to show Kelli as the extraordinary person she is: "The Status Woe: Rising above mediocrity one mishap at a time." Here is something from the last blog she wrote on her site:

> If there is anything I've learned in my relatively eventful life, it's that I'm not special or unique. If something has happened to me, I know it's happened to someone else. I have to admit that I'm suffering from a severe case of battle fatigue...

Describing her latest failed effort to get help with her daughter, she concludes: "I am devastated. My husband is gutted." She had tried everything:

> I'm a firm believer that you do not need to be a bitch to be an advocate. But there's always this: [Tina Fey's quote] Know what? Bitches get stuff done.

I am not the only one whose heart aches for Kelli. Yes, for Kelli first—because Issy has support that Kelli doesn't. The world would sooner listen to Issy's story than Kelli's. My friend Kate's mothers' group laughed at the black and blue leg of one of their own, but their kids were still little. A grown autistic youngster who has not had the good fortune to receive the best opportunities for treatment (Issy didn't) can be impossible to manage and in fact a danger to him- or herself and others. I read about a mother and godmother who tried to kill themselves and the tall and heavy autistic teenage boy they were left to their own devices to care for. I read about a doctor mother who succeeded in killing herself and her son. One very brave mother said of her son, "If he were a dog I would put him to sleep." Sacrilege! You may feel such things but you may never say them. Maybe I'm wrong again but I see the immensity of their love for their children in these women. I see their desperate cry that their children indeed are not "dangerous"; they are just difficult. Sometimes too difficult.

Did anyone hear the distress calls of these women before they did or said what they did? Their frequent requests and struggles for getting help are certainly well documented. Those desperate attempts are not sensationalized by the media but the mothers' final acts of anguish are. I think the bruised bodies and souls of mothers and fathers, the interminable red tape to get some assistance, the grief and burden of siblings—these should be on the front page of newspapers, not distortions of distress calls.

What is really obvious watching the clip of the mother elephant giving birth is that mother and child start out as one. If the calf does not show signs of life the mother is frantic. When I was shown my own baby the first time in the hospital I felt... nothing. I felt I was shown my heart, with arteries still attached, pumping away. What kind of emotional reaction would you have looking at your own heart? Do you "love" your heart? It seems like an irrelevant question, doesn't it? A healthy beating heart makes you feel alive; a child who cannot stand on its own feet makes you feel, like my friend said, half dead. That's when you let out your wail—a wail, that unlike in elephants, in human society goes unheeded.

There is a most cruel hypocrisy that women in advanced societies have to contend with. By "advanced" I mean the kind of societies that no longer have "villages" that help them raise children. While motherhood is revered in advanced societies in a sentimental and ultimately meaningless way it receives little actual support. Mothers are often left to their own devices to improvise, fight, and make do. If they have a particularly painful challenge, well then tough luck. And

God help them if they fall short, make mistakes, fall apart, or are simply up against circumstances over which they have no control.[1]

The blame—and the eternal debt

Back to random YouTube surfing... My childhood interest in detective stories, the way crimes are solved and criminals tried, is now amply rewarded by real crimes and real detectives on YouTube. Serial killers, of course, are most interesting because they elude capture for so long. Thus I came upon a number of documentaries about Jeffrey Dahmer, the notoriously gruesome serial killer in the 1980s. What particularly interested me were those documentaries that included interviews with his parents. There is a long interview with his father, who has the air of a man of clear conscience—you see, he's just the dad. The interview with the mother, on the other hand, is short and troubled. She has the air of a cornered and injured animal and does not go on and on like the dad.

Unlike his dad, Dahmer's mother was not an articulate person. She had suffered from mental illness for years and was certainly doing no better once her son was discovered to have committed unspeakable crimes. But her short interview was very interesting. She had been on the receiving end of the most hideous accusation: IT IS YOUR FAULT. Don't we all know that the mother/child bond is most formative? Don't we know that even healthy mothers can screw up their children, let alone mentally ill ones? Isn't it just self-explanatory that monster kids are made by monster moms? Jeffrey

---

1   My friend Cherie Takemoto responded most creatively after her special-needs son was born. She devoted her professional life to providing support and advocating for children with disabilities and their families. I never heard a distress call from her. She and her lovely daughter Margaret were always ready to respond to others' distress calls.

Dahmer's mother appeared on the interview with another woman who was the coauthor of a book she was writing: *The Assault on Motherhood*. It is a shame that she died before finishing the book. It would have been her defense against being accused of her son's crimes. It would have been a defense against the knee-jerk social assumption that mothers are responsible for the failures of their children. Mother and child are born as one but they don't remain one. You would think anyone understands that.

And yet, the Kelli Stapletons are jailed, not helped. The Joyce Dahmers are blamed, not pitied. Does anyone praise Mrs. Einstein for producing a genius son? Does anyone credit the mother of Paul McCartney for the good songs that her son wrote?

A while ago we went to dinner to the house of a colleague. Laura, a very bright, cheerful and professionally accomplished woman, has suffered an almost freakish fate. Her happy, healthy, intelligent son had been drawn to the lure of some "cool" and macho dudes in his neighborhood and had ended up in a very bad situation. He had been caught in a scuffle during which someone had been shot dead. Luckily Laura's son was not guilty of murder but he ended up in jail nevertheless. Next year when he will be released, he will have spent eight years in prison.

The night at Laura's house we talked at length about her son. She showed us pictures. She included my son in the conversation because she thought all boys should realize the dangers of playing with certain kinds of fire. I was very grateful to her. She lives and works in a community that has been very supportive of her and values her very much. And yet... I detected a distress call in her voice too. I heard it in the enthusiasm with which she wanted my son to understand certain dangers. I detected a flicker of a sense of responsibility, a sense of having to pay a debt to society by making an example of her son. "IT IS NOT YOUR FAULT," I wanted to scream. "You don't owe anybody anything. It was your son who chose to engage in utter stupidity, not you."

The kids themselves

Mothers suffer the consequences of their children's choices all the time. Self-destructive choices of kids can make mothers not just miserable but drive them nearly mad. Sometimes no amount of support given by family, community or society can help. One of my cousins died from cirrhosis of the liver following years of alcohol and drug abuse. Another cousin died from complications of a suicide attempt brought on by an obsessive relationship. A good friend of mine, an ultra accomplished and successful lawyer, died of drug overdose. Yet another friend died of AIDS which she got from her drug-addict boyfriend. I know the mothers of these friends and cousins and I know how they grew up. I don't know what more anyone could have done to prevent their self-destruction.

"I am like a train and will run anything over if it stands in my way," said one ten-year old boy to his mother. "Where is the train headed?" she asked. "To doing whatever I want," he answered. "I will run you over if you try to stop me, like I always have."

You can't stop this kind of train and you have no choice but to lick your wounds when it runs you over, and grieve if it eventually derails and crashes. As one of my aunts put it, "I'm always crying even when I'm laughing." Society adds to that wound the salt of blame.

My friend who died of AIDS said that she did not blame her boyfriend for giving her the disease. "What gave me AIDS was my own lack of self-respect," she said. During her last months she visited high schools to warn students about AIDS. She wanted them to see how ill she was. "This is what AIDS looks like," she would say to them. "This is also what not having self-respect looks like. If I had self-respect I would not have gotten involved with a drug-using, abusive boyfriend in the first place." Bless her soul, she did not blame her mother.

The website behind this book started on the note of taking

a close look at the "bad" boy problem. My goal was to expose the nonsense that creates the problem and help somehow rectify things. Little did I know that I would eventually hit upon the undercurrent of the "bad" mother. This river runs even deeper. "Bad mother," and its unspoken corollary "inadequate mother," accusations are silently rampant—a quick look at all the "how to" mothering literature shows this. Any mother's quick comparison of herself to the "good" mothers invented by these books is bound to make her feel inadequate and blame-worthy. Just as I found that "bad" boys are those who are made unhappy by the callousness and conformity of adults and institutions, "bad" mothers are those whose desperate attempts fall into the blindspots of society, whose cries for help fall on deaf ears, and who fail to meet the extra-human demands made on them. Bad boys and bad mothers are unhappy boys and mothers.

Many faces of unhappiness

Everything that grows is subjected to afflictions and then dies. And everything that is built crumbles or is destroyed. We bring our children into this kind of world and then are caught up in it together. We can't help but to try to fix things, to at least avert the worst disasters, to try to make our children safe and happy until they're able to take care of themselves. We yearn for the moment that we can say we are finished, the result is good, and now we can rest. There is a sadness built into the human parenting venture.

But unhappiness is different. It is anxiety, fear, shame, guilt, blame, sense of unworthiness, worry... My own unhappiness made me more attuned to the "extreme" mothers whose distress calls are either not heard or ignored. I was humbled by those calls; I allowed them to put my own life in perspective. I became aware that a gnawing unhappiness, a perpetual state of anxiety, is part of too many women's experience of motherhood. But this unhappiness pales in comparison to the helpless distress of mothers in the face of their children's unhappiness.

There is no question that mothers absorb the unhappiness of their children. Like the mother of the autistic child who absorbs her son's kicks, all mothers are challenged to withstand blind punches from their children, intentional or not. I will make the confession that I lack the fortitude to absorb attacks, neither physical nor mental. I fall apart. I tried to absorb my son's unhappiness as much as possible and I became exceedingly unhappy myself. I doubt that made him any less unhappy. You ask yourself, how can your tenderest feelings and your most selfless hopes be fraught with so much anguish and confusion? How does the extreme happiness of a new mother metamorphose into its exact opposite? How...? Why...?

The riddle of happiness is of course not easy to solve. If I were to offer a glib definition I would say that happiness requires the freedom and support to be oneself. I think that's true of both children and mothers. But in this case the chicken definitely comes before the chick. Mothers can do unspeakable damage to their children, which should make it obvious that nothing short of a great deal of the future of humankind rides on the health and happiness of mothers.

But "mother" is really just another woman; she has no magical powers nor extra-human strength. Who mothers are as women and how they live as free and equal members of society will go a long way toward the health and happiness of children, the future free and equal members of society. In an ideal world women retain their freedom and receive the extra support they need to remain who they are after they become mothers—with their strengths, flaws, moments of brilliance, and limits. And just like every other right women have earned, this will happen only with help from other women. Perhaps the place to start is with having patience, confidence, endurance—and actively reminding each other of the joys of motherhood. The rest is out of our control.

The gamble

"Mommy come swim."

Kate was telling me about Emma, now twenty-four, living semi-independently in a nice house with a group of autistic adults. Emma loves being in nature and her mother is almost always available to let her enjoy it. They were on the banks of Walden Pond when Emma asked her mother to join her in the water: Emma happy and energetic, Kate feeling lazy. If it had been her "normal" daughter, Kate said, she would have shrugged off the invitation and sat out her daughter's swimming, taking a quiet moment by herself. But Kate would never dampen Emma's good spirits. Joining her daughter in swimming, laughing and playing lifted Kate's mood. "I always end up refreshed and more cheerful when I join Emma in the delight she takes in nature and animals. We go to the lake together a lot." Walden Pond. How apt!

I know it has taken many years and gargantuan effort for Kate to make sure that Emma does not lose her capacity for happiness. It has taken Kate round-the-clock involvement in her daughter's life. Even when Emma was in an excellent boarding school Kate never left town for more than a couple of days, always on call if Emma wanted to come home—twenty-four years of it so far. It has also taken the full support and unsentimental dedication of her husband. This is a lucky family.

Elizabeth is a homeschooling mom whom I have run into at events for a number of years now. She is a beautiful and warm woman and her son and daughter have inherited those qualities from her. At a recent birthday party I sat for some time chatting with her son, Danny, who is on the autism spectrum, now a tall and handsome young man. I have always found it delightful to engage with people whose minds work differently, hence my long-standing interest in autism spectrum. Danny told me about a show he's following on the internet, how it has developed in an X-rated direction, and his argument with his parents over the permission to watch it now that he is over eighteen. I really enjoyed talking to him and he cracked me up several times. When Danny left to join the other kids Elizabeth and I talked about our own lives.

She is going through a divorce. I have not known her very closely over the years and have no knowledge of her particular circumstances, but in response to another mom who was enquiring about divorce laws, Elizabeth shared her experience. What she told us was that when her divorce is finalized she will be left with no financial support. After two decades of dedicating herself to her son, alternately trying schools and homeschooling, she is left with a dated résumé and dubious employability. Her husband had not earned much money during those years and was supported by his family, which had worked while Elizabeth was raising her kids and not "working." But now that the marriage has fallen apart, while her husband still enjoys the support of his family, Elizabeth is left out in the cold. "Go back to work," is such a facile and cruel remark.

The lack of a mother's financial independence may be negotiated in one family in a supportive and empowering way, and in another it could turn into hurt and humiliation. The role of the casting of the dice cannot be wholly dismissed.

"Maddy" Jordan Middleton

Sometimes no matter how hard you try, no words come out when you open your mouth, or if you're writing, your fingers freeze. An event that recently took place in Santa Cruz, CA, has put me in this state. On July 26, 2015, fifteen-year old Adrian Jerry Gonzalez lured eight-year old Madyson "Maddy" Middleton to his apartment, sexually assaulted and then murdered her. This happened in broad daylight while

Maddy was riding her scooter outside her apartment in an artists' complex where they were neighbors. It was an event that practically tore out the hearts of many in the community.

I don't have the words to describe all that has happened. I will quote from the news source, KSBW. A few days after the crime:

> Laura Jordan [Maddy's mother] heard crying near the memorial for her daughter at the Tannery Arts Center courtyard. There, in front of dozens of bouquets, loving cards, stuffed animals and candles, she saw Reggie Factor, Gonzalez's mother, on her knees, inconsolable.
>
> Factor wailed, cried to God and screamed that her son was a bad boy, a terrible boy... Why hadn't anyone told her? How could she not have known?

From the little that we have learned about Adrian Gonzalez, it is clear that he had had emotional problems for a while. Surely his mother knew about those but perhaps what she was trying to ask was how it could be that she was not able to guess that her troubled boy was capable of such an unspeakable crime. A smug blaming of the mother will not do. It was Maddy's mother who reminded us of this.

> Jordan sat next to [Factor], placed a hand on her back, and held her close: "I love you. I don't blame you," she repeatedly told Factor. "It's not your fault."
>
> Two friends, two mothers, forever tied by one heinous act... "I just love her, and we both lost our children that day. That's the tragic truth," Jordan said. "I don't fault her."

Maddy loved animals, especially wolves. She had wolf sheets, wolf bedspread, wolf wallpaper, and wolf pictures on her walls. The idea occurred to Jordan—"just in a flash as if Madyson had told her"—to howl at the moon the Friday after the crime, which was a "blue moon," the second full moon in July.

No one at the Tannery knew what the response might be, but at 8:30 p.m., on the dot, they could hear howling from across the city, reverberating off the hills and the Tannery walls. Men in business suits at a convention in town howled. [Others] joined in when they heard the town responding. "Everybody needs to release this pain," Jordan said.

The fact is, until we all join our efforts, the load carried by extreme mothers will never be lightened. It would be terribly sad if we stop at howling for Maddy.

CHAPTER 6

Monster Moms and Extreme Fathers

There is an Old Testament story about Solomon and the two mothers that is all too often relevant these days. The story is typically cited as a case of the wisdom of a judge but I think it is first and foremost an example of true motherhood. The story is that two women, both claiming motherhood of a boy, were brought before Solomon. Since he could not determine who the true mother was he asked for a sword and declared that he was going to split the child in two so each woman would get half. The true mother of the child cried, "Give him to her but don't hurt the child." Thus Solomon was able to determine who the real mother was.

The real test of motherhood is if a woman would rather give up a child than see him or her get hurt. What I call monster moms are women who put their own interests, or, worse, the chips on their shoulders, above the health and wellbeing of their children. As I've encountered a number of bitter divorces over the years I've seen a few of these monster moms. And contrary to what a wise justice system should do, the courts have turned a blind eye to true parenting. Sometimes it's the father who is the true mother.

Two extreme cases come to my mind. In neither case do I know exactly what the points of contention between the parents are; that's between grown men and women. But I have seen how the behavior of the women has negatively affected the children's lives and wellbeing and I find that beyond any justification. Coincidentally both these situations went to court in Chicago, which apparently is one of the worst places for custody battles—worst, that is, for the children.

When Jason and his ex-wife got divorced they shared custody, with the kids' principal home being their mother's. Over the years Jason's older daughter became increasingly unhappy living with her mother and begged to live with her father. The ex would not allow it. The girl got more and more depressed, was medicated, and even ended up being hospitalized a few times. All the girl asked for was to live with her father but the mother would not relent, no matter how unhappy her daughter became. The mother's relationship with her daughter obviously deteriorated as the case dragged on and on in court. As of this writing the battle is still raging, the daughter still suffering, and the court still ignoring the best interests of the child, who in this case is now an articulate teenager the court refuses to hear.

When Michael and his ex divorced she gave custody of her three sons to him. He moved his family to California and lost no time in creating a full and joyful life for them (and for our boys in the community in the process). In a year the mother changed her mind. Back to court she went and the two younger boys were removed from the care of their father. The boys went to Chicago to live with their mom and her boyfriend. They hated it. They became angry and acted up. At one point the eight-year old threatened to stab his mom with a pencil. Her reactions were so out of line that the boys were taken from her too. But they were not sent back to their father who was spending house and home to win back their custody. The boys became wards of the state (whatever the legal term is) and, since they had "violent" tendencies (hey, pencils are lethal weapons) they were medicated and even hospitalized for a time. Eventually Michael lost his case and the boys were sent to live with their mother. Very sadly, both boys have sunk into depression—but not Michael. He continues to build the life that he started with all three of his sons and has created a community that his sons' friends have the great good luck to be a part of. I will return to this story in the next chapter.

I know the children in both these families and it wrenches my heart to see them become victims of the nastiness of their mothers and the impersonality and cruelty of the courts. A certain hypocrisy is also quite enraging. While our current society provides very little meaningful support to mothers who would sacrifice everything for the health and wellbeing of their children, the courts are upholding some sentimentally blind notion of a mother's rights. Society's superficial reverence for motherhood has very little to do with the reality of raising children: children's rights and best interests must trump everyone else's, including the mothers'. It is heartbreaking to see the struggle that some men go through not just to protect their children but to salvage what they can of mother-child relationships. Women can act savagely and do irreparable damage to their children. Pity the man who has to take on such an adversary.

Sometimes, however, other circumstances than monster moms require extreme fatherhood. A couple of years ago I met one such father, Alireza Ansari, a military man and a fighter pilot from Iran. When Alireza's son was born with autism his world was shattered. After the family exhausted local resources they decided to make a trip to consult with specialists in the US. They found promising treatment here and their trip ended in indefinite stay. While Alireza's wife is a loving mother to their son, Alireza felt that he had the strength to face the challenge more successfully. A resourceful, irrepressible and hardworking man, Alireza took over the care of his son. Starting from absolute scratch in a new country (no money, no job, no family, no friends) he decided to make caring for his son his priority.

In the process of learning about autism and working with his own son, Alireza turned into a very effective teacher of autistic children. He ended up co-founding a nonprofit organization (castcal.org) offering after-school care for autistic children and young adults. While still struggling to fund the shoe-string budget of his organization, he is not the kind to be deterred. He was right in his judgment that he would do a good job at dedicating his life to his son, even if that meant going from flying airplanes to starting a new life bussing tables in restaurants. Alireza's idea of being a man was to tell his wife and daughter, "Go ahead and live your lives. I'll take care of things." He's ended up not only taking care of his own son but the sons and daughters of many others. In his book *Dear Oprah* Alireza Ansari puts a comic spin on what many would have experienced as tragedy.

I started my website inviting, even challenging, men to step up to raising their kids. With men like Michael and Alireza I see the creative and powerful force they are capable of contributing to raising children, especially boys. True equality between men and women would certainly reduce the need for extreme measures required of both.

CHAPTER 7

Community: The Body of the Matter

A child is born into an individual body and raised in a collective "body." This collective body is the community in which a child grows up: it can be healthy or disabled; it can be supported or undermined; it can thrive or it can self-destruct.

In the old times children did not "leave" their families and go to school. It's only been in the past couple of centuries that school has slowly replaced the organic community into which children were born. In United States of present time school is most often the *only* community children are brought up in. Unfortunately one quickly sees that school is no community at all. Community requires connection, communication, and continuity. I found very little of that in schools. Friendship is temporary acquaintance, happenstance, and dictates of convenience. Empathy and *caritas* are nothing but a random string of you-scratch-my-back-I-scratch-yours actions. Lack of trust and interest nip communication in the bud. And continuity is impossible when there is so little acceptance and perseverance, where people are constantly "shopping" for some better "deal."

The first question everybody asks you when you take your kid out of school is what the homeschoolers call the "S' question: the question of socialization. This question implies that children are wild beasts until they are "socialized" in school. I think what happens when you leave the deceptive vestiges of school "community" is not that you immediately connect to some other community. The first step is that you face the isolation in which we live more starkly.

Perhaps the homeschooling movement will be useful in redefining community. Maybe even homeschooled kids will be instrumental in inventing a whole new conception of community. Perhaps the children of today, freed from illusions of community, will build new and real ones for their kids. That's all in the future. As for now, families are lucky if they live in established and functional communities. If not, though, all is not lost. Even now we can create communities. I found that homeschooling families in our area have done just that. It was our great good luck that we were welcomed into a generous and growing community of homeschoolers in Northern California. I have organized aspects of this community into three groups: the organizers, the educators, the friends.

Organizers

M y search for other homeschoolers began with the simplest Google search: "homeschool san francisco." In 2010 when I did my initial search the biggest groups in the San Francisco Bay Area were the San Francisco Homeschoolers and Bay Area Unschoolers. Within hours of clicking on these groups' websites and shooting off some emails I was on the phone talking to a couple of friendly and helpful women who immediately invited us to the next gathering.

I will never forget the day Jack and I joined our first homeschoolers' park day. We met a bunch of warm and accepting people with kids ranging in age from infants to high school. Every new family was welcome because it swelled the ranks and enriched the group. My son ran off with a group of boys his own age and I sat chatting with the moms and the occasional dad.

It's hard to describe how I felt. It was as if a chronic fever with its accompanying body ache and throbs inside my head suddenly lifted. The hot and cold sweat gave way to a cool mist on my forehead that the other mothers gently wiped off with an understanding and playful smile: Homeschooling? No big deal. Actually pretty good.

While by nature homeschoolers are a diverse and eccentric bunch they all have one thing in common: the best interest of each kid. It is interesting how having this basic priority leads to so much harmony and collaboration. To this end generosity of spirit kicks in, with everyone sharing and passing around what might be of interest and use. Suddenly a random group of people starts feeling like a community.

There is a great deal of overlap between different homeschool groups in our area. Most of us belong to more than one group and our kids are welcome to join activities from any group. There are plenty of activities to join: regular park days often with dads coaching sports, annual not-back-to-school picnics, dances, "proms," game days, snow days, field trips, annual fairs, and plenty of ad hoc "classes" and activities. This list is off the top of my head right now; the number and diversity of activities as well as programs and classes are really quite vast.

I mention the groups below because these are the ones we have had the closest experience with.

San Francisco Homeschoolers

This is the first group that popped up during my initial search. These folks have an eclectic approach to education and come from different backgrounds. Some kids are school dropouts, others have always been homeschooled; some follow particular curricula, others follow their nose; some are in "charter" schools, others sign up for classes or group lessons here and there. All in all most of us in this group do a combination of things, sometimes adopting academic structure based on family philosophy and/or the kids' interests, and sometimes completely giving in to serendipity.

Bay Area Unschoolers

Unschoolers" are followers of the education philosophy of John Holt who believed that children are hard-wired to learn and attempts to steer them in proscribed directions are harmful to true education. "Fish swim, birds fly, and children learn," Holt famously said. Unschoolers are every bit as involved and busy as school kids or other homeschoolers but are completely self-directed and it is they who determine the presence or absence, or the degree, of structure in their lives. They organize awesome activities!

Marin Homeschoolers

We joined this group when we left San Francisco and moved to Marin County. Marin Homeschoolers is also an eclectic group, through which we connected with local families and activities. This community, in turn, overlaps with homeschoolers in Sonoma County.

By hooking up with just these three groups we found ourselves part of a vast network of homeschoolers from Santa Cruz to Sacramento, and communities from East, South and North San Francisco Bay. My son's best friends and some of my own most cherished friends have come out of the groups and our common experience.

Homeschool Association of California (HSC)

HSC, the overarching organization of California home-schoolers, is one of the first and most important resources you discover in your homeschooling journey. This is an extraordinarily informative and helpful organization that can hold your hand through every stage, from filing the right papers to finding friends. By California law in order to home-school your children you have to establish a "private school" whose only students can be your own children. Every year you have to re-register your school and update your records. HSC has answers to all the questions you may have about any of this. Their website is an enormous resource and networking tool and their newsletters inspiring and mind-expanding.

One of the first things we heard about when we joined the homeschooling community in our area was the annual HSC conference. This event, held over a long weekend at a conference center, is one of the funnest, whackiest, most serious, and liveliest experiences of a lot of homeschooled kids in our neck of the woods. I have blogged about this elsewhere so I won't say more. Suffice it to say that every year my son and his friends look tremendously forward to the conference and many of the teenagers are engaged the entire year in planning and organizing their events at the conference.

Over the years, even the kids who do not regularly see each other during the year meet up at the conference, keep up with each other and make new discoveries. They grow up together, get to know each other better, and make new friends. The families too stay in touch and share their lives and adventures. We have never missed a year and are not planning to—even now that my son is not a homeschooler.

A word on communication

Communication is very important for building community. I got confirmation of this fact comparing the San Francisco and Marin homeschool groups.

The main difference between our experience with Marin Homeschoolers and the first two groups I mentioned was the medium of communication. SF Homeschoolers and Bay Area Unschoolers both operated via an email list. We had volunteers who facilitated the list but everyone posted freely. Usually when a new family joined the group there would be an introductory note from the new family and an official welcome from the facilitator. Apart from questions posted to which members who had the answers replied, there would occasionally be links or information that would be of interest to the group. Every once in a while someone would raise a topic that would generate discussion, sometimes quite heated. Through these exchanges we got a sense of both individuals members and the community as a whole. There were times that people disagreed with each other and other times when they got on each others' nerves. These were times when you discovered you didn't like so-and-so so much, and times when your friendships deepened with others. In short, through the freestyle posts on the list you got to know each other.

When we joined Marin Homeschoolers they had just switched from an email list to setting up the group on Meet-Up. Some older members voiced their disagreement with the switch and I had sympathy with them. While MeetUp software has a great deal of organizational capacity it does not allow for the free-form, spontaneous and intimate communication that creates a real community. Software is a useful tool for organizing and spreading information but it does not nurture connection. Because of this, even though I spent most of our homeschooling years in Marin, I still have a better sense of the community in San Francisco.

Educators

A ll the world's an education of course. But not all the people in it are educators. Educators are those who know something, know that they know it, and want others to know it too. Education is the effort to share knowledge and expand its limits, and educators are those who make this effort. Being old-world and old-school at heart I revere true educators and am eternally grateful to those who extend their passion and generosity to my son. Among those, two top my list.

The Naturalists: Vilda Foundation

W e are connected to nature. Each day we stand on this earth, nourished by the light of the sun, refreshed by clean water, and breathing fresh air. Yet our current culture seems to have largely forgotten to acknowledge this connection, creating separation that has imbalanced our entire ecosystem.

This is the philosophy of one of the Marin homeschoolers' most popular programs called Dirt Time. Dirt Time and a number of other programs and workshops are run by Vilda Foundation (vildanature.org), founded by Mia Andler and run with help from a number of other outstanding young naturalists. Spencer Nielson has over time become my son's closest connection to the group. Dane Bowman shares with Jack the love of tea and lessons by a Chinese-Tibetan doctor and tea master.

This is what Vilda does:

We believe [connection to nature] is accomplished by actually spending time outdoors, with our hands in the dirt and feet on the ground, planting trees, clearing brush, finding frogs in a creek, making a meal out of wild plants, learning how to turn a piece of wood into an instrument, or creating natural dyes with berries. Through our programs, children can expect to:

- come to know their local environment as an extended part of their home
- feel a sense of belonging on the earth
- form lasting friendships and connect with other families

When we heard of Dirt Time through Marin Homeschooler network we immediately signed up. Jack ended up attending two years of Dirt Time, as well as joining Wild Farmers, a program held at the organic farm of Marin Community College where children learn about organic farming by helping with every aspect of it. Between these two programs the kids learned a great deal about nature in general and their immediate surroundings in particular. Even after some of the kids went back to school they joined Vilda on summer workshops and backpacking trips. This year it will be Jack's second week-long backpacking trip with Vilda and he will do three weeks of volunteer work this summer with the young children's day camps.

Connection to nature—this is the most vital lesson taught by naturalists, both young and not so young, who are dedicating their lives to educating children. I believe there is an added benefit here too. As (I hope) more consciousness is raised globally about the wisdom and need to respect and preserve our natural environment, I think this generation of children will grow up with opportunities to engage in this effort. In other words, I think smart kids (and parents) would do well not to waste time in imagining a professional naturalist future. Our Chinese-Tibetan doctor friend claims that children can start training to become doctors at an early age. I believe it. They can also learn to become naturalists at an early age.

I am so enamored of Vilda and its team of naturalists that I cannot help but to quote them again. Their words don't just ring true to me; I know from personal experience that they *are* true.

At Vilda, we facilitate the development of healthy relationships to the self, between participants, and to the natural world. We respect each child in our programs as competent and unique. Our instructor to student ratios are very intimate, allowing each participant to be known and cared for personally.

Having suffered through bullying in elementary school, when Jack joined Dirt Time he was still vulnerable to that kind of dynamic and I was weary of efforts to stop it. When Jack reported that he felt bullied by one of the boys at Dirt Time I frankly didn't know what to do. As it turned out I was not expected to do anything. Jack's team leader, Spencer, called us about it. His kindness, alertness, fairness and compassion for all the involved kids melted a part of me that had become hard and frozen after years of enduring the callous and dishonest ways of teachers and schools. I don't know what Spencer "did" while he was in charge of the situation. I felt no need to intervene. All I know is that he was the single most important person in helping my son put his bullying experience behind him.

I never enquired what steps the Dirt Time team took to separate the kids involved in the bullying situation and resolve the problem. I think part of it was encouraging Jack to be a mentor of sorts to a younger group of kids. A mixed-age group of kids offers great opportunities for all kinds of learning. At the end of the term I received these emails from the mothers of a couple of those younger kids. These women did not know me but got my email address through the group.

This is from Terry:

Hi Clara, I just wanted to let you know how much my daughter enjoyed meeting Jack at Dirt Time last fall. She won't be continuing this semester, so I know she will miss him. She always had stories about his kindness and enthusiasm. He is a wonderful kid.

This is from Dawn:

Hi Clara, I don't think we've met, but I just wanted to let you know what a dear Jack has been to my son Gabriel (7) at Dirt Time. He has been fun and respectful and polite. Gabriel really enjoys him, and I have enjoyed that when I have seen him interact with Gabriel, he has been so nice. At Mia's book release, Jack played with Gabriel outside. They were "being boys," but as I watched occasionally from inside the house, I noticed how kind Jack was, and then today, he specifically came up to Gabriel to say thank you for the trade they did today on the last day. He went out of his way to do that, and it was appreciated and noticed. Anyway, just wanted to let you know.

I reproduce these emails for two reasons. First, they still make me feel so good and proud! After years of hearing nothing but bad things about my son while he was being abused I still cherish others' observation of what a good kid Jack is. The second reason is as proof that the Vilda crew do indeed succeed in developing good relationships between the children and a community of all of us who have come together. I can't help but compare the outcome of this bullying incident with the bullying situation at Jack's former school. The Vilda crew proved that in the right environment, and in the care of adults driven by love and respect, life problems can be solved and nastiness somehow dissipates. (I can't help repeating: It's the environment, stupid!)

Mia has this "signature" that appears at the end of her emails:

Despite their artistic pretensions, sophistication, and many accomplishments, humans owe their existence to a six-inch layer of topsoil and the fact that it rains.
—Anonymous

I am a big fan of human accomplishments but the acknowledgment of this fact creates a humility that is needed to put the-world-according-to-humans in perspective. Mia's book *The Bay Area Forager* is a terrific place for losing oneself in this perspective.

The Sensei: Goju Karate

Imagine yourself walking on a dusty road on a hot day, hands clasped behind your back, eyes on the ground, absorbed in your thoughts. Suddenly you come upon a perfectly ripe, blushing peach that some hand has strategically placed in your path. You smile and pick up the fruit still covered with morning dew and pulsating from its attachment to the branch. You look up and find that unbeknownst to yourself you have walked under a magnificent peach tree laden with ripe fruit. It's yours, free for the picking.

This happened to us with Goju Karate (gojukarate.com) and the man behind it, Sensei Michael Darigo. I wrote about Michael as an example of an extreme father in the last chapter. He moved with his three homeschooling sons from New York City to Marin a few years ago. He and his ex had just divorced and she had moved to Chicago and given him custody of the kids. Our kids met in a math class and became fast friends. Soon Michael organized Friday afternoon (and well into evening!) Minecraft get-togethers at his house. From then on a whole posse of homeschooling boys spent their Fridays together, forging what shows all the signs of lifelong friendships. Parents got to know each other too and friendships developed there as well.

Michael's Minecraft Fridays sketched out a community for us. But he didn't stop at that. A powerfully built martial artist and a brilliant guy, it was written all over Michael that he was up to other things. Within a year he had built nearly from scratch the biggest and most beautiful karate dojo in Marin County. He himself, a fourth-degree black belt, teaches every single class, from seven in the morning till eight at night. Now, one has the sneaking suspicion that a guy who finances such a large and state-of-the-art dojo, charges a small tuition and teaches all day, must be financially independent. He clearly has no financial need to serve his dojo community over twelve hours a day, but that's what he does. He teaches kids (four to eighteen), adults, special needs students, workshops specifically for women, and meditation. He doesn't just teach karate, he is dedicating his life and resources to *karatedo*.

Karatedo is the philosophical aspect of the physical practice of the martial art. Karate is both development of body and cultivation of mind. Compassion, humility, discipline, hard work, living healthy—and the underlying effort to "Become Better," as Sensei Michael puts it—all of this is karate. The walls of the dojo are lined with explications of insights students can meditate on and incorporate into their training. There is one that is particularly relevant to raising children.

> *Soto no tera gakushu no* means "outside the temple, no learning"
> [It is] the notion that our environment deeply affects us, and can have a profound impact on many aspects of our lives... [It] is really a kind of mindfulness: an awareness of the people and things in our environment, and the way they affect us. We must, at the very least, be strongly aware of this effect, and we must also work hard to shape the effect so that it is in line with our goals and aspirations.

At the dojo Sensei Michael not only fosters mindfulness but has created an actual environment, a "temple," where kids are immersed in the values and experiences that develop the best in them. The hours that the kids spend at the dojo are not like hours spent at some gym. They are hours where they breathe, as it were, the very air of wisdom and strength. And as if this was not enough, Sensei Michael has hired a number of the older boys to help run the dojo. (In the beginning they helped clean the dojo, which is what I particularly appreciated!) In effect he is paying them for the great gift that he is offering them! (I insisted that the kids work for free but the Sensei would not hear of it.)

Now imagine a man of this level of integrity, competence and generosity losing custody of his two younger sons. Imagine him thinking about his two unhappy sons pining to be with him while he extends his dedication and gifts to our sons. I cannot go to the dojo without feeling a constriction in my heart, noting the absence of his two boys. I even feel a little guilty enjoying that which his own sons are deprived of now. But perhaps that's the most valuable lesson he is teaching all the kids—his own and ours—that you never stop becoming better even when you have every reason to quit.

This is real education. And it is an extreme father who is providing it.

Friends

Over the homeschooling years my son and I have made some very close and dear friends. I am not going to describe my son's friends; they are all bright kids and happier in their skins than we are led to expect from teenagers. What I do want to do is give brief descriptions of the basic circumstances of the mothers of these kids, for a number of reasons.

First, when is all is said and done, with extremely few exceptions, it is mothers who create community. Building a community takes time and effort, and it seems that women tend to make more of those two. Second, it also seems that women tend to value and depend on friendship more than men. As a result, the friendship that develops between mothers plays an important part in encouraging friendship in kids, and indeed models it for them. The women I list below are every bit as responsible for the friendship of our kids as the boys themselves. I myself have received not only love and support from these women but a kind of affirmation that I desperately needed. The bond that has developed between us is a particularly precious one because we have shared our children's childhood. What's sweeter than that?

I also want to bring up something that is a bit of a taboo: money. But, as my friend Anna points out below, we have to get over our sense of shame around the question of money. I mentioned before that homeschooling requires a degree of sacrifice. In a world where families increasingly need two paychecks to make ends meet, homeschooling can easily create a financial crunch. Homeschooling is a family affair and the family cannot continue with pre-children or pre-homeschooling days. But the problem is not that the family has to tighten its belts for a while—that's easy. The problem is that the parent who gives up his or her paycheck—and economic independence—is going to have a hard time returning to the job market. (I will leave it to the reader to guess the usual sex of the parent in question!)

Compiling this brief description of my fellow home-schooling moms I noticed a common element. Frequently it is with help from their own mothers (and/or grandmothers) that women are able to make children, and not careers, their priority. In the lives of most of the women I mention below, mothers and/or grandmothers help out with the raising of the kids, both financially and through sharing the caretaking. In fact, I have noticed that caretaking in general solidly remains part of the work of women. Mothers take care of daughters and their kids, and daughters take care of their kids and mothers (and grandmothers). Occasionally, where there is an elderly grandmother in need of care a minimal salary is involved. It is impossible to appreciate the "cost" of raising children without mention of the material aspect of the lives of generations of women.

Now, although none of the women I list below fits the skirt-suited, bulging-briefcased, booming-voiced image of high-powered "career" women, I think each is a superwoman. Each one not only performs above and beyond the call of duty for her family but gives of herself and shares her resources as though she was endowed with extraordinary privilege.

I am listing my friends below by the order of their appearance in our life. (Any similarity between them is strictly coincidental!)

Rachel and I met when our sons were in school in first grade. A year after I pulled Jack out of school she took her son out and we homeschooled them through middle school. She has three kids: the oldest my son's age, and a younger boy and girl. The younger kids have always been in school and her eldest returned to school in high school. She is divorced now but even when she was married her family lived at her mother's house. Her main source of income was through caring for her grandmother while she lived, and later by renting out a room in her mother's house through *airbnb*.

Rachel frequently takes in friends, acquaintances, even

strangers, who need help and/or a welcome place to stay. Just recently she nursed a distant friend who had showed up at her door desperately ill till the end of his life and then threw a memorial for him that his family wouldn't. She routinely shares the yard of her modest home for the massive cook-out project of a local nonprofit, Curry without Worry, who feeds the homeless and low-income San Franciscans. Rachel and her mom Lenore are community-kingpin superwomen.

Mona Lisa pulled her daughter out of school following a bullying episode in second grade. Her daughter was home-schooled through middle school with a most rigorous academic program, and later returned to high school. Her younger son started school but might be pulled out too. Mona Lisa is an attorney by profession but has not been able to dedicate herself to that fulltime. On top of being a sort of free-lance lawyer she has a successful safe-sand business (safesand.com, clean and natural sand for children's sandboxes) and has been the president of the San Francisco chapter of National Organization for Women. She also does a great deal of pro bono civil rights work. She created the San Francisco Rock School and hosts classes for that school in her house. She is now divorced and expanding her work as an attorney. She is a superwoman even by conventional standards!

Tamara has four sons. Her eldest sons are Jack's friends and have always been homeschooled. Her younger ones are toddlers. She and her husband live at her mother's house and run a day care center from their living room. Tamara's super-womanhood begins with giving herself completely over to almost a dozen children, her own and others'. Her house is a kind of anchor for all kinds of homeschooler activities, sleepovers, and lavish parties. Every moment of her waking life is dedicated to the needs of children. She has long needed a surgery that would release her from constant hip pain but even that comes second to her children's needs.

Robin's older son is Jack's friend and has always been homeschooled, though he might consider high school next year. Robin's younger son is in preschool but will probably go to school in the future. Robin is an attorney and though her family moved to California from New York a few years ago, she continues her work long-distance. She and her husband mainly work from home and she makes red-eye, one-night trips to New York when her job calls for it. I would bestow super-womanhood on her not just for her sacrifices but for her extraordinary powers of concentration! She does her complicated legal work in snatches of time sandwiched between the needs of her two boys, during naps, and late into the night. And, unlike some of us who kick and scream an awful lot, she never complains of anything!

Clara, i.e. yours truly, quit her higher-education teaching job when she moved to California from New York, and did not pursue it while her son was young because daycare would have cost more than her income. She and her husband had just started a publishing house when she pulled Jack out of school. Her husband remained in his day job to support the family. While their publishing venture produced a number of good books, the raising and education of their son took precedence over marketing, which meant that the publishing business did not thrive financially. They live in a house that Clara's mother helped them buy. Her claim to super-womanhood is writing three books, co-editing and co-publishing eight, producing a multimedia interactive website, helping take care of her aging mother, and homeschooling her kid while not officially "working."

As I was writing this chapter I ran these little excerpts by my friends for their approval and input. My friend **Anna,** whose son Misha is part of our group of homeschooling boys, wrote me an email that describes her unique but somehow not uncommon situation much better than I can. She is a superwoman not just because of her round-the-clock caretaking, performing, and producing art shows, but for her invariably positive attitude and her commitment to spreading joy. I gratefully share her email here:

> I am inspired by you and I totally agree about sharing information to help people visualize how they can empower themselves and how dreams can be achieved no matter what the circumstances. I have no shame any longer around the money part and I freely share with those who I can tell can benefit from it, yet I don't throw the pearls before swine... Kind of like I don't go on and on about homeschooling to someone who is not really curious about it and only wants to fight... Or with someone who would think nothing of taking away my rights because they don't agree. I think one of the reasons I'm writing this is that I would like more information going out to people.
>
> Misha started homeschooling in second grade when we moved to Northern California. In the October of first grade he had piped in from the backseat of the car: Ma, I want to be homeschooled! He had met and been impressed by what another kid had said about being homeschooled. So I said if things changed in our life, we'll do it. And by the next February, they had changed.
>
> When we moved to Northern California, caring for my grandmother was my fulltime job, becoming part-time in the last couple of years after she broke her leg, although I am available 24/7 for emergencies. Mostly it was the flexibility of being able to bring my kid to work and the feeling of family and the love that made me choose this job. The reality was a bit different from what I imagined, because caring for my grandmother and giving her my attention did take a lot of my time away from my kid. But at least he could interrupt me any time he wanted. I was still able to get my work

done and I was not penalized because of his presence as I might have been at traditional employment.

While I was still in Southern California and Misha was three I was self-employed, working at home in my somatic practice AND had started an organic/natural body care practice with my neighbor. I was always torn by how much time my two careers took away from my kid, even when I had the time flexibility. I was so desperately trying to make ends meet that when the opportunity came up with my grandma, I knew it would give me what I needed and what she needed too. She had enough money to hire me because my grandfather took care of their finances so well before he died. It was much more settling and stable to work for my grandma, with an income I could rely upon each month (unlike the somatic work where for instance, when 911 happened, I didn't work for something like 3 months!).

My parents gifted me some money for a down payment for a house and the rest is a mortgage with my grandma. I make monthly payments to her that cover the interest she would have received if she still had the money invested. If it was a regular mortgage with a bank, I probably could not afford to live here. These are the perks when family can help circumvent world economics!

When my grandma dies I will have to re-negotiate the loan because the trustees (mom and aunt) will take it over and her estate will have to go to the inheritors. I might inherit something but probably not to the tune of the whole mortgage.

I put in all these details because I would like it to be known that having been gifted some money has made my situation workable, that is, being able to achieve my priority of providing flexibility and availability for my child. Still, I have had more than fulltime jobs since Misha was two and I am not absolved of the basic mortgage reality that most of us have. Thank goodness my family is able to support my philosophy of child-first and thankfully I have something to offer in financial exchange. Still, my income is poverty level and it doesn't go beyond house payment, food, car, utilities, basics. But I'm alright with it because my greatest wealth is the time spent with my kid, on MY terms, as a happy, generally relaxed person.

So, the combined efforts of everyone are helping me raise this child with a momma present, even without a second income-providing partner. Misha's dad does contribute to certain things (e.g. he has gotten his mom to help pay for tutoring because she gives gifts towards the other grandsons' education) and he occasionally buys Misha clothes, etc... all on his terms and slow going. But with my financial stability, I can focus more on what he DOES do rather than focusing on what he DOESN'T and that seems to work in my favor towards more generosity from him and also less expectation from me—even though YES! I agree with all single parents who aren't getting help from the other parent. Both parents have a responsibility, yet MAKING someone do their responsibility is crazy-making and better to use that energy to empower oneself to live the life one wants—that's what I think anyway.

My mom and I were talking the other day and she totally gets it. My grandma too. I think it is that intense mothering love and support that is helping me realize my dream to stay with my kid—plus the choices of the men in their lives who make family a priority. I feel like I have had to claw and scream my way to it because my own partner did not have the same priorities, but it is worth it.

For all the sacrifices I have made, I don't dwell on them, yet I honor them and myself for making them. I need to appreciate myself!

The proof that I have made the right choices for us, came in an instance when I was musing to my son about a possible scenario where I could have worked with a dear friend in her business and that we would have had such a great time! He loudly and passionately protested that he WOULD NEVER HAVE GOTTEN TO SEE ME AT ALL! if I had done that! I think he was about 10 at that time. I think he was worried that I might actually go that route, pick up a career and let it take over our lives. His reaction set me straight, gave me all the appreciation I ever needed or ever will need.

CHAPTER 8

The Work of Modern Mothers (or is it Postmodern?)

Any account of raising children will inevitably bring up social and political questions that exert great influence on women's lives. The fact is that women overwhelmingly remain the care-takers and educators of children. Their influence as mothers is enormous. Their various labors lay the foundation on which any other kind of productivity is based. And unless we all turn into hermaphrodites or eliminate all sex and gender differences in one fell swoop, the role that women play in society is irreplaceable. Throughout this book I have touched on some of the social and political issues pertaining to women, but in this final chapter I would like to direct a more analytical gaze on the binds and double standards that affect all aspects of family life. I feel this kind of analytical look at women's lives is crucial if a certain kind of strain on family life and marriages is to be avoided. This chapter offers a case in point.

Unfortunately the minute you turn your attention to the inequalities between men and women, and especially if you use the word "feminism," you face the charge of being "anti-men." This book is written from the perspective of a mother and consequently brings up many legitimate grievances of women. Critiques of male-centered and male-dominated social realities are not attacks upon individual men, a mistake both men and women too often make. I have seen women taking out their personal bitterness on the men in their lives in the name of "feminism," and I have also seen individual men getting defensive as if a social critique from women's perspective is the cry, "Patriarchy, thy name is [Tom, Dick, or Harry]." I do not want to contribute to either of these tendencies.

Most of this book was written for a website, hence the breezy "blog" style. Here I want to offer some thoughts that might require a bit more effort in reading. It is perhaps sharper and more critical in tone. But, please, Fair Reader, try to get through this section. I hope by the end you realize it is in your interest.

The chronic family crisis

A while ago I got a call from a friend that prompted me to write this chapter. She had had a family crisis that in my mind was simply a flaring up of a situation that is almost always simmering quietly in some corner of modern family life. I think women, hence their families, have been operating within a sort of chronic crisis since the role of women in society has changed.

I think the question of work is at the heart of this crisis. To put it in a nutshell, there has been an inequality in the quantity and quality of expectations put on women versus men. These expectations translate into the work that is involved in raising and providing for a family. The responsibilities, which of course people take on voluntarily in the best situations, take center stage in women and men's lives when they have children. The inequity in what portion of these responsibilities falls to women is not just a personal issue; it is a political and economic one as well. I think it is time to stop talking pop psychology, and direct a more hard-nosed focus on the factors that contribute to this simmering crisis.

The personal and the political

The consciousness-raising of the 1960s "second wave" feminism was built on the premise that the personal and private are political. While the "first wave" feminism of the 1920s mostly concentrated on winning voting rights for women as citizens, the second wave earned a good deal of rights for women as women: reproductive rights, equal opportunity, equal pay, and other social and civil rights. I believe we are due for a third wave of feminism focusing on women as mothers.

The optimism and relative successes of second-wave feminism has had a few downfalls and shortcomings. One of the downfalls has been the emergence of the idea of the superwoman: strong women with boundless energy and resource who will do it all, have careers, bear children, raise and educate them, run households, deliver multi-generational caretaking and other traditionally female responsibilities—and do it all exactly right. Men, in exchange, have added to their traditional workload some additional tasks: change some diapers and vacuum the rug, make some meals if they happen to be foodies, and take women's acerbic asides about the paucity of their extracurricular contributions in good humor or hang-dog guilt.

The most important shortcoming of second-wave feminism, however, has been that in celebrating its victories its attention got deterred from one of the most life-changing parts of being a woman: motherhood.

The distress call

I don't know how to start," my friend Donna said when she called me, clearly shaken up. "I don't know where to begin."

There had been a family crisis following a meltdown between Donna and her son Leo. She had called me first because I understood a context that others did not: her experiences both as a professional and as a mother. That's where she had to begin and it was that context that I understood.

When you are distressed, when you feel ignored and abused and undermined, you face an almost daunting task in relating the actual events that created and reinforced those feelings over the years. It is always a long story. It is not easy to sit a friend down and claim their ears for hours on end—there is simply too much to say. And to do so in therapy would cost an awful lot of money before you even get to a point where the therapist understands enough to be of use. Donna told me her story in snatches and in fits and starts, but I was able to fill in the blanks because of our shared experiences and having been close for decades. We had similar careers before we took a few years off to have a child and had to extend those few years on account of our boys having trouble in school. Eventually we both became homeschooling mothers.

Donna's distress had everything to do with what I have written in this book—raising a challenging boy—and is also a glaring and urgent example of the overlap of the personal and political in being a mother. But let's begin with the personal.

"Have I been living a fiction?"

Donna's recent crisis had started like this: She had decided to write Leo a letter, setting a few goals for him to achieve by the end of the year. The goals were to cover certain academic material, spend a certain amount of time outdoors and/or in physical activity every day, and complete household chores. She had also written in the letter that if by the end of the year Leo had not kept his side of the bargain they would have to look into alternatives. She told him that traditionally when kids could not muster enough self discipline by Leo's age (14) they were sent to military academies to have discipline beaten into their heads. Since they were not a family to try that option they would look into enrolling him in a nature immersion program where kids are taken on expeditions as a group to learn the lessons of nature and also to learn to work together to get through challenges. I agree with Donna that for our computer-addicted children these are fantastic programs. But they are quite costly. Donna had stipulated in her letter that if Leo makes it necessary to be sent on these expeditions the money will have to come out of his college fund. She gave the letter to Leo after running it by her husband Adam. "I support you," Adam had said.

Leo had mulled the letter over and accepted its conditions. But a few days later there had been a blow up. Donna was driving him to a park for his outing after a battle prying him away from the screen, as a result of which they were both in a bad mood. "You are not holding up your end of the bargain," Donna had said.

"I never made a bargain," Leo retorted. "I just went along with your stupid letter to keep you quiet. Dad and I don't believe in what you said. You're always coming up with one bullshit or another."

The car came to a screeching halt as Donna pulled over: "What did you say?"

"I said that Dad and I don't agree with your letter."

Donna let the "bullshit" part go for now. "I showed dad the letter before I gave it to you. He does agree with me."

"No. He later came to my room when I was upset and said to just say yes to you. He's your yes man. He and I just say yes to keep you from making a scene."

While Adam had never called Donna's ideas "bullshit" it looked like that was the message conveyed to Leo.

"Dad and I need to talk," Donna said.

"Yes. You need to talk to each other. I'm tired of keeping your secrets from each other."

"What secret have I told you about dad?"

"You say that he gets stressed out and he can't relax and have fun."

That evening Donna and Adam had a talk which opened a whole can of worms.

To backtrack a bit, almost exactly two years before this crisis Donna told me that during another argument with Leo he had told her that she was a bad mother and that even Adam agreed: "Dad said you're an inexperienced mother." Donna had been very hurt. She and Adam had had a talk and he had said that it was a stupid comment and that he had not meant it in a bad way. Donna had let it go. She figured that after all, every kid being a new person, we are all inexperienced parents, she and Adam both. But apparently there was more to it than that.

This time Adam was not able to brush off his comment as a spur-of-the-moment stupidity.

"When you tell Leo to 'just say yes to Mom' it implies that you condone not going along with what I say," said Donna. "Two years ago you told him that I was an inexperienced mother. Leo assumes that you don't have the courage to say to my face that you don't agree with me, so you contradict me behind my back. This can't lead to him having a good opinion of you and it undermines what I try to do."

This time Adam had to admit to his disapproval of Donna's mothering. "You are never satisfied with Leo," he said. "You have been disappointed in him since shortly after birth." The minute he heard himself saying this he added: "I'm sorry. That was a clumsy way of putting it. The minute I open my mouth I say the wrong things."

"The minute you open your mouth you reveal things

about yourself. You can't write this off as clumsiness any-more," Donna said.

To me she went on: "To say that I have been disappointed with Leo since 'shortly after birth' is such a strange and confusing thing to hear that for a moment I got literally dizzy. The years we had lived and raised a son together suddenly seemed to me like a fiction.

"I was disappointed in Leo? I was not satisfied with him? I, who fought tooth and nail, repelling all those judgments against him at school? I, who spends hours with him every day nurturing the copious talents that he has? I, who believes most kids who are called ADHD are actually too smart and are bored in traditional school settings? Yes, we do fight. I can't just give in to his rejection of things that he must do for his health and his education. Anyway, clashes are inevitable between any two people who are together 24/7, especially when one is a child who is given to pushing limits.

"Now, Adam himself has no tolerance for Leo's pushing limits. He does not put up with his resistances. When Leo refuses something Adam simply gives in. His homeschooling responsibility was to work with Leo on science. That's when he saw how hard it was to get Leo to do anything. So he simply gave up. He even gives up when Leo drags his heels doing his chores. If Leo tries to put off putting out the garbage, for instance, Adam just does it for him. He doesn't like the fights, the battles of will, any confrontation. He's an avoider, I'm a fighter.

"Giving in to Leo's resistances is not an option for me. I might kick and scream but I work with him no matter how much he pushes my buttons. I believe in education and I cannot give up. Last year when I was away for a few weeks I made a step-by-step assignment sheet for Adam and Leo to complete together. When I came back no effort was done to even try. And no apologies either, no acknowledgement. It was simply, Oh, we didn't get around to it. I cringed but said nothing–I'm always accused of being critical, so I shut up. I did my best to catch up, but there's only so much I can do. Now Leo is way behind in science.

"So, yes, Adam is the good guy as far as Leo is concerned. He just simply doesn't make the demands that I do. To me it is giving up on someone that is a sign of being disappointed in them, thinking them simply not capable. But lo and behold the tables are turned on me: I am the one accused of being disappointed in my son. I am the bad, inadequate mother, the 'inexperienced' one...

"And that's not all," Donna continued. "I said to Adam that I felt all these years that we have talked about Leo, that I have described and complained and discussed the various things about our life, he had not really been listening to me. I felt that he had had his own ideas about how things were and without sharing them with me he had just tuned me out, just nodding to keep me quiet. Leo was right. He had been a yes man in the sense Leo understood it. 'Have you even been taking what I say seriously?' I asked him. 'Have I just been blabbing to you all this time? About Leo, about work, about everything?'

"'I guess the problem is that I don't really trust you,' he said. 'You're always talking about things that you don't do. You have all these great ideas but none of them have panned out.'"

Donna explained that the "great ideas" that he was referring to mostly had to do with finding work. The bottom line was that Donna had not "worked" and had not brought in money. That meant that she was not trustworthy in keeping her word about finding a job while not even doing a good job as a mother.

"I knew that Adam was unhappy about me not earning money," Donna said. "But I had no idea about the level of mistrust and resentment that he harbored—was it not bringing in money that made me a bad mother or vice versa? 'Maybe it is you who has been disappointed in me since shortly after Leo's birth,' I should have had the presence of mind to tell him.

"All these years, like a blabbering fool, I have been talking to him and sharing the good and bad of my daily life with Leo and my efforts to have a career. I have been thinking that Adam was in this with me, or at least that he was hearing what I was saying and was half interested in them. It turns out that he was just tolerating my 'many good ideas' and secretly drawing his own conclusions. He has been holding grudges. How can you pretend to go along with something you don't agree with without building resentment?

"What is really hurtful is that every time Leo had complained about Adam I had taken Adam's side. 'You have to see what you did that made dad so angry,' I would tell Leo. Even when Adam had once smacked Leo on the behind which had really frightened him I had not coddled him. I told him that sometimes I get so angry that I want to do the same thing. No wonder the worst secret that Leo revealed about me is that I had said Adam gets so stressed out that he can't have fun. I never brought him down in Leo's esteem or undermined him.

"And another thing," Donna said. "I have been under a gag order. Whenever I have pointed out something wrong that Adam has done he has told me to stop criticizing him. He himself doesn't 'criticize'; he nods in agreement while secretly disapproving and disparaging me to Leo behind my back. This is bad enough for a couple's relationship but it's awful for my relationship with my son. Once on a rare occasion that Adam made dinner I commented that more tuna in the casserole would have been better. 'Stop criticizing Dad,' Leo snapped at me, 'we're tired of you criticizing us all the time.' Adam had assented with his customary no-response response. After a few of these episodes I was very careful not to say anything even remotely 'critical' about Adam.

"But what has Leo really learned? That Adam is beyond criticism? That being the 'inexperienced' one I could and should be not only criticized but written off and ignored, even insulted. No wonder Leo called my letter bullshit."

I understood what Donna meant by feeling that she had been living a fiction. It is very confusing when you think you know what's going on in your life to realize that there are things happening behind your back of which you are totally ignorant. You feel like you have been made a fool of. "You know," Donna said, "I often even told my mother that I thought there was something weird about the way Leo resists and contradicts me. Now I wonder what Adam's role has been in this. I can't in good conscience deny that there's a streak of adversarial tendency in Leo's character—something like his existential predicament I'd say—but has that gotten reinforced over the years?"

I mentioned earlier that Donna and I understood each other's situations. She had also assumed that her husband understood too. When Donna gave me her distress phone call she kept repeating that she was confused. "I don't know what to think," she said. "This is so confusing. What has Adam been thinking?

"Adam's not a bad guy. He's intelligent, kind, a good father. How did things get to this point? I feel that I've been rowing a boat as hard as I can while Adam and Leo have been throwing their weight in the opposite direction. Of course I'm disappointed. I'm disheartened. I'm discouraged. I'm tired. I feel I was set up to be the bad guy—to fail."

The professional background

Of all my fellow mom-friends I am closest in background to Donna. She and I shared an office while we were adjunct faculty members in the English Department of a college in New York City. We were both PhDs from an Ivy League university and had just started out on our teaching careers. We had a great deal of intellectual interests in common but we were also both concerned about the changing political and economic circumstances of academia, hence our careers.

Adjuncts are part-time, non tenure-track faculty members

who comprise the increasing majority of faculty in American colleges today, both private and public. Some 70-80% of college courses are now taught by adjuncts. In the 1990s when Donna and I started our careers there were no adjunct unions. At our college there had been some activism in the distant past as a result of which the adjuncts at our campus enjoyed health insurance. This was a City University of New York campus, we loved our students, and we were grateful for our positions. After all, we were still bright-eyed and bushy-tailed young professors. Our plan, like most other PhDs, was to adjunct while we prepared our dissertations for publication, continue to publish articles, and keep applying for full-time positions.

But... adjunct pay at state colleges was about $2,500 per 3-unit class per semester and less than $2,000 at private. Summer courses being practically never an option, we had to teach five courses per semester to earn a maximum of $25,000 per year. (For permanent faculty three courses was considered a full-time schedule, for which the median pay was some three times more than our five-course load.) We spent an awful lot of time commuting between college campuses in Manhattan, Brooklyn, the Bronx, and New Jersey. We eked out a living and could only barely afford to live where our jobs were. Writing, giving talks at conferences, courting publishing possibilities, and keeping up with the PR of the academic job market required the kind of time that we simply didn't have.

After a few years of this life we realized that the trend of replacing full-time faculty positions with part-timers was here to stay and no matter how hard we tried at becoming great teachers and producing good books, a decent academic position was quickly turning into a pipe dream. I lucked out by getting a consulting job with the United Nations and left teaching. My new job as "communications consultant" was no more than a string of freelance writing gigs which paid well and were interesting enough, but were equally a career dead end. (I found that just as the majority of the teaching was done by the contracted labor of adjuncts in academia, the most valuable work at UN agencies was performed by the contracted labor of consultants. It was the 90s; the whole world was swept up in an orgy of outsourcing.) Donna stayed in her adjunct position while I worked at the UN. She was a native New Yorker and a teacher at heart. She became very active in forming an adjunct union. I moved to California and about the same time we both got married and had our sons. Here the second phase of our parallel lives began.

Losing our careers

The idea was this: for the first few years of our children's lives we'd quit our jobs and devote our lives to our little ones. What mother doesn't want to do this? Our husbands made enough money to sustain the family through these years, and frankly childcare cost more than we would make as adjuncts.

In California I tried my hand at freelance work but outside of New York and Washington, DC, there were no consultancy jobs like the ones I had left teaching for. I assessed the adjunct situation and being discouraged decided to work on building a publishing business that would someday sustain both me and my writer-cum-engineer husband. Donna kept on working on an academic career. During the period that our kids were in preschool and then school Donna and I went back to writing, if for different purposes.

Donna revised and published her dissertation with a decent publisher and joined the bona fide academic job hunt. Full-time, tenure-track positions (paying a little better than adjunct rates in the beginning, but offering better working conditions and a fighting chance for a future) were not only rare, but required temporary relocation to rather far-flung places. Donna, now no longer single, could not uproot her family for that kind of pay with an uncertain future. She started looking for adjunct positions but because this time she was not available anytime, anywhere, her chances of landing even adjunct positions were significantly reduced. Her reputation as a union activist certainly did not help. Every time she got excited about a possibility her hopes were dashed.

The wild card: the kid

While Donna was trying to revive her career her son Leo was having trouble in school. It started in kindergarten where he would not sit still and by first grade the teachers wanted him "evaluated." Donna started volunteering more and more at the school to keep an eye on things and before she knew it she found herself fending off teacher after soccer-coach after principal who found faults with Leo: he's ADD, ADHD, ODD, he doesn't stay put, he draws pictures of guns, he is not a team-player, he doesn't want to work, he tunes out the teacher—*maybe he has Asperger's syndrome?*—and unanimously: *he has to be evaluated.* "Leo's classmate Nick takes medication and it really helps him," teachers said. "Maybe it will help Leo too?" "Help whom?" should have been the reply, "you or him?" But we always think of the best answer too late.

Absolutely no medication, Donna and Adam agreed. Leo was a high strung and complicated kid who was sometimes hard to figure out. He was only five when Donna told me that while listening to some virtuoso pianist Leo got frustrated and blurted out: "I'll never be able to play like that." Nobody was forcing him to play anything! Another time he woke up from a dream and said, "Dreams are like delicate art projects. You have to wake up slowly or they'll break." So clearly the kid had imagination and an artistic sensibility. He was also advanced academically. Donna and Adam were not going to dull his imagination and stifle his intelligence with medication. So when the pressure and harassment from the school made life miserable and took up more time than it was worth they pulled Leo out of school. Donna and I started homeschooling our sons at pretty much the same time—and found that neither of them were easy to "homeschool."

The "schooling" part of homeschooling is not hard in itself. People always told us that it was easy for us because of our teaching background. While having teaching experience gave us a certain degree of confidence, neither of us thought that when you have kids with normal learning ability (the vast, vast majority of kids) teaching is hard. The young of any species are wired to learn, especially the human variety. Individual differences, eccentricities, strengths and weaknesses are nothing compared to the inexplicable drive of the human species to learn. We have both seen plenty of homeschooling parents with very little formal education and no teaching experience who produced fabulously educated children. Anyone who is willing to learn can "teach"—that is, you can always learn with your kid. In addition, as college teachers we had seen plenty of kids who when motivated enough quickly caught up with all kinds of educational deficiencies.

The hard part about homeschooling is the absolute dedication it requires of at least one of the parents. It's a "lifestyle" choice, homeschoolers say. Donna and I may not have chosen that "style" for our lives but we had no choice but to submit to its demands once we found ourselves in it. In our case, and the case of many parents whether or not their kids are in school, one of the most frustrating aspects of the "lifestyle" of all kids of this generation is the amount of time they spend in front of the computer screen. Homeschooled kids sometimes end up living in front of them. It is up to the "homeschooling" parent to make sure they don't. Prying your kids away from the screen is harder than pulling teeth. I know from personal experience that it can be the source of a battle of wills that can ruin your life, day in and day out.

Not all homeschoolers are *unschoolers*. Unschoolers believe that children should be left alone to follow their spontaneous interests and that their learning leads have to be followed even if that means spending practically all waking hours in front of a screen. Neither Donna nor I nor our husbands share this belief. We think excessive hours in front of the computer screen is an addiction that kills motivation and who knows what else. But it was up to Donna and me to battle the screen every day with Leo and Jack. We both think that this has been a simply dreadful part of our homeschooling experience. I honestly don't know how others do it but it has been positively painful for me to observe, and fight, the fact that the number one pleasure of my son is to sit in front of a computer screen. I know Donna has shared this daily torment with me.

Both our bright and head-strong boys challenged us daily, refusing to participate in any other life than their electronic one. Motivation, enthusiasm, cooperation, went out the window—no degree of extra motivation and excitement and encouragement on our part seemed to help. It just drained us on a daily basis. Contracts were written, "consequences" established and enforced, patience and impatience got tried, rewards given—but nothing worked. It was a battle of attrition and I know from experience that kids always win at these battles. They simply give it all their unfettered might whereas adults are limited by the restraints of experience and maturity.

During our phone calls over the years Donna and I shared our stories, vented our frustration, got mad, cracked up, analyzed and criticized, and generally gave each other moral support. She also often mentioned that she was feeling the pressure of bringing in income. In addition to being stressed out by his demanding job Adam was growing tired of being sole bread-winner and wanted relief. He had been a musician before having a family but now with his job as software engineer he could not devote as much time as he wanted to music. Who could blame him for missing music. But this meant that as Leo's demands on Donna's time and energy—her very vitality, I understood well—grew, and her marketability as a professional declined, the clock started ticking louder and louder on when she would be able to make financial contributions to the household so Adam could have a break.

Dollars and cents

One of the biggest taboos in our lives is the question of money. Having struggled to make ends meet while in graduate school and then working together, Donna and I never kept financial secrets from each other. As a labor union organizer Donna has always been particularly matter of fact in calculating the dollars and cents of everyday life. So here are a few relevant facts of her life.

Donna's parents owned a roomy if run-down apartment on the Upper Westside in Manhattan which had been bought by the hard work of her immigrant grandparents. By the time Leo was born Donna and Adam could not afford a bigger apartment than their own studio in Manhattan, especially since Donna had to stop working. Donna's parents, who were getting on in age, decided to sell their apartment and have all of them move out of New York City. They chose Bergen County in New Jersey for its good public schools and proximity to Manhattan, where Adam worked. Thanks to the outrageously inflated real estate prices in the City, with the money for their Upper Westside apartment Donna's parents were able to buy a small apartment for themselves, give Donna and Adam a down payment for a house, and set aside money for Leo's college education. Donna and Leo were their only child and grandchild.

By the time Leo was school-age, adjunct salary was up to about $3,000 per course. Adam easily made four times more than Donna, working similar hours. That's when Donna decided that instead of adjuncting, it would be better to rework her dissertation for publication so as to increase her chances of getting a "real," full-time teaching position. But as it turned out taking Leo out of school coincided with the publication of her book and she became a stay-at-home mom again, this time a homeschooling one. Her career got put on the back burner again. Adam, feeling the numbing and depleting demands of a job and hours of daily commute, was becoming increasingly unhappy. From his point of view he was the "working" member of the family.

Mothers' work: gender inequity

Prostitution is often referred to as the world's oldest profession. If this is indeed true it is the world's oldest *paid* profession. Motherhood must be the world's oldest *nonpaid* profession. In recognition of the former's labor and participation in the economic activity of their societies, prostitutes are now called sex workers. Perhaps women's mothering and other caretaking labor deserves some recognition too?

Economic activity is defined as actions that involve production, distribution and consumption of goods and services. The calculation of GDP (Gross Domestic Product, the measure of economic activity and growth in a country) has significant ramifications for the economic policies of a country and the economic wellbeing of its citizens. Every now and then there are reports and policy papers put out by organizations such as the World Labor Organization or the World Bank acknowledging that the labor of a vast segment of the population, namely women working inside the home, is routinely left out of the GDP equation. Now, surely women's work falls into both the "production" and "services" category of economic activity: stay-at-home moms, "housewives," are unpaid laborers who produce (literally) and give service to the citizens of a country. Ironically, this group is indeed acknowledged in their contribution to economic activity as consumers; advertising can show you this. This suggests that those who define economic activity, based on which GDP and other economic indicators are measured, are aware of the existence of mothers; they just don't consider them productive members of society. Consumers, yes; producers, no.

Let me clarify something right away. When I say women "produce" citizens I don't mean just that they conceive, carry and give birth to the young of the species. What I mean is that quite apart from the biological function, which may or may not be part of motherhood, women continue to play the bigger role in caring for and bringing up children. "Bringing up" children involves looking after their physical and psychological well-being, socializing and teaching them, nurturing their talents and interests, and generally being available to them to the maximum extent you can muster. In short, raising children, in the best case scenario, means producing decent citizens by giving them the best services you are able. Isn't this kind of providing "production and services" worthy of the GDP?

Another interesting fact. I recently read in an ILO policy brief (there are many of these but here I cite one by Debbie Budlender, "Measuring the Economic and Social Value of Domestic Work"—you can search it online) that "a general assessment of law and practice on domestic work across the world is that it is 'undervalued, underpaid, unprotected and poorly regulated' in spite of the contributions that domestic workers make to the care and welfare of millions of households." Most researchers point out that the undervaluation of domestic labor—unpaid mother-workers or minimally-paid domestic laborers—has something to do with the undervaluation of two groups of people: women and racial/ethnic minorities, since it is they who overwhelmingly perform this labor. So the question is, in the race for exploitation, which comes first: sex or race? Did human communities have female members first or racial/ethnic minorities?!

(I can't speculate on that. But once I took an unofficial poll of my students that may shed some light on the question.

I asked my students, well over 90 percent of whom were from racial and ethnic minorities, whether they thought we would sooner have a black or a woman president. The overwhelming majority said a black president. Their prediction came true!)

What's encouraging is that what these stodgy old international organizations have been hashing out for decades (without any noticeable result) is now taking on the savvy polish and articulation of a new generation. The interesting site salary.com recently published its "13th Annual Mom Salary Survey" (salary.com/mom-paycheck). Based on their research the salary that a typical mother is estimated to earn is an annual $113,568, based on a 94-hour work week. The itemized breakdown of hours per occupation that mothers fulfill is interesting: Housekeeper 14.4 hrs; Cook 14; Day Care Teacher 13.08 [substitute school-related activities for older children]; Facilities Manager 10.8; Computer Operator 8.9; Van Driver 8; Janitor 7.8; Psychologist 7.3; Laundry Operator 6.2; CEO 3.3. The salary calculation for this work considers 54 of these hours as overtime, which is the work that "working" mothers put in at home in addition to their outside jobs. This is what is missing from Gross Domestic Product calculations of the world. Not exactly insignificant when we're talking about half the world's adult population.

The ILO policy brief that I cited earlier concluded that domestic labor is "under-valued in societal terms in that its economic and social value is not adequately recognized by governments, citizens and others." It is especially sad to realize that the "citizens" who undervalue the work of mothers often include their own families, starting with their husbands and children.

Adding insult to injury: gender inadequacy

The injury is that our work as mothers is not considered real work. This means lack of economic independence in the present and lack of economic security in the future (social security does not count the years of a woman's domestic work as years of employment).

The insult is that caretaking being an indefinable activity, a caretaker's work is never done, nor good enough. Meeting the minimums of physical needs is not hard; providing quality of life is hard. Making people happy is hard. Caretaking is very difficult to define; it is of the moment and pertains to the individual. It requires that the caretaker go out of her way, sometimes way out of her way. It requires that she make her very self available: her time, energy, strength, personal resources, freedom. You cannot quantify quality of life or happiness, or how far is "out of your way." You certainly can't quantify what the worth of a woman's self is. This inherent impossibility to define these aspects of caretaking can easily lend itself to negative assessment of women's work. A caretaker's work can easily be never enough, nor good enough. Given that the great majority of caregivers are women this is a big part of what I call gender inadequacy.

This attitude is what's behind the old "it's the mother's fault" syndrome. We all remember the days when mothers were blamed for the autism of their children by being called "refrigerator mothers." Thank goodness that's not the case anymore. But how much progress have we made exactly? If all these "how to" books that continue to be written for women are any indication, I'd say the progress is far from enough. Maybe mothers are given a break in extreme cases such as autism, but not in everyday life. If we were seen as adequate mothers we would not be in such need of various experts pointing out our shortcomings and offering corrections. From psychobabble to political-correctness-for-dummies to half-baked and semi-literate theories about everything having to do with children, we are reminded that we don't know what we're doing in every best-selling genre. We are reminded that we must change our evil ways.

We all know that parenting requires sacrifices. This will

always remain true. But should sacrificing your self-worth and confidence also be required? "You are not a good mother" is a message that is drummed into our heads where ever we turn. Some of it has the purpose of "selling" us things: from consumer products and advice on how to change our inadequate ways, to drugs. But I think it has an even uglier and viciously misogynist side. To entertain the possibility that all your (already unacknowledged) life effort to do well by your children is woefully inadequate and actually hurting them is the most misogynist blow I can think of. It causes grave injury—and it is below the belt, at that. It is devastating.

Against this backdrop, when a father tells a child that his mother is "inexperienced" and instructs him to ignore and undermine her, both in words and by example, the hurt and humiliation he causes the mother is beyond what can be caused by one individual. I completely understood how stabbed-in-the-gut Donna felt. It was a reeling blow, hence her repetition of how confused she felt. She not only was not bringing in money but she was not even doing a good job as a mother; she was simply an inadequate member of the family.

But how had this happened to her? How could her intelligent, kind partner have dealt her such a blow?

The answer has to do with the inseparability of the personal and the political. Adam perhaps had not intended grave injury but a little insensitivity on his side (caused by an attitude of curl-up-and-take-a-nap-in-your-own-moneymaking-virtue) had been amplified by the societal message on the inadequacy of mothers. Kids, bent on having their way at any cost, simply lap this up: Take it out on the mother; it's her fault for not doing enough or being good enough.

If family or school or society does not sanction the result of the care-taking of a mother—i.e. it does not approve of the child—then the mother is inadequate. And things being as they are, if the child is made aware of this "inadequacy" in his mother any unmet demand of his simply confirms it. The child internalizes the gender inadequacy. If the mother's efforts do not meet the equally indefinable requirements (the "wants") of the child then she is not a good mother in his eyes. The kid learns to sit in judgment of the mother from early on—and just as bad, the "wants" avoid any scrutiny and turn into entitlement.

Our generation of women grew up believing in our own inherent value and our equal rights. But we have learned that what we think of ourselves is after all not all that matters. "Self- esteem" is far from the sole issue here. How society "esteems" us is equally important. If what we contribute with our being in the world is neither enough nor as good as it ought to be, then where does that leave us? And worse, what does it teach our children?

It is impossible not to notice the proliferation of a certain kind of kid these days—the self-centered, entitled monster. If the person who does the most for a kid is never good enough nor does enough, how do we expect him to have respect for her? And worst of all, if the mother is always at fault how will a kid ever learn to take responsibility for himself? If in the old world kids were punished for their transgressions, in our new world they are spared at the mothers' expense—until they grow up, that is. If they're lucky they are rudely awakened at some point; if they're unlucky they better be rich.

I often wonder how much of the teenage attitude problems that we take for normal in this culture originate from the internalization of society's devaluation of mothers. (In the case of girls it is especially ironic; I see the monster of misogyny snickering.) Perhaps as children get older they extend to others the disdain they have learned to harbor toward their mothers. Fathers, teachers, figures of "authority," all fall prey to this attitude. The typical "teen" behavior of looking-down, undervaluing, ignoring, and undermining adults—an all around lack of respect—must start somewhere. It is no wonder that in cultures where mothers are revered the concept of the "teenager" does not exist.

Furthermore, the undervaluing of mothers' work and the

accompanying gender inadequacy undermine everything we think we are teaching our children about freedom and equality. I grew up hearing my father say "liberation of women is liberation of men": advanced for half a century ago but unfortunately having taken on a sour note of cynicism over the decades. If we want our boys and girls to grow up to deeply care for equality and freedom for themselves and others it better start early.

What's postmodern about it?

Let's call the period of the second phase of feminism the modern. It was the time when we asserted ourselves, we raised awareness, we won rights, we worked on ourselves, we proved ourselves—and we thought there was nowhere to go but up up up from there. Hah! Turns out our personal selves progressed much faster than our social, political, and economic circumstances. Our main Achilles' heel proved to be the question of having children. While we were busy negotiating the circumstances of having babies we lost sight of the bigger question: raising them. Here we regressed at least a notch or two. What was expected of us kept piling up while society acknowledged our work less. This is our postmodern predicament.

Part of the postmodern expectation overload has to do with the myth of the superwoman—and we ourselves are guilty of having contributed to its creation. Giddy with winning new opportunities, independence, and professional success we wanted to prove that we could do it all: get great education, make good money doing what we are as good as any man, turn ourselves into Martha Stewart, and raise happy, healthy, "well-adjusted," over-achieving superkids.

Unfortunately even when mothers rid themselves of their own expectations to be superwomen, getting rid of the expectation that they produce superkids is often out of their control.

All too often understaffed schools and over-hassled teachers are looking for faults in the kids and their parenting to blame for their own frustration and lack of success. Anything short of a superkid who performs brilliantly in everything and is mostly seen and not heard is a problem kid—and part of that problem is the inadequacy of the mother to be a supermom. And the remedies offered by society are inevitably commercial ones, from consumer goods to psychopharmacology. It's about time to realize superwomen and superkids are as much marketing fiction as Martha Stewart.

But not all the postmodern demands on us are fiction. I think children, especially in more "advanced" countries, are growing up in increasingly unhealthy, culturally impoverished, and unhappy societies. I did not grow up in United States so I do have grounds for comparison. The fact is that raising children in America has become more and more difficult. The support network is not there, and I'm not talking about the good old days of extended families and the "village" that helped you raise your kids. Support would be nice but it's almost too much to ask for now. Now we spend most of our energy and time on warding off assaults on ourselves and, worse, on our kids.

Take the question of health. It takes a gargantuan effort to battle the assault of junk food advertising and their almost forceful availability on a daily basis. My son tells me that I'm a "health freak" for not keeping candy, chips and soda in our house. For a while when he was at school, eating dry Top Ramen was what the cool kids did. In fact, he would often say that one reason kids bullied him was that he did not bring Top Ramen or Lunchables to school for lunch; he said they saw him as a goody-two-shoes for his healthy lunches. School lunches were despicable; suffice it to say that the globs weren't even defrosted properly when they were handed to the kids. Even the junk-food junkies did not eat that. Once when I accused Jack of trading in his healthy lunches for junk food he said, "Get real mom, who would trade me stuff for *that*?" I don't understand why with all this talk about obesity nobody asks that junk food be taxed the way tobacco is? Wouldn't that be an easy and profitable investment in our future? The things that the tax revenue could do... like, say, support farmer markets and urban gardens.

Another assault on children's health is the dwindling of outside play time. Even recess is starting to disappear from schools. But more importantly, the lack of safe public space for children to play is an atrocity. When my son played soccer in San Francisco about half the city traffic on weekends was comprised of parents hauling children to parks across town to play soccer. Neighborhoods had their own parks of course but the hyper-organized "leagues" that defined soccer for non-Latino kids in San Francisco assigned teams to fields. Getting together with your buddies to kick the ball or shoot hoops in your own neighborhood was not good enough for truly dedicated (read "white") parents and their kids. Parental adequacy required expenditure—of time, money, and gasoline. Needless to say I never became a soccer mom.

With lack of safe public space free play is seriously curtailed. The days of just "run outside and play" are long over for most of us. But outside play is natural exercise. It does not require equipment, supervision, structure, or expenditure. It does not require social secretaries to arrange "dates." It does not require mothers' organization, coordination, transportation, and killing time waiting for the kids to be done. It does not require the micromanagement of the kids' and mothers' time.

Speaking of micromanagement, it is not just physical exertions and presence that is required of mothers now. Anything less than full and constant engagement with your kid is considered inadequate. Every moment is a "learning" moment. We must lose no opportunity to coach the kid in "conflict resolution" and "impulse control" and "team work." An accepting and relaxed approach to parenting is very difficult to pull off when kids choose their friends based on the kids and not their parents.

Then there is the assault on children's mental health.

A big part of this book describes the absurd demands put on mothers to control and indeed subjugate their boys to the wills of others. Some kids will simply not bend to the will of others. The mother who can't or won't crush the stubborn independence of her children, no matter how much she might suffer from it herself, cannot be a good mother. She is inadequate. Endless how-to advice, professional intervention, and even medication become necessary. It is when she is sufficiently beaten down with reminders of her inadequacy that she will do anything for a little sympathy, a little lifting of the guilt over her evil ways: "It is not your fault," the professionals soothe the mother's ruffled feathers. Then they offer: "It's the fault of your kid's brain chemistry. Here, make him take this pill. It will make him sit down and shut up." Schools are quick to identify "problems"; the medical establishment is happy and vested in prescribing drugs; and psychotherapy is always ready with the justification: If you don't drug your kid you are hurting his self-esteem, compromising his success, refusing "help."

While the grip tightens on kids and parents wriggling to free themselves of unnatural and irrational expectations, other influences are given absolute freedom. Media, the "entertainment" applications of technology, the trash that is labeled culture—this is what is given free and increasingly profitable reign. Let's take the question of sex and violence for example. I sigh to recall the days when people complained about "sex and violence" on TV and in the movies. That was child's play compared to what's available to kids now.

When I was a kid it was a milestone when a boy first laid his hands on an old, dog-eared issue of Playboy. Now I don't even want to know what kids watch on YouTube. At a birthday party when my son was in fourth grade the girls ran to us and reported that the boys were watching "porno." Heck, at day camp in second grade my son told me the boys were talking about a site called bigboobs.com. He thought it was funny but when I looked at it out of curiosity later it was anything but. (Hint, it wasn't just big boobs.)

What's equally shocking in its ramifications is the violence kids are exposed to now. There has been a frightening shift from watching violence to taking part in it in games. In the guise of fighting terrorists or aliens kids routinely spend hours and hours committing the most gruesome acts of violence, complete with blood and gore and even rape of women and murder of children. The same boys who started life identifying with Batman and Superman and Ninja Turtles in their tireless fight against "bad guys" turn into proud bad guys themselves. This is not a case of discovering anti-heroes. In the past anti-heroes were Robin Hood at best and Bonnie and Clyde at worst. Now anti-heroes, if we can call them that, are actually gleeful about "bad guys" just to have an excuse to kill and rape and pillage.

Pornography and violence are of course extreme examples. Frankly I consider what passes for "culture" in the media equally pernicious. TV shows full of dolled-up girls and empty-headed boys, gossip about the details of the lives of imbecile celebrities and "artists," framed by endless advertisement peddling poison to put in your body and mind is what passes for culture now. This is what I mean by the cultural impoverishment of our society. I am not talking about Socrates and Beethoven and Kandinsky missing from our everyday lives. I'm talking about a decaying popular culture. Where are the artistic standards that made Fred Astaire, The Beatles and other popular, rock and roll, and jazz cultural icons? The Beatles worked tirelessly to perfect their art and craft, even after they were already global sensations. The virtuosity of Jimi Hendrix and Miles Davis was not just talent nor drug-induced; it came from hard work. Auditions for Hollywood required acting skills. The aspiration that "culture" now instills in kids is to achieve some random fame that makes their hair color stuff of evening news. They think "making it big" is just around the corner; all they need is attitude.

This is the cultural assault that we postmoderns are up against. How can you blame the overworked mother micromanaging her kids' lives dragging them from afterschool class to soccer to piano lesson to gymnastics to playdate, just to fill up their time with something a little more enriching than what the media offers? How can we not do our darnedest to shelter our kids from the powerful and cynical forces that want them to buy, eat, learn, take pleasure, and find meaning in what can best be described as poisonous trash?

Then there is schoolwork—and not just for the kids. When women first started working outside the home they were not expected to help run their children's schools. I myself worked harder doing volunteer work at my son's school than I did homeschooling him. While I was volunteering at my son's public school I took satisfaction in knowing that I was contributing to the education of some kids whose parents had to work too hard to be able to spend time at the school. The volunteer work required of parents in private schools charging exorbitant tuitions, however, is beyond absurdity. Nevertheless, it is work expected to be performed predominantly by "non-working" mothers.

Much of the schoolwork that is expected of kids is homework that requires the engagement of parents. It used to be kids learned whatever they did at school and homework was to reinforce that learning. Now kids come home with homework they have no clue how to do. A great favorite of schools are "projects" of dubious educational value that in a don't-ask-don't-tell fashion get done by parents and turned in the next day. Only God knows what happens during the over six hours that kids spend at school. Six hours is a very long time in a child's day. I hardly think that if they learn during that time there would be any need for parents to be doing projects for them at home.

Finally, a word about the changes in postmodern fathers. It is wonderful that they have discovered the pleasures of spending time with their children and being more involved in raising them. Supporting the aspirations of the mothers of their children, they understandably hesitate to accept sole breadwinning responsibility. Men certainly have the right to reject breaking their backs earning bread for their families. They are no less entitled to having their own professional and nonprofessional ambitions and interests. I just wish that salary.com would calculate the overtime that men put in doing caretaking and domestic work when they get home from their jobs!

I think the continuation of our postmodern condition threatens to make motherhood not just labor-intensive and stressful but joyless. I think mothers should revolt against this. We really do deserve the joys of motherhood.

To love and to work: A crisis of value

Freud said the purpose of life is to love and to work. I'm pretty sure he was talking about professional males like himself. It also seems that he experienced those as two distinct aspects of life. The work of the women of his time and social class was to run households, cater to their husbands' needs, and raise and educate children, and/or oversee all this. That was their "job" and it was performed inside the house. (I'm not talking about poor women; they always worked outside as well as inside.) The prevalent myth of Victorian womanhood was the "angel in the house." Still, the myth notwithstanding, what women did inside the house was considered work even if on "angel" wages—that is, living and dressing as nicely as their husbands could afford. The true reward, however, was that their work and love were one and the same. Poor professionally-splintered men!

In our modern times the myth of the angel in the house got replaced with the myth of the superwoman. The part that did not change from the Victorian era was that mothers' work continued to be labor of love; that will not and should not ever change. What did change, however, is that once women (middle class women, that is) started working outside the home their domestic work became invisible. Some progress! Once women started earning cash their "angel" work became even more devalued; indeed, by earning their own keep they become not more but *less* angelic.

A fundamental thing that has changed since the Victorian times, however, is our notion of what is valuable. If back then nurturing life was what was valued in women's work, now earning cold cash is. Add to this view a certain "work ethic" that prides itself on its moral virtue, and the combination is problematic. Work ethic is certainly not a bad thing but I'm not sure how much of a good thing it is to see earning cash as a moral virtue. A sense of virtue leads to sense of superiority to entitlement. Not good.

Freud also said biology is destiny. Insofar as most mothers are still biological mothers his observation seems still true, even if we now see it ironically. He also asked a famous question: What do women want? I'm not going to speak for every member of my sex, but I would bet anything that many members of my sex would agree with this answer: Why don't we start by acknowledging and equitably remunerating women's caretaking work?

Love at work: Donna and Adam upshot

After Donna's distress phone call to me she went through a bad period. She got very depressed. But a growing kid cannot be put on a backburner while parents sort things out between themselves. So first, they came up with some practical solutions. The truth was that while Donna was depressed Adam was at breaking point with the stresses of his commute and job. He was lucky that he could negotiate a shorter work week, with less pay of course.

Donna cut back on her domestic labor. Quality of life did suffer but so what if the kid doesn't eat fresh organic food every day? So what if a clean house and warm dinner do not await Adam upon his return from work every night? Donna decided that by now Leo was literate enough to be left more to his own devices on educational matters. So what if he was behind in some subjects? She knew from her teaching experience that kids have lots of time to catch up; it's up to them to want to do it. She gave up trying to spur motivation and enthusiasm in anyone—no more rowing against dead weight. She spent more time going into the city, spending time doing things she missed. So what if Adam and Leo stayed home while she was out enjoying herself? Let them entertain themselves and each other.

As for her professional future Donna gave up on an academic career. She started writing again, but not with an eye toward landing a job. She wrote from that place inside herself that just had to write. But mainly she decided to concentrate on exploring the new world that has dawned on us—too new for us to quite grasp yet.

The key to opening the doors to this new life, however, was offered by Donna's parents. The fact was that Adam's reduced pay was not enough to live on and now that Donna had faced the reality that adjuncting would probably never lead to a full-time position she needed time to explore new professional possibilities. Her parents could not bear to see their daughter depressed and her family-life threatened, so they mortgaged their house and gave her the money to sustain them until Donna had found herself a new profession and Leo was out of the house so she could devote her time to it. It was also their way of acknowledging the caretaking that Donna offered them now that their health was declining. (I don't mean to be petty but I can't resist pointing out that Adam's sister took care of his aging parents, without any acknowledgement other than lip service.)

"I'm cashing in my inheritance," Donna, the old labor activist, told me. "This is one of the ways the middle class is being eroded. Unemployment forces them to cash in family assets so they have nothing to leave for their own children. That gets everyone a notch down on the social ladder: if our parents became upper middle class on account of the real estate bubble, we are struggling to remain middle class, and our children will turn into corporate blue collar. Adam and I may maintain our middle class quality of life now but Leo might not have anything to fall back on if he ever needs it in the future. He'll be back to the level of his working class great grandparents—except that he will never afford to buy an apartment on the Upper Westside!"

But back to the present.

"The happiest words I utter everyday are 'good night,'" says Donna. "After Adam and Leo go to bed I go downstairs to my office and check out what's going on in the world. I read, I watch movies, I spend hours and hours on the internet and YouTube. I actually have quite a life in cyberspace: friends, kindred spirits, unimaginably knowledgeable people with a generosity of spirit that makes life worth living..." I know what she means. The resources out there are mind-boggling. What we need is the intelligence to sift through the deluge of information and the imagination to create new things. We can start with reinventing ourselves.

And the future?

The problem being both on personal and political levels, so must the solution. Step one is acknowledgement: from the ground up, starting with our life partners and offspring all the way up to those who make macro-economic decisions for our lives.

We need consciousness raising and activism. We need to step up the efforts suggested by the bumper sticker we occasionally see: "All mothers are working mothers."

But let's be idealistic for a moment. Let's say that society should come to a consensus to take care of all caretakers. I am quite aware that this is a vague statement. It begs the questions, What is caretaking and how much is it worth? No one person can come up with answers to questions like that. There must be both private and public discussions to sharpen our focus and define our options and strategies. Perhaps by taking on this discussion, caretaking will finally be valued both on personal and political levels. Maybe even by looking at those questions squarely there will be no need for concrete answers. One can never underestimate the power of creative decency.

As for the third wave of feminism and the possibility of fair appreciation of mothers' work, here's a clue. It is now customary to refer to pregnancy as a state achieved by a couple: *We* are pregnant, people say. If that's not ridiculous enough here's a headline I saw in a gossip magazine recently: "Swedish princess and her American husband have decided to give birth to their baby in New York." *They* give birth?!

It seems that now even carrying a baby and giving birth are not considered exclusive domain of women. If the labor of our bodies is not considered our labor, who exactly do these working bodies belong to? (Sounds familiar?!) It seems that now instead of more of our labor being counted as work, even less of what we do is considered labor. If going through pregnancy and birthing is now something a couple do together, can we also please share the morning sickness and labor pains?

On that note, Fair Reader and Modern Mother, good luck. And good night.

www.ingramcontent.com/pod-product-compliance
Lightning Source LLC
Chambersburg PA
CBHW021038090426
42738CB00006B/145